PASSENGER PRINCESS

MORGAN ELIZABETH

To all of the girls who have been told they don't belong somewhere.

I hope you have the time of your life proving them wrong.

PLAYLIST

Espresso - Sabrina Carpenter
Guy on a Horse - Maisie Peters
Guilty As Sin? - Taylor Swift
HOTTOGO - Chappell Roan
Who Says - Selena Gomez
Gorgeous - Taylor Swift
Sue Me - Sabrina Carpenter
Bodyguard - Beyonce
Quarter Life Crisis - Taylor Bickett
thanK you aIMee - Taylor Swift
all-American bitch - Olivia Rodrigo
After Midnight - Chappell Roan
Mean Girls - Charli XCX
Crazier - Taylor Swift
You Look Like You Love Me - Ella Langley
Fearless - Taylor

A NOTE FROM MORGAN

Dear Reader,

This book wasn't supposed to be the next one I wrote. In fact, this book was a silly voice memo I sent randomly then I remembered at the perfect time. I was supposed to write book two in a different series, but when I sat down to write it.... Nothing came.

So after a few days of panic, I went down stairs to my husband and had a Kim Kardashian style *yeah, I'm great, but can you talk for a minute?* Melt down where he told me to just *write something else.*

I, a people pleaser to my core, thought that was impossible, but of course, he was right. I started plotting this book out with little more than a title (the title came first, if you're wondering) I slipped into this new world with these new characters and fell in love.

All this to say, thank you for picking up this book when, I'm sure, your *to be read* list is a mile long, because I wasn't sure how anyone would feel about a silly, goofy, rom com.

While Passenger Princess is a romcom (and honestly it might be one of my favorites yet!) it does touch on a few topics such as: a stalking, unwanted touch from a stranger, explicit sexual situations, foul language, and a fight scene with hair tools.

As always, please take care of your mental health first and foremost!

I love you to the moon and to Saturn,

Morgan

ONE
AVA

I think I'm going to vomit.

That's the only thing going through my mind as I stand under bright lights in a dress my best friend made that weighs as much as a small child, my makeup a full centimeter thick, my feet numb from towering heels, and my hair sprayed within an inch of its life.

I'm going to vomit, and this is the most fun I've had in a *long* time.

"Third runner-up is...Miss Oklahoma!"

Kristie McGee is sweet, but she stuttered during the interview section, and, from what the girls in the dressing room whispered to me about, that's worse than a death sentence. Her fake smile doesn't crack as she gazes at the camera before her light goes out, leaving just three women lit on the stage.

My hands robotically move in small, gentle claps—the only acceptable kind on this stage. It's small enough, you're barely even moving, and no real sound is made, but like everything else on this stage, it's for show. To say, *look what good sports they are!*

And although I've been framed many ways over the last four months, from a trailblazer to a disgrace and humiliation to the apparently sacred world of pageantry, no one can say I'm not a good sport.

I breathe carefully, trying not to splinter the dress Harper *literally* sewed me into or show my nerves on my face. At least three cameras at different locations are pointed at each remaining contestant, and any tiny shift in my face holds the opportunity to be picked apart and made into a clip or a meme.

What's worse than losing Miss Americana?

Becoming a meme *and* losing Miss Americana.

So my entire body remains stiff, my smile wide and plastered in place

"Second runner up..." Third place isn't bad—you still get a cash prize, but it's not as much as second or first, and you don't have the same sponsorship opportunities thereafter.

And you don't go on tour.

"Miss New York!"

I allow a hint of disappointment to show through my mask, a frowned upon move someone will probably be annoyed by. What else is new, considering nearly *every* move I've made since getting into the Miss Americana pageant has been against the grain? But since everyone knows Lily and I are friends, I think it's worth the slight show of emotion.

Making friends here was, admittedly, a surprise to me. Part of me thought all of these women would resent me—the idiot amateur who somehow made it to the big times, the woman who joined just to try to drum up business for her friends. And yes, a handful here feel *precisely* that way about me, but there are even more women who I would call a true friend now.

Lily is one of them, and her coming in third saddens me. If someone was going to beat me, I'd want it to be her. I wish I could hug her, tell her she did amazing, and we'll get drunk together later and talk shit. Instead, I'm gliding (pageant queens don't simply *walk*, of course) to the center of the stage, where I grasp Anne's hand between mine and smile wide at her.

It's a fake smile, of course, because she's the absolute worst—the kind of pageant queen that's a cliché of herself. Snotty and unkind to everyone in her orbit behind closed doors, but shining and perfect to the audience.

Her answers are always about girlhood and team spirit and cheering on one another, but as soon as the cameras are off, she's all underhanded gibes under her breath about extra weight or what people are wearing.

She's toxic.

She's also part of the reason I decided to take this pageant seriously.

When I somehow made it past the auditions to become Miss Americana New Jersey and thus entered the nationwide Miss Americana pageant, I fully intended to just have a good time. Another crazy experience I could tell my grandkids about one day and an opportunity to scream about my friends' businesses from the rooftops.

Until the first joint press event introducing the official Miss Americana contestants for the year when Anne gave me the most wretched once-over. "Strange that they're letting *anybody* into this pageant these days."

If there's one thing about me you should know, it's that I *love* proving people wrong. Because of that *single moment*, I worked my ass off and spent the three months between being accepted and the actual pageant learning everything I could about the industry, about what it would take to beat her. I didn't care if she got last place and I was second to last, I just wanted to beat *her*.

It wasn't a one-sided beef, of course. From that moment, Anne has done everything and anything in her power to discredit me. She talks shit about me in the underhanded mean girl way she's perfected in public and straight up *ignores* me in private, acting like I was invisible and not worth the dust under her red bottoms.

But now her eyes are gleaming and hopeful, and she's smiling wide at me like we're long-lost sisters, a look reflected on my face as well.

Again, it's what's expected from the show and what we're contracted to deliver. If there's one thing the Miss Americana pageant respects, it's tradition, and we all had to sign a mile-long contract threatening legal action if we stepped out of line.

The rules and guidelines range from how we should address hot topic items to the press (i.e., divert and ignore) to promising to uphold the vow for the reigning Miss Americana to remain single for her entire term, since apparently a dating or, gasp, *married* Miss Americana is just unsightly.

"First runner up is..." Regina, the pageant runner, says, holding a thick white envelope. Last year's Miss Americana stands beside her with a broad smile, holding a near-comically large crown on a pillow for the first-place winner.

It should be noted here Regina Miller also hates my guts.

It wasn't like with Anne, where she hated me from the very start. No, I think she thought I'd be a fun way to get press, the "normal" girl they could promote as a, *See! Even* you *could be Miss Americana!* I was a novelty, a novice who was fun to watch but never going to win.

Until the public fell in love with me.

The largest chunk of points in the final top ten of the pageant is a public vote, accounting for just over one-third of your total score. The contestant with the most votes gets the full thirty-five points, second place gets twenty-five, and so on. When social media and news outlets found out about the *refreshingly authentic* (their words, not mine) contestant, people became interested in the pageant, which has been waning in popularity since the early 2000s. According to one article, the advertising costs for this final competition are on par with the fucking Super Bowl.

So, while Regina believes I'm making a mockery of the pageant and going against everything its decades of tradition stand for, I've also sparked interest in the dying industry, so she's had to learn to play nice with me.

Begrudgingly.

Regina cracks the golden wax seal on the envelope with a wide smile, pulls out the expensive card stock, and gazes at the name on the paper.

And for a split second, I can see it.

The tiniest crack in her well-practiced pageant face reveals the truth: disappointment and irritation.

My stomach flips.

Then it's gone nearly as quickly as it appeared, and she's turning towards the main camera, smiling wide and saying, "Miss Utah!"

This time, I don't have to fake the look on my face as it goes slack, my jaw near the floor.

Anne's smile falls, and she clearly mouths *what the fuck*, but I can barely focus on that, instead filing it in a mental bank I'll open later and watch when I need a good giggle.

Because if Utah got second place, that means...

"Making our winner of the Miss Americana pageant, Ava Bordeaux!"

The shaking of my hands held in Miss Utah's isn't part of the facade. Instead, it is unbearably real as reality crashes in: I'm about to go on the craziest adventure of my life. I'll travel, explore, and meet so many amazing people, all because I took a chance on myself and wanted my best friends to succeed.

My body goes into autopilot as I bend at the knees a bit for someone—I can't even focus long enough to know who—to slip on the bedazzled sash as last year's Miss Americana secures the crown on my head and another assistant hands me a bouquet of flowers.

I try to remember what I'm supposed to do, how I'm supposed to act, and how not to let imposter syndrome creep up. I didn't plan for this. In my hyperfixation-studying of the pageant, I never thought I'd actually *win* this thing.

The panic creeps in because, *what am I doing?* How did I get here? How do I tell them they've made a colossal mistake, I can't—

But then my best friends in the very front row catch my eye, cheering like absolute psychos, Jules sobbing, and Harper jumping excitedly.

And I remember what I've been saying for the past three months: inspiring the followers I accidentally accumulated and using it as a platform to encourage women and girls to bet on themselves, take a chance on themselves, and do one thing that scares them every day.

Shoulders back, tits out, bitch.

You were born for great things.

TWO
AVA

After hours of interviews, a healthy amount of tears, and a quick outfit change, I'm at an exclusive club in Atlantic City celebrating my win with my favorite people and a shit ton of strangers, wearing the most gigantic crown ever. (I took off the sash because it's a bit much, but I *earned* this crown, and I won't lie, it looks *good* on me.)

Thursday is my first official event as the reigning Miss Americana, and that's when I have to start playing by their rules to be the perfect pageant queen version of myself while going on the trip of a lifetime.

But tonight? Tonight, we're celebrating.

This means I'm a little past tipsy, my feet ache from dancing too much, and I'm feeling on top of the world.

"Did you hear Atlas Oaks is here?" Jules yells over the bumping bass while we're getting a drink of water in between dances.

"What?" Harper yells, jumping up off her chair. Jules nods and tips her chin to a VIP section.

"Atlas Oaks, the band Jeremy likes? They're here."

"No way! I told him he should have come," Harper says, pulling out her phone to text her asshole boyfriend.

"We should see if I can get you guys a hello!" I shout over the music, grabbing her hand and standing, moving toward the rope doors.

"It's not—"

I shake my head with what they call my signature, *Ava has a plan,* smile.

"No, we're doing it. I went to high school with Stella Greene. She was a few years ahead of me, but it's a small town, and she was on cheer with me, too. I bet she'd, at the very least, help you get a picture with them." I look at Harper, who is dragging her feet. "You can send it to Jeremy and rub it in his face."

I shift my gaze from Harper to Jules, and we roll our eyes. Harper is dating the most intolerable asshole of a man who, if I didn't know better (and to be so honest, I don't really; it's just what she *tells* us), I'd think he hates everything about her. But also, he has a strangely all-consuming obsession with the band Atlas Oaks for someone with absolutely no personality.

"Ava—" Harper starts, exhaustion in the words.

I hold my hands up in surrender. "I'm just saying! He didn't want to come tonight because he's a fucking loser—" I start, but she cuts me off with a sigh.

"He has an early day—"

"Yeah, yeah, yeah, he has a super important job he has to see to on a fucking Sunday morning. Got it." I roll my eyes but continue. "Now we can meet his favorite band and make him feel stupid for always thinking he's too good to hang out with Jules and me."

"He doesn't—"

"You can get their signature, maybe," I say because I'm absolutely *loving* this idea now, and I know this might be the only chance to get her on board. "Have them sign a cocktail napkin or something and give it to him."

"He would really appreciate that," she says, biting her lip, slightly less hesitant now, and allowing me to move her in the appropriate direction.

"Perfect, let's go," I say, grabbing my drink and making my way toward the VIP section.

"Ava, no. Ava, I—" Harper shouts, following me as I move with determination. Jules follows behind with a smile and a slight shake of her head, knowing there's no stopping me once I get an idea in my head.

Stopping in front of the big man at the bottom of the steps of the VIP section, I give him my best smile (what I can now call a *pageant-winning* smile) and speak. "Hi, I'm so sorry to bother you. So my friend over here—"

"No," he says, thick arms crossed over his chest, sunglasses on even though we're in a dark night club, and an earpiece in his ear like he's watching over the president rather than a rock band.

"What?"

"No," he says in a similarly deadpan voice.

My smile widens, and I shake my head. "I'm sorry, I didn't get a chance to explain. I'm—" I start, but he looks over my head past me like I'm not worth even having a conversation with and cuts me off again.

"Don't care who you are, you're not getting in there."

"I just—"

"Don't care."

Okay, so this man is the absolute worst. I'm sure so many people try to sneak in here with wild stories, but he hasn't even given me the grace of letting me *say* who I am, much less trying to verify I do, in fact, know the band.

I put my hands on my hips, taking a step closer and glaring up at him. It's then I realize how tall he is—six foot two, maybe six foot three—and he towers over my five feet two inches in five-inch heels. And *how* handsome. He's the kind of handsome man who definitely knows he's hot but doesn't care about it.

Close-cut brown hair and a small diamond stud in each ear that somehow looks like he tries and is utterly effortless at the same time.

A strong jawline with a hint of a five o'clock shadow shading it. Full pink lips I just *know* could do wicked things to me.

Except his attitude is utter trash.

"You know, I could be someone very important, and you're just pushing me aside."

"You're not," he states, blunt and asshole-ish as ever, and my eyes go wide, my mouth dropping open.

"Ex*cuse* me?" Harper's hand goes to my lower back, and she murmurs something about leaving, but I don't even process it because the big man is speaking again.

"In this world, in *my* world, you are not important. Sorry, princess, blondes with hot bodies wearing crowns celebrating their birthdays are a dime a dozen." His eyes shift from the crowd to me for a split second, and I hate to admit his eyes are also incredibly attractive as they scan me. "Nothing special."

My mouth is opened in shock and irritation, and I'm about to snap back, but I'm stopped by Harper tugging at my hand.

"Come on, babe. Let's get you out of here," Harper says, looping her arm through mine and pulling me away. "It's not worth it."

"He's being a self-righteous ass," I say with a wave of my hand in his direction, now determined not to back down.

"It's my job to keep uninvited people out of this section. I'm simply doing my job," he says, not an ounce of apology in his words.

"Does doing your job include calling me a *dime a dozen*?" He doesn't get a chance to answer because, when he opens his mouth, we're interrupted.

"Ava!" a voice says from behind the big guy, and when I look up the small set of stairs, there's a familiar smile. "Ava Bordeaux! Is that you?" Stella Hart, now Stella *Greene*, comes down the stairs, and the man steps to the side as she puts her arms out.

"Stella! Yeah, it's me!" I hug her, and over her shoulder, I glare at the big bodyguard, but he's unfazed, looking at the crowd once more.

"What are you doing here?" she asks, looking me over.

"Celebrating!" I say, pointing at the crown.

"Oh my god, that's right! I heard! Congratulations! Okay, you *have* to come up." She turns to the big guy, patting his shoulder. "They're cool." And then she grabs my hand, tugging me and, in turn, Jules and Harper up a couple of stairs and into the small area where people are sitting on cool, low couches before turning to face us.

"Guys, this is Ava Bordeaux—she went to Ashford High a few years below me, but we were in cheer together for a bit." A man I recognize as her husband, Riggins Greene, scoffs, and she glares at him.

"It still kills me you were in cheerleading," Reed, the guitarist with floppy, curly brown hair and a sweet smile says.

"She won the Miss Americana Pageant," Stella says to Riggins, who has stood and put an arm around her waist, pulling her in tight like he can't bear to have her out of arm's reach for long.

"Wow, you don't say," he says, looking impressed only because his wife is impressed.

"Yeah, but to be honest, we only came over here to say hi to Stella because Harper's boyfriend is a boring loser and refused to come here to celebrate with us." Stella wrinkles up her nose, and I give her wide eyes and a nod, conveying exactly how I feel about Jeremy. "But you guys are his favorite band, and I just thought it would be so hilarious to send him a picture of us all seeing you."

"Oh, diabolical," Stella says with a laugh. "Yes, yes, absolutely! Guys, picture!" she shouts, hands waving at the guys, and I half expect all of them to glare and say *fuck off* since, before we came up, each was involved in their own conversation. Instead, they instantly obey, standing while I hand one of the servers my phone to take a photo.

Stella Greene is a power of nature, so really, I shouldn't be surprised. The photo is taken, and my phone is returned to me.

"Oh, my god, this is perfect," I say, looking at the shot with Harper in the center, Wes, Reed, and Jules on one side, Riggins, Beckett, and me on the other. Jeremy is going to shit his pants. "You guys *so* made my night."

"Oh, anytime. We love revenge over here," Wes says with a smile and a wink at me.

"My kind of guy," I say with my favorite sassy smile before turning back to Stella. "Seriously though, we just wanted to stop in and say hi—this was so much more, but we absolutely don't want to intrude. It was so good to see you!"

"Oh, my god. No way, you're not intruding at all! Please, stay! I'm getting so bored with the guys here."

"Hey!" Riggins says from behind her.

She looks over her shoulder and rolls her eyes at him. "There's only so much of them I can take. Sometimes I need girl talk."

"Oh my god, that's so true," I say, even though I absolutely do not —I haven't had a real boyfriend in years, much less one whose friends I hung out with so often I got bored of them.

By choice, I've been single, going on a never-ending series of one or two dates before deciding they weren't for me. Sometimes, I'll keep a guy around for a few weeks, but never for anything serious.

Life is too short to spend giant chunks of time with anyone who doesn't hold your interest.

Turning to my best friends, I give them the *wanna stay for a bit, or should we make our excuses?* look, before Jules looks to Harper, nods, and takes a seat. Then, I make formal introductions. We catch up briefly, and the night continues with dancing, drinks, and laughs.

As the night winds down, Stella looks at me, intrigued. "So, you know Jaime?" Stella asks, pushing my shoulder gently.

"Who?"

"Jaime, do you know him? He keeps looking this way." She tips her chin towards the entrance of the VIP area, and when I turn to look, the only person there is the hulking man. I let out a loud laugh and shake my head.

"Oh, god, no. He thought I was some crazy fan girl and absolutely hates me."

"Uh, he very much does not hate you," she says, looking from me to Jaime. "He keeps looking over his shoulder, sneaking glimpses of you."

"I'm sure he's just doing his job, ensuring you are safe."

Stella shakes her head, disagreeing, but doesn't answer before Wes comes up, putting his hands on her shoulders and standing behind her.

"Are we talking about how our big ol' Jaime has a hard-on for the princess?"

"A queen, thank you very much," I say with a wink and an adjustment of my crown. "And he very much can't stand me."

"Jaime doesn't give anyone a second glance. He absolutely has a thing for you." Wes steps back and gives me a generous once-over, a mischievous smile spreading on his lips. "Though anyone would happily give you a second glance. Or a third."

I reach up and pat him on his cheek. "Rock stars aren't my thing, but thanks for the offer."

"All right," Jules says with a laugh. "You are past the point of being allowed to be in public without making a fool of yourself."

I glare at her before smiling because, even in my state of inebriation, I know she's right. "Why, are you afraid I'll dance on a table?" I ask. "Again?"

It's a reference to two years ago at a cowboy bar I dragged us to because I saw an ad for it, and it looked like a fun time. About three minutes in, before we'd even had a drink, someone played a song that seemed to indicate to all the regulars it was time to dance on a bar.

I'd never done it before but always wanted to, so before Jules or Harper could even try and stop me, I had tapped on someone's shoulder and had two strange men helping me up.

Life is too short to date men who can't hold your interest, but it's *definitely* too short not to dance on a bar if you get the opportunity.

"Yes, exactly," she says, standing.

"All right, all right," I say, standing and getting a small head rush, making me giggle.

"We're going to head out in a few, too," Stella says with a yawn, snuggling into her husband's chest. "But we need to swap info! Meet up next time you're in town."

I nod, then exchange numbers with Stella, promising to hit her up at the end of my tour before moving down the steps and exiting the VIP section.

"See ya later, big guy," I say as I teeter on my tall heels in front of him and pat his chest. "You know, you'd be a lot hotter if you were just a smidge." I hold up my pointer finger and thumb, pinching them so there's a tiny gap between my fingers. "Less grumpy."

"Noted," he says, and even though he fights it, I can see it: the tiniest hint of a smile, the whisper of it on the edges of his lips. "Get home safe, princess."

THREE
JAIME

Monday morning, I wake before the sun as usual, fitting in my normal workout, coffee, and a protein shake before I head to the Five Star offices in downtown Evergreen Park.

I live my life incredibly regimented, something I maintain even while on the road with assignments. Growing up in a family of chaos and unpredictability, creating a routine was the one thing I could count on. With age, the need for control and order has not changed. If anything, it's gotten stronger.

I use my mornings and near-meditative routine to clear my mind and prepare for whatever the day may bring.

Unfortunately, much to my irritation, all my mind can think about is the tiny blonde out celebrating her birthday with a tiara as big as her entire face at AfterDark on Saturday.

It's unexpected.

It's inconvenient.

But it's also the only thing I've been able to concentrate on since. Two whole days and a total stranger has taken up residence in my mind. The way she walked up to me, all sass and confidence, with not a care in the world. The way she wouldn't back down, the triumphant grin on her lips when Stella confirmed she wasn't some random weird fan.

The way she looked over her shoulder while walking up the stairs, her big blue eyes shining as she winked and wiggled her fingers at me, the way she patted my chest and called me "big guy" when she left.

And most damning of all, the way I watched her ass sashay away in that tight, short bubblegum pink dress until she was out of sight and the way I regretted not getting her number.

If I can't shake her from my mind by the end of the day, maybe I'll figure out her social media and contact her. Even though she seemed to know Stella and the guys, there's no way in hell I'm giving them any ammunition to be assholes and bother me about it until the day I die.

But I'm hoping it won't even be necessary since today I'll get the details for my new assignment, which is the exact thing I need to distract me from the princess.

Four months ago, my former boss and mentor, Hank, sold the private bodyguard company he had formed forty years prior to a larger security firm. Nothing about my job changed except for I no longer reported to Hank. I've had the same assignment for nearly eight years, working as the head of security of Atlas Oaks, and I was still on that assignment while the company changed hands.

The band is working on their next album and laying low for the most part, so I'm being reassigned to a new temporary position. This isn't the first time this has happened. During past reassignments, I've protected senators and dignitaries, higher-stakes jobs to keep my skills sharp. Hank always made sure to give me something interesting when I had a break, for which I was thankful. But now that he has sold the company, I have no clue who they will assign me to.

Hank took me under his wing when I was just eighteen and fresh out of high school, helping me to get the certifications needed for the job and training me personally. Since then, he's been my mentor and closest friend; even though I don't work for him, I still talk to him at least once a week.

Walking into the Five Star building, I tip my chin to Donna, the executive assistant, before shifting my bag over my shoulder as I walk.

"Hey, Jaime. Greg wants you in his office when you get settled," she says with a smile.

"Got it," I reply, moving in that direction, tightening my jaw, and taking a deep breath to try and clear my mind.

Unfortunately, Greg, the new owner of Five Star, and I don't necessarily get along, so it's made my life more difficult. But at thirty-five, I've only got three more years before my retirement sets in and I can retire and live in the small cabin I bought in a secluded part of Pennsylvania, living a life of peace, quiet, and solitude.

When Hank owned the business, he made sure all of the body-guards had the option to retire after working with the business for twenty years with a full benefits package and a pension, a condition put in place to ensure loyalty to the firm as well as making sure everyone working for Five Star was in top physical shape. He didn't want anyone hanging onto a job their body could no longer fulfill just to keep the lights on.

Just three more years, I remind myself as I push open the door to Greg's office, not bothering to knock. I've been doing a countdown of sorts for the past two years since the business sold. *Only have to deal with this bullshit for five years, and I can retire. Four years, and I can retire.*

Now I'm down to three.

"Hey Wilde, how's it going?" Greg asks with a wide, fake smile, gesturing for me to sit in the chair in front of his desk.

"Not too bad, not too bad," I say, rubbing a hand on my neck. "How are things with you?"

I've never been good at small talk, always feeling awkward and uncomfortable. It's fake, useless, and a waste of time, but Greg loves it and spends the next five minutes telling me about the boat he just bought and his golf score.

"Hear everything went smooth at the club with Atlas Oaks—anything to report?" he asks, finally moving on to work conversation.

I also hate the way he expects me to give him lengthy reports on my every move when all I did was stand in front of a VIP entrance for five hours, making sure no one bothered the band. Hank never gave a fuck about the minutia, so long as the job got done with no issue, I was free to do it however I wanted with no reports.

"Nothing out of the ordinary. The club was understanding, and accommodating and the band kept it pretty low-key."

"Good to hear, good to hear. Want to make sure they come back to Five Star when they go back on tour, you know?"

I give him a strained smile and nod, and he waves a hand at me with a laugh.

"But you're here for your assignment, correct?"

"Yes, sir," I say.

He lets out another jarring laugh, making me grind my molars together before he nods and pulls out a manila folder, placing it in front of him but not opening it.

"So your assignment is a short-term one until Atlas Oaks goes back on tour," my boss says.

"Perfect," I say, leaning back and crossing my arms on my chest. "What are we looking at? Guarding a senator? Some undercover shit? A dignitary?" Short-term assignments used to be some of my favorites. Hank had so many connections, there was always someone looking for bodyguards for anywhere from one day to a few months.

Unfortunately, since Greg has taken over, I've gotten nothing but people with too much money and self-importance hiring a bodyguard just to feel special. There is nothing more tortuous in this world than having to follow around some self-absorbed asshole who expects you to spend every waking moment kissing their ass. I'm tired of watching over some CEO's rich wife while she spends hours shopping, primping, or going to a salon.

When Greg laughs a bit, his face shifting to a look almost apologetic in nature, I know I'm not going to love this assignment.

"Not quite," he says. "Look, I know you were hoping to get something dangerous and exciting, but it is what it is," he says, and suddenly, I'm not nearly as optimistic as I was when I woke up this morning, and I wasn't exactly what one would call *hopeful*. "As a business, we go where the money is, not the excitement. Besides, those kinds of jobs don't pay nearly as much as the ones you've been taking."

Another thing I can't stand about Greg is his hyperfocus on money rather than the business of keeping people safe.

"This contract is incredibly important to the firm, and you're the only one with all the required certifications for every state." My brows come together, trying to pinpoint what that could mean. "They've agreed to work with us on a trial basis. After this trial assignment, if everything goes well, we'll settle on a more long-term deal, ensuring all of their security needs are met by us for the next five years." Suddenly, the happy and carefree look is gone from Greg's face, and he leans forward, putting his forearms on the desk and glaring at me.

"What I'm saying is I really need this contract to go well. I know you're up for retirement, and it would be a shame if we lose work and have to let any men go."

The threat rings clear between us, deafening like a shot fired.

Do well on this assignment, or all the time you've invested in this company will be for nothing, and you'll lose everything you've been working for.

"Of course, sir. Whatever you need, I've got it," I say with a nod. "You've chosen the right man for the job." Suddenly, the fierce look is gone, replaced by a smile again.

"Great to hear. It's a three-month contract, and it's imperative we do well. This contact has connections with presidents, Jaime. Presidents, CEOs, and celebrities—that's what they pump out. We nail this, and Five Star is set for life. We need this contract to go well."

My shoulders straighten, and I force myself to jump into focus, to sway from the all-consuming dread swirling around me and move to reality, to focus on the here and now.

"Let's back up for a second. What are we talking about? What kind of company has that kind of reach and no security in-house?"

He smiles wide, and somehow, I know I'm not going to like the answer.

"The Miss Americana Pageant."

FOUR
JAIME

I should have called Hank.

That's what I'm thinking hours later, sitting in a meeting room with Greg, an older woman with the stiffest posture I've seen in my life and a gentle, well-practiced smile on her face, sitting across from us.

I should have called Hank and asked how to handle this bullshit. But if I did, he would have gotten stressed about a business he got rid of to reduce said stress, so I decided against it.

Regina Miller is an older blonde woman who, as soon as I walked in, gave me a head-to-toe look and then sneered, clearly not impressed with what she saw.

"We're incredibly excited to work with you," Greg says after we go through the basic niceties of introducing each other and asking how the drive was and whatever other bullshit is required.

"Well, we're just happy you could fit us in in such a short amount of time," she responds pleasantly, a tiny smile on her lips.

"Anytime. I know we talked a bit before we set this up, but why don't you fill Jaime in on his assignment?"

"Well, of course. You see, every winner of the Miss Americana pageant goes on a three-month tour to support whatever platform she decides to champion during her reign. Usually, things like healthy eating, the arts, or animals. This year, the *winner*." She says the word winner with bitterness, as if it's something she's still coming to terms with and isn't happy about it. "Chose women-owned businesses."

"A great cause," I say.

She lets out a puff of air, which I suppose could be interpreted as a laugh, but she doesn't smile.

"Yes, just...wonderful. As I was saying, we'll be sending her to each state in the continental United States, where she'll meet with the Miss Americana contestant from there and visit a woman-owned business."

"Interesting method. It's a great way to spotlight small businesses and a great match for an organization such as yours," I say.

She gives me a tight smile that screams *I would like you only to speak when spoken to,* before giving me a fake nod and continuing.

"Yes, well. This year's winner was a bit of a surprise."

"How so?" I ask, crossing my arms on my chest and leaning back, trying to take in the whole picture.

"Well, this was the first pageant she's ever won, for one," Regina says. "I'm sure you don't know much about the pageant world, but that's never happened before. Women dedicate their entire lives to being a contestant on the Miss Americana stage, winning pageant after pageant to prepare for the biggest moment of their lives."

Condescension twines in her words, making it clear she does not like this year's winner. Strange, since she runs it.

"We have a very specific image and branding, and we expect all of our contestants to abide by those guidelines, but especially our reigning queens. Unfortunately, Miss Bordeaux has not done this so far, and I am hoping you and your company will be able to help with that while guarding her."

"I don't think I quite understand," I say, even though I think I do, and I don't like what she's saying at all.

Suddenly, any semblance of kindness leaks from her face as she leans forward. "What I'm saying is your job is less to keep her safe and more to keep her in line."

"What?"

"My priority and the reason I've brought in Five Star is to maintain the image of the Miss Americana pageant."

My brows furrow. "Not her safety?"

She waves a hand like it's a non-issue, then sits back, some of the hatred leaving her eyes. "Well, of course, we don't want anything to happen to our Miss Americana," she says, and I don't miss how she refuses to call the girl by name, only referring to her by a title rather than... whatever her name is. A smile creeps over her lips. "Though, a little bit of a martyr situation could be good press, you know?" She smiles and looks at me as if I'm also going to smile and agree, but I'm baffled and appalled by the strange direction this conversation has taken.

"I'm joking, of course," she says when she realizes I won't agree with her.

"Of course," I say, taking in Regina better in this new light. She's pretty at first glance, older, but clearly someone who takes care of herself, but when you look closer, you see it: the ugly creeping under her skin. It's not anything to do with her looks but from greed and envy, and probably a bit of the other five deadly sins as well.

Her smile drops as she leans in, resting her hands on the table before her. "We're looking for someone who will travel with her, make sure she gets from place to place safely, but know that we're also retaining your firm to keep her in line."

I sit up straighter with a shake of my head. "No."

"No?"

"No. I'm not a babysitter. I'm a bodyguard. My job is to protect, not stop some spoiled brat from causing trouble." I turn to Greg, whose face is a mask of irritation or frustration.

"Excuse him, Ms. Miller. He's not used to dealing with the clientele end of things." He turns back to me, the politeness there moments before melting away instantly. "You'll do whatever the assignment requires of you, Mr. Wilde, as we spoke about earlier."

My jaw goes tight, but I reluctantly nod when I remind myself of what's at stake.

So I get to follow around some brat for three months, keep her in line while she smiles and pageant waves or else I lose my job. It's a waste of my skills and my time.

"Plus, there's more to it than that, Jaime, don't worry." Greg starts. "A little something for you to sink your teeth into. It's not just babysitting. You see, she's got fans." I raise an eyebrow, waiting for him to expand. He looks at the paperwork in front of him, flipping through it until he finds what he's looking for. "It seems she won because she went viral on social media and then did it again and again. She's built a rabid fanbase, and some of them are...intense. You won't just be following around some pageant queen and be bored out of your mind. In the past month, she's filed three police reports due to the messages she's received."

"What kind of messages?" I ask, sitting straighter.

"One death threat, two admirers sending candid photos of her out and about," Greg reads from the paper. "And last week during a practice, someone attempted to break into the event space to meet her."

Well fuck. That's the kind of shit Atlas Oaks deals with, the shit Willa Stone reports regularly. Just how popular is this pageant queen?

"Interested now?"

I sigh, then nod reluctantly.

Greg looks at Regina and smiles, and she nods.

"Perfect. I'll meet you at the Miss Americana offices in two hours to meet your next assignment."

FIVE

AVA

Sitting in the Miss Americana offices in South Jersey, for the first time since I filled out the application, I feel completely out of place, and no level of false bravado can knock the feeling from my mind.

The walls leading to the meeting room we're in were lined with photos of past winners with their perfect teeth, hair, smiles, and outfits. I know someday soon my picture will be in this hall of fame, with my too-wide smile, the slight gap between my front teeth, and probably too much mascara because I decided when I was sixteen that going natural just wasn't in the cards for me, and the more blush, the better.

It didn't help when the receptionist led me to the meeting room, the women we passed whispered to each other, hums of, *that's her*, and, *I just don't get it*, and, my personal favorite, *it should have been Anne*, drifting to my ears on sharp winds.

I'm not bothered, not really. I've always been a bit of an outcast, despite my unending desire to fit in. Raised with two brothers and a single dad, I spent a long time being too boyish, and then I was too girly when I grew into my curves and leaned into my love of pink, cream, lace, and bows.

Too much, too gaudy, trying too hard.

When I won the Miss New Jersey Americana pageant, a dark horse no one expected to get far, the whispers started again. They only continued when I used my knowledge of social media to go viral multiple times while preparing for the final pageant, drawing intrigue from all angles.

Some welcomed me with open arms, fans and viewers called me a breath of fresh air, and media outlets noted how my participation in the pageant has sparked new interest in the seemingly dying industry.

But still, there are always a good handful of haters at every required media outing, every practice, or get- together for the pageant. The people who look at me like some kind of outsider, a wolf in sheep's clothing who shouldn't have even made it through the doors, much less allowed to participate. The disapproval came strongest from the actual organization itself, which, at first, saw me as a way to jumpstart public interest, probably by using me as some punchline, but then regretted letting me in at all when I gained the popularity they were craving.

It seems that disapproval hasn't changed much with the glares I'm getting right now while I sit at a round conference table, a dozen eyes staring me down like some kind of failed social experiment.

Across from me sits Regina, her blonde hair perfectly blown out, the ends perfectly tucked under her chin in a style that, from what I could see when I did my minimal research, she's had for at least twenty-five years. Her posture, like most of the pageant women I've met, both current and past, is absolutely immaculate, and her black tailored skirt suit says professional.

And the glare on her face screams hatred.

I expected that part, at least, since she's hated me from the very start.

To her left is a lawyer with long, pin-straight dark hair and a boring dark suit, and to her right, for some reason I don't think I want to know, sits Miss Utah.

If I thought daggers were coming from Regina, full-blown nuclear missiles are aimed at me from Anne. She fully believed she had the crown on lock, only for me and my silly little self to come in and throw everything to the wayside.

Oops.

When no one speaks after a few beats, I take a sip of my water and sit back with my well-practiced, easy-going smile. "So, can I ask why Anne is here?" I tip my chin toward the curly-haired redhead with perfect posture and a glare that could kill me.

"Because." She pauses, swallowing as if the next few words taste terrible or physically pain her to say. "I am the first runner-up. I won't be at all events, but I will be at some over the course of your tour."

"As you know," Regina starts. "Your tour representing the Miss Americana pageant starts on Thursday."

This is why I was excited about the win: the tour. As someone who loves adventures, traveling the entire country on someone else's dime sounds like a true dream. Add in the opportunity to showcase women-owned small businesses while I do it, and I'm more than willing to play whatever part they want me to for a year.

A fair trade, in my opinion.

"I'm excited to get on the road. My followers are so excited to hear all about my travels and learn more about the businesses we're going to highlight."

A tight smile tightens Regina's lips before she nods, her eyes going cold.

"As a reminder, we ask you to maintain a professional composure at all times, since you will be so directly linked to the pageant and the Miss Americana brand. Any violation of the core tenants of this organization could result in you forfeiting your crown to the first runner-up," she says, the threat obvious.

Stay in line, or we'll rip that pretty crown right off your head.

"And wouldn't that just be so convenient for you, Anne?" I ask the woman who would love nothing more than for me to fail.

"At least someone who deserves it would have the title," she mumbles.

Now that? That pisses me off.

"I worked my ass off, same as you. I answered my questions, performed my talent, and modeled the swimsuit just like you. I'm sorry you have the personality of a wet carpet and you think you're above putting yourself out there and letting the plebs get to know you, so no one voted for you—"

Something in Anne snaps, and she leans forward, her beauty turning to ugly venom before my eyes. "It's a stupid loophole! All that should matter is if you're pretty and if you're pageant queen material. Just because people felt bad for you—"

"Enough," Regina says, the words firm and menacing, and instantly Anne sits back like the obedient dog she is. I have to roll my lips between my teeth to stop from laughing while Regina closes her eyes and sighs deeply as if she's trying to grasp onto one last strand of her patience.

"All we are trying to say, Ms. Bordeaux," the buttoned-up lawyer starts. I wonder if she's also a former pageant queen with her calm decorum and flawless posture. "Is that you signed a contract agreeing to act within the realm of the brand or risk losing your title and potentially being sued for damages made to the Miss Americana brand. Of course, that won't be an issue if you act in a way befitting your new position."

I give the poor woman a sweet smile before turning to Regina, the real person who needs to hear what I have to say.

"And as I told all of you many times since I signed on, I will continue to be myself no matter what. That means on stage, on social media, and on this tour. I'm not going to do anything to violate my contract or make the pageant look bad, but I also won't be anything but myself, which is what everyone has come to expect from me."

Her smile goes tight, like she's unhappy to hear my response, but I won this pageant being myself, and I'm not changing just because they want to maintain some false narrative for what the "perfect Miss Americana" is.

Finally, Regina leans back and puts on the fakest of her smiles, one I haven't seen yet.

"You know, Ava, if it's too much for you to follow our guidelines, we can easily avoid all of these pesky headaches now. We're happy to give your crown to Anne and let you keep the prize money." She gives me an exaggerated sigh and smiles before reaching out to touch my hand, and I have to fight the urge to pull it away. "We understand this isn't for everyone, the pressure, the expectations..." Her words trail off like she's expecting me to agree, to nod and accept her offer with gratitude.

Something tells me they've never met a woman like me.

What a disappointment for them.

"You know, Regina, I think I'll be okay. I'm very excited to show the world that a Miss Americana contestant doesn't have to be picture-perfect, that they can be a normal, everyday, down-to-earth girl. I'm excited to represent a version of women not often exemplified in the Miss American pageant before."

"How very not like other girls of you," Anne says with venom, and I turn to her with a sugary-sweet smile.

"Funny thing is, unlike you, I'm exactly like other girls, and I'm grateful for that. I love being relatable and approachable. I like pink frilly things, bows, and makeup. I love getting my fancy coffees, reading my silly little romance books, and listening to the same music as other girls because it's fun. The only difference between me and other girls, like, say, you, is I don't judge people for what they do or do not like. I just let them live their best lives and cheer them on."

Next, I turn to Regina.

"Which is what I hope to show everyone on my tour: how anyone can be a Miss Americana so long as they are themselves. I'll make sure I'm not acting in a way that would hurt the image of the Miss American pageant, but I'm not changing who I am. I won this title because of who I am, not who I pretend to be, and that won't be changing any time soon."

Suddenly, the kindness leaves her eyes, and she leans forward, a viper preparing to strike. For the first time, I'm seeing the real Regina —the rotten trash beneath the glittering facade she shows everyone else.

"Now listen here, you little brat. I—"

Before she says whatever threat she's looking to throw my way, someone knocks at the door before it cracks open.

"Regina, Five Star Security is downstairs and will be upstairs in a minute or two," the receptionist says, poking her head into the door.

"Perfect, send them in when they get up." She turns to me, her previous threats have melted, and neutrality is now on her face. "That's your bodyguard for the trip."

My head shifts a bit in confusion. "Bodyguard? Why do I need a bodyguard?"

"We wanted to make sure we had someone on staff reporting to us on how you're doing," she says before pausing, the unspoken threat hanging in the air before us. Someone following me around and reporting back to them on my every move, looking for some reason to say I've broken my contract, some reason to take my crown and give it to Anne.

And just like that, I decide I'm going to do everything in my power to toe the line but stay well within the bounds they drew for me. I *will* prove them wrong while never giving them whatever they need to get rid of me, because doing so would mean they win, and once I set my mind to something, I never lose.

Will I change myself?

Absolutely not.

But will I play the game they've started with perfection and look good doing it? Absolutely.

They've never met a woman who can play the game as well as I can, that much I can guarantee.

"And, of course," Regina's condescending voice continues,

breaking through my thoughts with a small smile in the words. "We want to keep you safe from all those admirers you've acquired. Some of them seem quite...attached to you, and of course, we wouldn't want anything bad to happen to you."

Something about how she says it sounds like a threat rather than a reassurance.

"Who is it?" I ask, leaning back.

"A..." The lawyer taps on the screen of a tablet and then looks at me. "Jaime Wilde? He is new to working with us, but not new to the firm he works for. Impeccable recommendations."

"Hmm," I say, trying to place the name somewhere. It's familiar, though I've met so many people in the last six months, and all names are starting to melt together.

Another knock comes before I can dig too far into my subconscious, the same pretty brunette popping her head in. "Regina, Five Star Security is here."

"Perfect, send them in, please."

SIX

AVA

A moment later, the door to the meeting room opens, a gruff-looking older man walks in, and, for a moment, I think he's who my security for this event will be. That I could deal with. A cute old man who won't give me too much shit? Perfect.

But then a tall, broad man walks in behind him, scanning the room like he's looking for a threat, and my entire body goes cold. I know that man, that build. And when his eyes finish scanning the room, stopping when they land on me, I realize I know the face, too.

The asshole bouncer from AfterDark.

"You," I say, my lips tipping up into a small smile as he walks in, the pieces falling into place. What fun kismet this is.

The man stares at me, thoughts moving behind his shuttered eyes. "Princess," he says, the words ricocheting in his mind nearly visibly.

"A pageant queen, technically," I say, tipping my chin up with pride because it might not have been my life's goal, but I worked hard to win my title. Plus, something tells me this man is not impressed by that title. If anything, he's a little annoyed by it, and if there's one thing I'm good at, it's pushing people's buttons.

I stare at him as his boss sits, and the man—Jaime Wilde, a great name if I've ever heard one—sits as far from me as possible, eyes still locked on me, trying to read me, to understand the mess we've gotten into.

"Do you two know each other?" the older man at the table asks, salt-and-pepper eyebrows furrowing.

We both simultaneously shake our heads.

"No, not at all," Jaime barks out with a fevered shake of his head. My lips tip up in an entertained smile. He says it as if I'm a serial killer, and he's trying to deny any kind of connection to me for fear he'll become a suspect next.

"No, not really," I say, smiling my perfect pageant smile at the older man. "He was working at AfterDark when I was celebrating after my win. I tried to say hi to Atlas Oaks since I went to high school with Stella Greene, but he was kind of grumpy about it and didn't really want to hear what I had to say. Honestly, he's very good at his job."

The older man looks at him with a semi-satisfied look. "Small world."

"Yes, well, as I mentioned earlier," Regina says, clearly over this exchange. "Jaime here is going to be following you on tour, keeping an eye on you, and chauffeuring you from place to place."

"So he's a school chaperone?" I say with a bit of a snort because it's laughable. Is this real life?

Let's backtrack:

One, somehow, I'm suddenly a nationwide pageant queen.

Two, the pageant I won hates me and wants me to resign so my newly founded archenemy can take the crown.

Three, I have a chaperone for the next three months because they want to watch my every move and force me to resign.

And four, my new buddy system friend is the grumpy bodyguard I drunkenly flirted with when he stopped me from entering a VIP section a few days ago.

I know God has to be a woman because no man has a sense of humor this good.

"Actually, chaperone is a good way to help you understand what he's doing here," Regina says with a more threatening than friendly smile. "He's going to be keeping you safe but also, as I stated before, making sure you stay within the organization's code of conduct."

"Or else I get your crown," Anne blurts like a small child who can't contain herself, her smile dropping when Regina kicks her under the table, her entire body jolting with the move.

You know what would definitely not be within the code of conduct?

Punching Anne in the face.

But it might be worth it....

"On that note," the lawyer says with a glare at Regina and Anne. "We're going to let you two get to know each other and talk about any needs or preferences either of you might have since you'll be together for so long. Please let us know if you need anything. Ava, when you're ready, we have a few forms for you to sign, so just go to the front desk."

I smile genuinely and nod. "Thanks so much, I will." I watch everyone but Jaime file out and close the door before turning to my new bodyguard with a smile.

He's standing, looking down as he packs a notebook into a backpack without even looking at me.

"Uhhh," I say, trying to figure out how to start this conversation.

It's clear this man isn't a fan of mine, and our initial meeting wasn't exactly ideal. Still, we'll be forced together for the next three months, so I might as well attempt to get things back on the right foot.

"So about the next—" I start, but he stands straight, slinging the bag over his shoulder. His eyes, no longer covered by glasses or the dim lighting of a club, are, in fact, handsome as can be, a green hazel with thick, dark eyelashes I'd kill for.

"My rules," he says briskly, cutting me off. No, hello, how are you? "You listen to what I say. You do what I say. You do not deviate.

We put safety first, and we'll get through the next three months without too much of a headache."

A beat passes, and I blink a few times. He crosses his arms on his chest and continues to glare at me.

"Excuse me?" I ask, mouth open.

"I don't have the time or patience to deal with some spoiled brat for the next three months. My job is to keep you safe. I am not a babysitter. Don't act like a fucking idiot, and I'm not planning to report your every move to her."

Well, that's a relief, but...

"I appreciate that," I say. "But I'd also like to be friends. We're going to be spending a lot of time together, and—"

"No," he says, brusque again, and now it's starting to annoy me.

"What?"

"No. I don't want to be friends. I don't want to play get-to-know-you niceties. I know your type, and I'm not interested."

"My *type?*"

"Self-absorbed, only cares about appearances. The type that smiles and flips her hair and thinks that can get her anything in life, while the rest of us have to follow the rules."

"You think you know me so well, you think you have me *so pegged*, but you don't know a thing about me, Jaime."

He sighs like he's tired of this back and forth. "Look. I'm here to do a job, and even though I'm not exactly fired up to have to follow you around for three months, this is just that—a job for me."

"Okay... and it's one for me."

"No, it's a fun little getaway. It's you playing princess and waving at your royal subjects."

I blink at him a few times, utterly shocked, before I speak. "Excuse me?"

"You listen to what I tell you to do, and we'll be fine."

"What is wrong with you?" I ask, getting annoyed now. I didn't think we would be besties, but we're going to spend a lot of time together, especially if he's driving me from stop to stop.

"I find this assignment irritating and a waste of my skills. Having to follow some self-centered princess around sounds like misery, but we all have jobs to do, and I'm going to do mine."

"I don't get it," I say as he moves towards the door, trying to decode him.

"Get what?" he asks, turning back towards me, that same look of irritation on his face.

"Why you hate me. I did absolutely nothing to deserve this."

He lets out a small sigh, a tiny crack in his mask. "I don't hate you, particularly. I just have no interest in following a beauty queen around. This assignment is essentially me being a glorified babysitter for a grown woman, and it's a waste of my time. I'm annoyed that I've been ambushed by walking into this with you because, if we're putting it all on the table, I find you kind of irritating, and, from what little I saw the other night and what I've heard so far, you seem like a disaster waiting to happen. I'm not looking forward to pulling you out of trouble every five minutes because you can't listen to directions, so I'm trying to be the adult in this room and set guidelines ahead of time. I'm so sorry you don't like them, but that's life, Princess."

He finally stops speaking, and I stare at him before inspecting my nails.

"Are you done?" I ask with a slight smile on my lips.

"What?"

"With your little tirade about how annoying it will be to be my bodyguard. It sounded like you had some really big feelings about it, and I want to make sure you let them all out before I interrupt. So, are you done?"

His jaw goes tight, and in that moment, I realize this will be so much fun.

"Yes, I'm done," he says through gritted teeth.

"Perfect, great. So, here's the deal: I don't really like rules. In fact, the more rules people give me, the more I want to break them. I'm going to do my absolute best to make your job an easy one, but I'm going to be me, regardless. I won't do anything crazy dangerous or stupid, but I'm not going to be some little subservient thing doing exactly what you say at any given moment." He looks at me, then lets out a soul-deep sigh. "This is going to be a disaster," he says under his breath.

I walk around the table towards the exit, stopping in front of him and smiling up at him. He's too handsome for his own good, that much I know.

And much, much too serious. I'll have fun forcing him to relax a bit.

"One thing," I say.

"What's that?"

"Don't fall in love with me, big guy, okay?" I ask, reaching up and patting his cheek. His jaw goes tight.

"I promise that won't be a problem."

"Is that a challenge?"

For the first time, he smiles back. From here, I see one dent in his cheek. A dimple.

"Do your worst, Princess."

"God, you don't even know what you just did, do you?" I ask, my smile spreading as I shake my head in disbelief, moving my purse over my shoulder. "If there's one thing I love, it's a challenge. Literally won an entire pageant just to see if I could. But you? You might become my favorite challenge yet."

I almost don't hear him mumble under his breath as I walk out "And you might just be mine."

SEVEN
AVA

Harper sits on the loveseat in my bedroom, filing her nails, while Jules lies on my bed, head in her hands, watching me frantically try to fit three months' worth of clothes into two giant suitcases. Unfortunately, the pile is looking like there's no way it's not going to take up at least three. I still need hair and body products, pajamas, workout clothes, underwear, makeup...and *shoes*.

"Oh my god, I'm so fucked," I say, looking at the mess scattered around us. "How am I going to bring all of my clothes?"

Harper sighs, putting her nail file on the side table and standing. "You're not. This new collection means you just need the bare minimum, and we can add accessories. Each is double-sided, so there are really two items in each. And these tops"—she lifts two tops with multiple straps and ties—"can be worn a thousand ways and never look the same. I've sent you a document with what to wear at each stop. Based on what I prepared, you only need four pairs of shoes and a pair of sneakers."

My anxiety melts.

"I could kiss you," I say with a sigh of relief. "Can you help make sure I pack the right things?" She rolls her eyes, and I smile when she starts lifting and folding, acting like it's an inconvenience, but really, her type A personality means she secretly loves this shit.

"So your bodyguard is that hot guy from the club?" Jules asks, picking up the nail file and rounding out her own nails.

"If by *hot guy* you mean the grumpy asshole, then yeah. And he can't stand me because he thinks I'm some self-centered princess."

"Well..." Harper starts, but I throw a bra at her, making her laugh right before promptly folding and packing it.

"Nothing out of you," I say.

Tomorrow is the very first event at the Atlantic City Boardwalk. Even though I'll be spending one last night in my bed tomorrow night, I won't be getting back until late and leaving super early, so I have to pack tonight, hence the chaos.

"I don't know, I feel like I could get over him thinking I was spoiled if he looked like that," Jules says.

"What?"

She turns her phone, and shows me a photo of Jaime, arms crossed on his chest, glaring at the camera. I grab it and see it's from the Five Star Security website.

It's absolutely unfair to look that good and be in *that* bad of a mood all the time.

"Grumpy or not, I bet he'd be absolutely amazing in bed," Jules says like she's reading my mind. I shrug, handing her phone back even though I want to continue to stare at that screen indefinitely.

"I bet he would," I say with a smile.

"You know, if this was a movie—" Jules starts, her common refrain, before Harper cuts her off.

"Jules, no. This is not a movie, this is reality." Harper glares at me, pausing her packing. "Ava, you're not allowed to date."

I scrunch up my face in faux confusion. "You know, it's so funny, because I don't remember saying *anything* about dating that man."

Jules lets out another laugh before fist-pumping the air. "Yes! I say you fuck him into a good mood."

"Jules! We're supposed to be the voice of reason," Harper chides, folding up a skirt. She's used to our antics, though.

"I think I'm being reasonable! Sexual tension is bound to build the way sparks flew between you two."

I think about how he looked down at me in the office, the tiniest hint of a smile on his lips, just a few inches between us. The way his eyes moved to my lips before they shifted to my eyes. His quiet *"Get home safe, princess"* the night at the club.

Obviously, I'm reading too far into things, tearing apart tiny moments in time that don't actually matter in the big picture.

"If by sexual tension you mean he'd like to leave me on a deserted island and never see me again, yes."

"Bullshit. *Everyone* loves you, Ava. You win literally everyone over. Why would he be any different?"

"Well, for one, I think he hates me."

"Bullshit," Jules says with a laugh, not believing me in the least. Fair, since I'm definitely exaggerating but...

"Okay, at the very least, he hates that he *doesn't* hate me." I shrug with a small smile playing on my lips, remembering the last words I said to him. "Maybe he hates that he wants into my pants."

Silence takes over as Jules and Harper mull that over before Jules speaks with a shrug. "I mean, maybe, but we can work with that."

"Jules!" I say with a laugh, throwing a makeup brush at her now.

"I'm just saying!"

We both continue in fits of giggles before it dies down and Harper, the logical one of us, speaks.

"Can I just ask why he would even hate you?" Harper asks, as confused as I feel. "He doesn't even know you. "

"I don't think he *hates* me, per se," I say, suddenly feeling like I have to come to his defense. "I just think he wants to do his job. He values...keeping the lines clear. He's very professional, and there was tension between him and his boss. I don't know. I think he just wants to do his job and move on."

Jules snorts. "Then I wish him all the best, having to deal with you for three months."

"What is that supposed to mean?" I ask, throwing a pair of socks at her head.

She tucks it into my suitcase without even wavering before answering. "It means the lengths you will go to make someone your best friend are extreme."

"Who, me?" I ask, hiding a smile.

They're not wrong. But is it *really* a crime to want people to like you?

"Fine, it's not that I want *everyone to like me*. I simply love proving people wrong. Just because I look like an airhead doesn't mean I *am* one."

"Well..." Harper says.

"Shut *up*, you guys are the worst," I say with a laugh, and Harper laughs too. Taking another sip of my drink, I place it on the bedside table and fall back onto my bed with a groan. "I mean, why do I even *need* a bodyguard? Isn't that a bit of overkill? It's not like I'm a political figure or anyone important. I know they want to keep an eye on me, but can't *anyone* do that? I'm not Willa Stone or something, needing a security team."

Harper and Jules take that moment to exchange a look, one I'm very familiar with. It's the *do you want to tell our sweet, delusional friend the truth, or should I?*

Jules takes the lead this time.

"Honey, have you seen your messages on social media?"

I roll my eyes. "Oh my god, please. It's just idiots with more time than brain cells to rub together."

"Ava, you've had to file no less than six police reports in the last four months."

I groan, putting my head in my hands. "It's not that serious!"

"Ava," they say in unison, giving me a *be-so-real* look before I sigh.

Okay, so there was the guy who tried to get into the Miss Americana dress rehearsal, proclaiming he loved me and that we were meant to be together. It was a little weird, but he didn't even get past the entrance of the building. I didn't even *see* him.

And yeah, I've had a handful of weird messages on various social media platforms, but doesn't everyone? Jules and Harper have to deal with those, too, and all of the other Miss Americana contestants get them, too. They're harmless. Any messages that contain anything particularly alarming gets reported to the proper authorities, but that's just for a paper trail.

Just in case.

"I hate being under a microscope even more than I already am. I wish I could bring one of you and have you as my bodyguard. Then I'd at least have someone in my corner."

For the first time since the meeting, I let the reality of everything crash into me: Regina and Anne's apparent goal to kick me out, Jaime's irritation with having to follow me around, the idea that this dream is slowly turning less and less enticing. "What if all of this is just a waste of my time? What if I'm miserable the whole time?"

A long beat passes where neither of us speaks, making me nervous.

"You could just quit, you know," Harper says, finally breaking the silence.

"What?" My head moves with her words, but when I look at my friend, her smile is soft, her hand reaching out to pat my leg. Looking at Jules, there's a similar expression on her face.

"You could quit. It wouldn't hurt Jules and me—what you've done for us, Ava, it's...it's been amazing. Life-changing. We'll never be able to properly thank—"

"I don't want a thank you, you know that. It was fun. It was...an adventure. And this trip is going to be an adventure, too." Harper smiles at Jules like they knew this was the decision I'd make. "I'm not letting these dumb bitches scare me out of this trip of a lifetime."

I sit up, pulling out of the momentary pity party with a smile. "I won fair and square; I played by the same rules they all did; just because whoever they thought would win didn't, doesn't mean I didn't earn this."

"There's our girl," Jules says, clapping. "Don't let those assholes win. You're going to have an amazing time no matter what." She sits up, smiling at me. "Okay, so let's talk about all the fun souvenirs you're going to bring us home."

EIGHT

AVA

My first official event for Miss Americana is at Atlantic City Boardwalk with the mayor and the Governor of New Jersey.

Yes, the governor.

This is my life now, I suppose.

But this is also the start of one of my oldest daydreams. When I was young, I read an article about someone who traveled the entire continental US in an RV throughout the summer. They went to every state, seeing all the sights and documenting them all the way. As someone who had never traveled outside of New Jersey, taking all of my childhood vacations at the Jersey Shore with my family, someone who daydreamed about adventures and travel, it seemed like the most fantastic thing someone could ever do.

And now, somehow, this pageant I joined as a bit of a joke is allowing that dream to come true.

How fucking cool is that?

"Okay, so next, we're going to walk over to the oldest restaurant on the Ocean View Boardwalk," the PR manager for the Miss Americana pageant says, looking to the assistant to the governor, who nods in agreement.

"This way!" she says, waving her hand.

Our crowd begins to walk: Regina is up front with the governor, Anne is walking as close to whatever press she can beg to give her three seconds to gab about herself, and Jaime and I trail toward the back of them. He has dark black sunglasses on, his jaw tight as he stares forward, on the lookout like someone is going to pop out from behind one of the dunes and snatch me away.

"Nice day," I say, looking at the sun before sliding a pair of brown tortoiseshell glasses down onto my nose, the lenses in a cat-eye heart shape.

"Mmm," he says, his head never looking toward me as he continues to scan the area as if someone is going to jump out at any moment and try to kidnap me.

I let out a small laugh, pressing on his arm to give him a friendly shove, but he doesn't even move, not the tiniest sway. "You know you can relax a bit, right? We have security for the Governor of New Jersey up there. If someone was a safety risk, it would be him, not me."

Jaime's face doesn't move to look at me when he speaks. Instead, he stares straight ahead, scanning. "My job," he says.

"Did you magically forget how to use full sentences when you realized I was your assignment, or do you just hate me?"

"I don't hate you, I'm just doing my job."

I roll my eyes again, looking at the blue sky with exhaustion. My mouth opens to say something before my name is called.

"Ava!"

It's a kid's voice, and when I turn, a girl, maybe twelve years old, is quickly walking my way with her dad. I slow my steps.

"Ava! I'm a huge fan!"

I turn away from Jaime and the group, moving to the girl with a wide smile.

"I'm so sorry, I told her you were busy," her dad says, an apology written on his face.

"Goodness, no!" I say. "I'm so happy you stopped me to say hi!"

"I'm a huge fan. You're so cool! I've been watching you since you won the New Jersey pageant! I can't believe that was your first one!" She's cute, with wide green eyes and brown curly hair pulled back in a ponytail, a pink T-shirt, and a purple skirt with a pair of white sneakers.

"Oh, god, don't remind me! Did you see me trip up the steps?" I ask with a self-deprecating laugh because I did trip up the stairs during the New Jersey pageant during the interview section. I laughed it off, making a joke about it to the announcer. Some articles attributed that "real" moment to the start of my becoming the sweetheart, fan favorite of the Miss Americana pageant.

Some have even speculated I did it on purpose, and it's pretty fucking embarrassing to have to tell people you aren't nearly as smart as they think you are, just a total klutz.

The girl laughs and nods. "I did, but it made me like you more. I'm pretty clumsy, too." She lifts a pink cast on her arm, which I hadn't noticed before, with signatures all over it.

"Clumsy girls are the best girls. We're having too much fun to worry about silly things like gravity."

She smiles wide before nodding. "I'm starting dance lessons at First Position next week because of you!" she says.

"No way! Oh, my goodness, you're going to have so much fun! Make sure you tell Jules I said hi!"

"I will!" She looks at me and then at her dad, suddenly nervous. "Can we get a picture?"

"Only if you let me sign your cast, too," I say, pulling a Sharpie from my pocket. Giving out signatures has been one of the strangest parts of this new change in my career, but I'm more than happy when it's for cute girls like this one.

Her eyes go wide before she jumps up, clapping. "Oh my god, my friends will be so jealous!"

I laugh, signing my name to the cast before taking a photo. "Can you send me that photo?" I ask, and her eyes go wide as she nods. I give her dad my email so he can send it.

"Bye!" I say with a wave. "I can't wait to hear updates from Jules on your dancing!"

"Thank you, really," the girl's dad says, genuine appreciation in her eyes. He lowers his voice. "She's always being made fun of for her clumsiness—she has dyspraxia, and it makes things a bit harder for her. You just made her day."

My heart warms at his confession. "I'm more than happy. If you ever need anything, you have my email now," I say with the tip of my chin toward his phone. He gives me a smile, and the two return back to where they were before she ran my way.

Jaime and I make our way back to the group. We've almost closed the gap when Jaime initiates a conversation for the first time.

"That wasn't safe, Ava," he says, low and irritated, as we reach the back of the pack.

"What?"

"That wasn't safe. You have no idea if those people had good intentions."

I stop walking all together and look at him, and he keeps walking until he realizes I'm not following. He turns to me, and there's five feet between us as I stand with my hands on my hips. His are crossed over his chest, and for a moment, I wonder what we must look like. It has to be a fun sight—a woman in pink wearing a giant tiara glaring at a burly bodyguard wearing all black.

"Jaime, it was a twelve-year-old girl in a cast and her father. In broad daylight. With the governor a couple yards away. I think I was pretty safe."

"Thinking you're safe is how people get killed, Ava."

"God, you're so dramatic," I say with an eye roll and start walking. "You said it yourself, this is a glorified babysitting job, right? So there's no real danger."

He sighs audibly. "I need you to make my job easy, Ava. Approved people only; if you want to stop, you need to let me know, and I'll decide if it's allowed. That's how we're both going to get out of this without any major issues."

"Yeah, I'm not doing that," I say, flipping my hair over my shoulder to ignore how annoyed I'm getting.

"They could have hurt you."

I give him a look of irritated disbelief. "You're joking, right?"

"I don't joke about safety."

I stare at him, mouth open, before laughing.

"I don't see what's so funny," he says

"Uh, the fact that you saw a twelve-year-old girl and her dad as some kind of crazy security threat?"

"You don't know the shit I've seen, the way people will fake shit just to get close to someone. Not everything in this world is sunshine and rainbows, Ava. Dangerous people are out there."

"I'm not an idiot. I know I look all cute and pink and silly, but I do have two brain cells to rub together. I know there's danger, and believe it or not, I've survived twenty-six years without any major issues. I know you're used to following around mega rockstars, but I'm just a girl who won a contest. Put the crazy away for a bit, use your common sense, and we'll have a grand time this trip, okay?"

"Ava—"

"No. I'm excited for this trip. It's the opportunity of a lifetime for me. I won't let some crazy, overzealous bodyguard ruin that." I take a deep breath, refusing to let this grumpy fucking man ruin my excitement.

"I know you're some kind of stoic asshole, and I know you've been all over the world, but I haven't. I'm going to say hello to people. I'm going to hug little girls who tell me they're inspired by me to start dancing or try their hand at a pageant. Get used to it. Figure out how to work with it—to work with me—because I won't change who I am just because you have some chaotic idea of what is safe and what's not. I'll take common-sense steps to make sure I'm not making your job more difficult, but I need you to do the same." I stare at him, waiting for a response, but his face remains hard and unmoving.

I raise an eyebrow, crossing my arms on my chest. I'm not the kind of girl who backs down. In fact, I'm the kind of girl who fights just for the fuck of it. The kind who will hold onto a grudge just for shits and giggles. Fuck, I won the entire pageant just because Anne was a bitch.

He must see my determination, because eventually he closes his eyes and sighs. "I'm sorry," he says, his voice low, almost too low to hear.

I force myself not to smile. "What was that?" His jaw goes tighter, and I lose the battle of the smile.

"I'm sorry."

I put a hand to my chest and gasp as if he's shocking me. "The big macho Jaime Wilde apologizing? On day one? Did I break you this early?"

"I'm sorry. I'm being a dick. You don't deserve that. You're right; a twelve-year-old girl isn't a threat, and you're here to do a job, just like me. We can set up realistic rules that we both agree to. Just...give me some slack because I'm not used to this."

"This?"

"All of this," he says, waving his hands at me. "The sass. The stubbornness."

I stare at him for long moments, trying to decode the sincerity of his words to better understand what he's saying and what he means, before I decide it doesn't matter. He's making the effort, and I should, too, if only to make this tour easier for both of us.

"Okay, okay. Look, let's make a deal. I'll do my best not to give you too many heart attacks by going off plan with your crazy, neurotic schedules, and you'll give me some slack when it comes to being, well, me. Deal?"

He stares at me the same way I stared at him moments before, assessing me behind those dark glasses before, finally, he nods. "Deal."

A wide smile paints my lips, though it's not a fake pageant smile; it's my real one. "Okay, now, big guy, let's catch up with everyone and eat. I'm starving." I loop my arm in his and start to walk towards the group, and begrudgingly, he follows. When he tries to disengage himself, I hold on tighter. "Nope. You're stuck with me," I say with a wide smile. "You wanted to be glued to my side; now you are. Fish fish, you got your wish."

"You've got to be fucking kidding me," he grumbles. Still, I don't miss how he doesn't continue to fight my hold, instead giving in and shifting to make the grip more comfortable for both of us.

God, this is going to be a fun summer.

NINE
JAIME

This is going to be a miserable fucking summer.

Everything this woman does rubs me in a way that makes me want to simultaneously strangle her and drag her into a room to fuck her until she can't argue with me anymore.

I have no fucking clue why, with everything she does or says, I feel the need to push back and give her a hard time. It's like I *want* her to pull out that sass, to flirt with me and make my dick hard.

When she stopped to talk to that girl, I knew there wasn't a threat. The group ahead of us was walking so slowly that it was not like we were going to lose them.

But something about her complete disregard for her safety makes me want to argue with her. And then she gave the girl's father, who had no ring on his finger and wouldn't stop staring at her tits, her email, and the rage boiled in my veins.

It makes no sense, the way it irritated me, and I should have buried it beneath all my other emotions and kept my mouth shut, but I couldn't help it. It's like some kind of gut instinct to fuck with her just to get her riled up. I can see how Ava fired up, ready to prove me, or anyone, for that matter, wrong about her, could quickly become my favorite thing in the world.

The uncomfortable truth is that no matter how annoyed I am by her, I met Ava Bordeaux in a crowded bar and haven't been able to stop thinking about her since.

But, of course, I can't have her. I can't have the gorgeous, curvy blonde who seems to enjoy pushing my buttons because she's my assignment. Mixing business and pleasure is never a wise decision, and my job is all about weighing the pros and cons of any given action.

Standing in the back of the restaurant, I watch as she sits before looking in each direction with a confused furrow on her brow and then smiling when she finally spots me.

"Come on, Jaime, there's a seat right here for you," Ava says, tipping her head next to her at the end of the booth, an extra plastic-coated menu in front of the seat.

"No, I'm good," I say, leaning against the wall, arms crossed on my chest, sunglasses tucked into my shirt.

"Jaime, sit," she says. When I shake my head no, she scoots out, giving a one-minute finger to the fucking *Governor of New Jersey*, then walks over to me. "Come on. It won't kill you; you can get something other than pizza. Salad or a cheesesteak or sausage and peppers or—"

"I'm not here as a guest, Ava. I'm here to be in the background, to watch your back." She fights a smile before putting on a firm face, and I groan internally, seeing the determination in her eyes.

"You're *my* guest."

"Appreciate it, really, I do, but my job is to be in the shadows and ensure you're safe. Nothing more."

"You can sit with me like a normal human. You're not some kind of dirty secret, Jaime."

"I have a very clear job description."

"To make sure I don't do anything stupid. If you're hiding in a corner, you can't stop me from slandering the company. And I have a conscience. If you're going to be following me around, you're going to be part of the crew, not some weird creeper hiding in the background."

"Ava—" I start with a sigh, but she cuts me off.

"No," she says, hands on her hips. She's cute like this, all bossy and indignant. "Come on, sit at the table."

"I'm not—" I start but don't get the chance to finish because she's tugging on my hand, dragging me back to the table where I very much do not belong.

"Hey, guys, this is Jaime, my driver, bodyguard, and chaperone. You're cool with him eating with us, right?"

Everyone nods, smiles, and continues their conversations like it's not weird that I'm here.

She looks at me, all smug, before elbowing me in the ribs. "See? No big deal. You're not combusting just because you're eating dinner with us, and no one is taking it as a sign that I'm unguarded and coming to get me."

I want to continue to argue. But there's something about Ava that makes me want to do whatever I have to to get her to smile at me like that. Something about her is enticing; she is the kind of person who is having a good time just being alive and makes you want to have a good time as well. The type of person who won't have a good time if *you're* not having a good time. The kind of person who makes it her mission to ensure you have a good time, too.

I sigh, resigning to the fact that this summer is going to be the strangest assignment I've ever been on. This will be a season of firsts, of challenges, and most of all, of her getting under my skin.

"You're going to be a pain in my ass this summer, aren't you?"

"You say pain in the ass, I say fun."

After dinner, when everyone starts to leave, we walk out onto the boardwalk. Ava looks at me, looks at the water, and then bites her lip.

"What is it?" I ask.

She sighs before rambling. "I know you'd rather chew glass than help me—" Ava starts, and I groan.

"Jesus, just spit it out."

"I need help taking pictures. For my social media."

I sigh, but considering I was an ass earlier, starting this trip off on the very wrong foot, I sigh and put out my hand. "Give it to me. You'll have to explain exactly how you want me to do it, though," I say.

She jumps and claps her hands. "Really? You're the best!"

Instead of handing me her phone, she stands close to me so I can smell her sweet perfume and shows me her screen.

"Okay, so hit this," she says, tapping a button to change the dimensions on the screen. "And then hit this to take a photo. But we need angles." She lifts the phone up in the air, then center, then down, miming what she wants me to do. "Literally, just don't stop taking pictures until I tell you, okay?"

I nod, and she moves to the railing of the boardwalk before saying, go, and beginning to pose. She shifts over and over for a minute, and I do exactly what she asks of me before she comes over to me, grabbing the phone and checking them. "Ugh, you're a natural. You've got the job."

"The job?"

"Of being my official photographer on tour." Then she taps the screen again, leans in, and moves her arms out until both of our faces are reflected on the screen. "Smile! Day one of the tour!" She smiles but I stay stoic, confused and utterly uncomfortable in front of a camera, and she laughs after taking a series of photos. "We have to work on that," she says. "You're like a British guard. I've gotta see if I can make you crack."

"Good luck with that," I mumble.

She steps back and smiles wide at me before gently tapping her hand on my cheek. "Oh, big guy, I don't need luck. Trust me."

That is exactly what I'm worried about.

"What's your handle?" she asks, tapping at the screen as we start to walk back down the boardwalk toward the parking lot.

"What?"

"What's your handle?" she asks without looking up, but I look down at her confused, no idea what she's saying. Eventually, she stops walking and looks up at me. "Like for social media?"

"I don't have social media."

"You don't have social media!?" she asks like it's some kind of great offense.

"No," I say, starting to walk again. "No need. It's a giant time suck, and I don't need to see people so into themselves and who needs the world to know their every waking thought."

"But social media is *more* than that! It's amazing. It connects people and inspires and teaches."

"I'm sure it does. It's just not for me."

"Wow. You're like an anomaly. The last person on earth without social media." She steps back, taking another picture of me. "I'm going to submit this to Guinness. You have to be a world record."

I snort out a laugh and shake my head, and she gasps, putting a hand to her chest.

"Oh, my. God. Did I make you laugh on day one too?!"

I roll my eyes at her but don't bother fighting the smile as she places her hand into the crook of my elbow and walks alongside me.

"We are going to be *great* friends, Jaime Wilde."

TEN

AVA

Jaime picks me up bright and early from my apartment and helps me haul my shit down to the SUV. I ended up fitting it all into the two suitcases and one smaller duffel, a purse, and a "car bag" stuffed to the brim. I did my best, really, I did.

When everything is in, I grab my car bag and start to set up the passenger seat for myself, pulling out my fluffy pink blanket.

"What are you doing?" he asks, his hand on the top of the car door, watching me as I drape my blanket over the seat just in case I get chilly.

"What?"

"Get in the car. What are you doing?"

"I'm setting up my seat. We've got, like, a four-hour drive."

Reaching into my bag, I pull out my water bottle and place it in the pocket on the side of the door, followed by a few snacks for easy reach. Finally, I take out a book, my clear and pink pouch with a letter *A* on it stuffed with pens, tabs, and highlighters, my headphones, my Nintendo Switch, and my phone before finally sliding into the seat and buckling in. He continues to stand here, hand-on the doorframe, showing off arms I definitely should not think look delicious.

"A real passenger princess, aren't you?"

"The only real way to travel," I say with a smile.

He rolls his eyes, checking to make sure nothing is hanging out of the car before slamming the door shut.

And then we're off on our adventure.

Jaime is silent as we drive to our first stop in Connecticut. Each time I attempt to start a conversation with him, he grunts out the most basic reply before going completely quiet again, the only noise in the car being the sound of the GPS giving the occasional direction.

Finally, I set down my game and sigh. "I'm bored."

"We've only been in the car for an hour."

"But it's been a *boring* hour."

"You're in for a boring summer if you can't entertain yourself for an hour on a road trip. We'll be doing a lot of driving in the next three months. Weren't you just playing a video game?" he asks, and I frown.

"Yeah, but I need to make a pink flower, and I can't figure it out."

"What kind of game are you playing where you need to make flowers?"

"A cozy faerie game," I say with a smile.

"No wonder you're bored," he says under his breath. and I roll my eyes before shifting in my seat, smiling at the big man beside me.

"Let's play twenty questions."

"What?"

"Twenty questions. I get twenty questions to ask about you."

There's a pause before he responds. "I don't think that's how you play that game."

"We're playing twenty questions, *Ava's version*." He sighs, and it makes me smile wider. Something about knowing I'm getting under his skin makes me giggle and fills me with sunshine.

"Why do you want to ask me questions?" he asks.

"I've decided I want to get to know you, Jaime Wilde."

"What?"

"We're going to be stuck together for the entire summer, a lot of it will be spent with just the two of us. Shouldn't we know a bit about each other?"

"I'm good. I think I know all I need to know about you, and I don't think you need to know anything about me in order to do your job."

I roll my eyes and reposition myself in my seat, staring out the windshield away from him. "God, who hurt you?" I say under my breath.

"What?"

"Clearly, some woman hurt you, and you're taking it out on me. Did she like to do her nails and wear makeup? Was she a girly girl who broke your heart or something?"

"No."

I cross my arms on my chest and shift to glare at him.

"Then why do you hate me so much? What did I do to deserve this overarching generalization that I must be the worst, most irritating person on the planet? I know this isn't the most exciting assignment, but I promise I'm not trying to make your summer a living hell. I'm not *actually* the worst person on earth."

He shakes his head, his eyes locked out the windshield, but I can still see his thick, dark brows furrowing. "I don't... I don't hate you, Ava. I just don't know how I'm supposed to act around you, okay? I'm trying to be... professional."

"Well, I don't think being *professional* is being a dick from day one, but what do I know about bodyguarding? I'm just a...what did you say? A self-centered pageant queen?" I say, quoting his earlier words about me, and he shakes his head gently.

"I shouldn't have said that. It wasn't nice, and now I know it's not true. You just...you get me all kinds of scrambled. My normal assign-ments pretend I'm not there. I'm used to blending in and being with my own thoughts. And then there's you."

"Then there's me...." I start and then smile. "And by that, you clearly mean a wildly beautiful, distractingly witty, and unbearably interesting woman you want to be best friends with?"

"Well, let's not get too far ahead of ourselves now, Princess," he says, and a small smile tips his lips.

"A smile! He smiles! Look at that!" I gasp.

"You've seen me smile, Ava."

"Yeah, but mostly only when I pick on you."

"Is this not you picking on me?"

"No, this is me flirting with you. It's kind of my specialty."

"Probably shouldn't be flirting with your bodyguard," he says.

I reach over, patting his hand. "Oh, you sweet, sweet boy. You have no idea what kind of summer you're in for, do you?"

ELEVEN
JAIME

Our next stop is in Stafford at an ice cream shop. Apparently, it was Miss Vermont's first job and owned by her mother. While we're there, Ava works the counter, scooping ice cream and serving fans. A portion of the proceeds goes to a local cause that Miss Vermont fundraises for.

Ava is smiling and joking the entire time while scooping ice cream terribly. I know ice cream server was *definitely* not ever on her apparently long list of previous jobs. But she is great with balancing it all—joking with the customers and serving them—while managing her Miss Americana duties.

I know she said she'd never been in the pageant world, much less the public eye before, something I confirmed when I researched her after getting the assignment, but she's a natural. It's like she was made to be watched.

I've seen many people trip into the public eye in my years as private security to the stars, and not everyone does it gracefully. Even less do it with minimal issues when it comes to handling the press or answering questions meant to embarrass or catch her in a bad light.

But not Ava.

Eventually, it's time for a taste test. I watch as everyone orders, with Ava forcing me to get a double scoop of chocolate. I don't miss how she diligently looks at the menu before she shakes her head with a small smile, declining. She mumbles something I can't hear—I'm standing far enough to stay out of the shot of cameras, something Ava begrudgingly agreed to.

I've noticed she does this each time we're out to eat, staring at dessert menus with longing, probably calculating calories or whatever, before shaking her head and getting nothing.

It's a reminder of why I *don't* like her and why I *can't* like her. She's too obsessed with appearances—how people will see her—if a single scoop of ice cream will somehow transform her slim body into something the cameras will hate.

While everyone eats, she moves away from the group, sitting next to me and my double scoop. I tip the cup her way.

"Want some?" I ask.

She looks at the chocolate ice cream dripping off my spoon with that same longing before shaking her head. "No, thank you."

"It won't kill you, you know. A few calories."

Her head cocks back in confusion. "What?"

"Ice cream. Or any dessert, for that matter. It won't make you gain a million pounds or whatever it is you've convinced yourself of. I know you're probably used to pageant diets, but—" I don't finish because her laugh fills the area, making heads turn our way, as tends to be her way. Ava's humor and joy are like a flame, and the world is full of moths.

Lately, it seems like I'm the one most willing to get burned.

Her head is tipped back, hair trailing down her back in soft waves as she laughs, the sun bouncing off her skin like that's it's entire job, and I'm enthralled by her.

Finally, she stops laughing and looks at me. "I have a dairy allergy, Jaime."

I sit there, blinking at her, and she shakes her head, still smiling.

"It's relatively new, I found out in the past year or so. It makes me break out in hives. Unfortunately for me, I love ice cream and desserts, but most have some kind of milk, obviously." Her hand lifts, patting my cheek like she finds me entertaining—a sweet little boy who has no clue.

To be fair, it's absolutely how I feel around her.

"I know we keep joking about it, but I'm really *not* some self-centered pageant queen."

Suddenly, I feel like an ass.

She's not wrong: I've been judging her since the very beginning, assuming she was some diva who only cared about herself and her appearance, but never once has she actually reinforced that belief, other than the amount of time she spends getting ready. But even that, she explains, is just something she does because *she* likes it. Not for anyone else.

I think I keep trying to cling to that, to believe it, because if I decide she's not that, I have no fucking shot of keeping this professional.

"I've been trying to tell you I'm not what I appear, Jaime. You just refuse to open your eyes."

A moment passes with her soft hand on my cheek, looking into my eyes, a small smile playing on her lips before I open my mouth to say...I don't know, but I don't have to stress about it because, in that moment, she's called off by someone. She stands, winks at me, and literally skips off to the reporter who called her name.

The woman is a puzzle.

And I am a giant asshole.

TWELVE
AVA

A knock comes on the door of my hotel room, and knowing it's probably Jaime giving me the plan for the next day, I shout, "Come in!" The door clicks with the sound of the digital lock undoing, and I set my book to the side as I sit cozied on the couch, looking up as he enters with three giant bags from different grocery stores.

He walks in silently, looking at me and tipping his chin at me in that cool guy way before moving to the small kitchenette and putting the bags on the counter.

"What are you doing?" I ask as he starts shuffling through the bags I can't see into from the couch. Finally, his head comes up, and he looks at me, a shy smile on his lips as he starts to remove things.

"The chocolate and vanilla from this brand are supposed to be solid," he says, placing two pint containers down, and my brow furrows. "And I got a few from this brand since they make normal ice cream, too, but I think it's going to be kind of hit or miss." He stacks up three more pints from a familiar brand I used to eat before we pinpointed my allergy. Cookie dough, peanut butter chocolate, and a cherry vanilla flavor.

"This brand is really fancy," he says, grabbing it from the bag of a specialty store. "And the flavors are kind of weird, but the reviews are great." He pulls out a few pastel-looking pints. I stand, walking his way and watching as he keeps going.

"And these are sorbets, which are fruit or whatever, so not really ice cream, but I figured it was worth a shot." He puts those next to the others and reaches into the bags one last time.

"These are ice cream bars. I like this brand, not sure if the bars are any good, but they sounded decent. Whichever you like, we can get more of at the next stop. Or we can try more. Figure out what's the best replacement."

He stands there for a long moment, looking at me before he starts shuffling things around, shoving the bags into each other, and stepping away. Looking at him, though, I see it.

A light blush crosses his cheeks, a bit of discomfort but also eagerness, like he hopes I like this simple gesture he just gave me.

"You got me ice cream?" I ask. He nods, but doesn't speak. "Why...why did you do this?" He shrugs, but I don't fill in the awkward silence.

Eventually, he sighs before answering. "You said you like ice cream. You said you *missed* ice cream." I stare at him, not believing it, and eventually, he keeps talking. "I didn't know you had a dairy allergy," he says, beginning his verbal vomit. "I thought you were just a cliché, watching your calories and wishing you could have dessert, but it didn't fit into some kind of contrived diet. I judged you, and I was an ass. Now I'm making it right."

"How were you supposed to know, Jaime?" I ask with a small smile, trying to alleviate the guilt he very clearly feels. "I never told you, never told your firm or anything. I don't really tell many people, really, because I don't want to be difficult. It's not life-threatening or anything, just uncomfortable."

"If we're being honest, I've judged you on a lot of shit, Ava. Not just the ice cream."

"That's not—"

"We both know it's true, and it's fucked. This one? This one I can make amends for. Let me," he says.

Silence takes over the small kitchen as I look from Jaime to the dozen or so pints of ice cream and boxes of bars, then back at Jaime, trying to piece it together to understand what this all means.

But it's so obvious.

"Oh, my god," I say with a realization, leaning against the counter, arms crossed over my chest.

"What?" His face goes slack with panic, then he looks around the living area, suddenly on guard.

"It's just...you really like me, don't you?"

I expect an eye roll and an irritated scoff, but I'm surprised when I don't see it. Instead, another shy smirk comes to his lips, the slight dent of a dimple hitting his cheek.

"You're a pain, you know that?" he murmurs, but it's not a denial.

Progress.

I'll take it.

My hand moves to his shoulder, and I shift to my tiptoes, pressing my lips to his cheek where his dimple is still. "Thanks, big guy," I whisper, meaning it. People don't do this kind of thing for me, and this man being the one to do it feels...special. Jaime let me past his tough guy exterior by doing something as simple as buying me ice cream.

"Anytime, Princess," he says, shifting away to grab spoons, a light blush on his cheeks.

"Will you stay?" I ask, suddenly nervous. "Taste test with me?" I feel silly asking, but I really, really want him to say yes.

And when he nods, starting to open the containers and meticulously lining them up, I let myself imagine that he does it because he wants to spend time with me, too.

THIRTEEN

JAIME

"Ava, we've gotta go," I shout, knocking on her door.

While I wait in the hall, I remind myself that no matter what she says or does, I need to act professionally. I've come to the realization Ava will do whatever it takes to push my buttons, and I have to stop showing her that it works.

Tonight is dinner at some fancy restaurant with Miss Massachusetts, some press, and Anne.

"Come in!" she shouts.

When we arrived at the hotel two hours ago, I got a key to her room as well as mine, just in case of some kind of emergency, before we each went to our own rooms to unwind and get ready for the night. I use it now to let myself in, the door slamming shut as she steps out of the bathroom.

"So," she says with a twirl. "How do I look?" She's wearing a slinky cream-colored dress with light pink silky bows tied on her shoulders as straps and high heels with matching pink bows at the back.

Instantly, my mind wonders if I tug on one of those bows, would the top slip down, revealing her full tits?

"You look…" I sigh, trying to wipe my mind of these uncontrollable thoughts and say something appropriate. *What the fuck is happening to me?* "You look very pretty."

She pouts. "Pretty?"

"Yes, Ava. You look very pretty."

She moves, heels clicking as she walks to the full-length mirror and takes herself in.

"Hmm," she says, turning left, then right in the mirror. "Not good."

"Not good?"

"Not the vibe I'm going for."

"This seems like your exact vibe, Ava."

"On your arm, I'm going for hot, big guy, not pretty."

I close my eyes and take a deep breath before speaking. "You're not going to this event on my arm, Ava."

She rolls her eyes at me, and I think about all those mothers who tell their kids if they keep doing it, their eyes will get stuck that way. I hope they never meet Ava Bordeaux, irrefutable proof that's a fucking lie, considering it seems she does it every five seconds in my presence.

"Okay, listen, we have to have a talk about this bullshit," she says, standing in front of me, face fierce, hands on her hips, and glaring up at me.

It takes everything in me to fight the smile because, fuck, she looks adorable like that, like an angry pixie. I bet if she put on the costume, she'd look like a dead ringer for Tinkerbell.

Instead, I raise an eyebrow in a *go-on* way and wait for her to continue.

"I don't care how this job normally works for you. I don't care if you normally just sit in the shadows on the lookout. That's not how *I* roll. I already told you you're not following me around for three months like a creep. You're not sitting in a corner when we eat meals. You're going to have a fun summer, too, do the fun stuff with me." She stops, thinking, before adding more. "Maybe think of yourself as my companion more than anything. You're here to keep me safe, yes, but also to keep me company. Be my friend."

"That's not how this job works, Princess," I say as soon as she's done with her tirade. "I know what I signed up for, and that's not it."

"Well, you better prepare for something new and different."

"My boss pays me well to be invisible. Clients want it, and I promise it's what you want."

Something in her face changes in the blink of an eye, going from joking and assertive to self-conscious and nervous.

"Look, Jaime. I got into this by accident. This isn't some goal I've had in my life. Now, don't get me wrong, it's an adventure, and I'm so excited to be here. I love to travel, love to see new things, so getting *paid* to do it is absolutely insane and crazy and fun. But I'm going to be lonely. I also don't really know *any of* these people. At all of the events before the actual pageant, I was the odd man out because all these girls knew each other ahead of time; they'd been in these pageants together for years. I didn't know a single one of them. Having someone—anyone—that I know and can talk to when it gets weird would really make me feel a lot better."

The sincerity in her face cracks something in me, as does the pleading in her voice that, against my best judgment, I give her an offer. "You get nervous, you feel uncomfortable, you come back and hang with me until you're ready to go back, okay?"

"Great, appreciate that, really, I do, but again, I'm not having you sit in the corner like the hired help while I eat or have fun. That's weird as fuck and makes me itchy."

"Ava, my boss would never approve—"

"Let me talk to him," she says.

My brows furrow, and her face has somehow become even more determined and stubborn. "What?"

Her hand goes out like she is asking for something. "Give me your phone; I'll call your boss and talk to him."

"No," I say firmly. She is *not* talking to Greg. The man will eat her alive.

"What's he going to do, bite? I just want to talk to him, explain my side. If he insists you're not allowed to hang with me, I'll accept it. I'm a pain in the ass and pushy, but I wouldn't put your job at stake," she says, like it's obvious.

I weigh my options for a moment in my head before shrugging, unlocking my phone, and handing it to her. "His name's Greg. Probably my last call."

"God, your phone is so boring. You don't even have fun apps or a background," she says with horror, then taps the contacts icon and finds Greg easily. "And there's only like five contacts in here."

"Can we stop hyperanalyzing my phone and just call my boss so we can get to dinner?"

She smiles wide before hitting call and lifting the phone to her ear. It rings for just a moment before she smiles again.

"Hi, Greg, is it? Yes, my name is Ava Bordeaux, Jaime's new assignment, we met briefly. No, no, he's totally fine; he's standing right in front of me." She looks down at her feet, blonde hair sliding down to cascade around her face. "So we're on our way to our event for the day, but we had a bit of an argument in Jersey that I want some clarification on." A deep, throaty laugh leaves her chest, and her head tips back with it.

Greg, asshole Greg, is making Ava laugh like that?

"No, he's a total gentleman, no need to worry. It's just that when we were all sitting to eat, he refused to sit at the table with us, saying he needed to lurk in the corners to watch us."

"I did not say that exactly," I say loudly, hoping Greg can hear me.

Her smile widens. "Yes, that was him. But personally, I think it's kind of weird to be enjoying myself and have him just being a bored rando in the corner, you know? So I politely requested—" I scoff, and she rolls her eyes at me. "He sit with me or partake in whatever event is going on. Otherwise, it feels weird and very diva-like, which I totally am not, you know?"

I raise an eyebrow at her, but then she laughs out loud, and once again, I wonder what the fuck Greg said to make her look like that.

"No, exactly! He's so hard-headed. He told me if he *ate pizza* with us, it would be unprofessional, and that was why he had to hide in the corner. I told him he was being ridiculous." She listens with a smile, eyes locked on me, and I think, somehow, she's won over Greg in three seconds.

How the fuck does this woman do that?

"Okay, so to clarify, Jaime has to do whatever I say within reason and participate in activities, or, God forbid, eat with me, which will not put his job in jeopardy?" I close my eyes and breathe in deep. "Perfect, thank you so much for clearing that up for me!" A pause before she shakes her head, twirling a lock of her hair around her finger. "He's a complete gentleman, Scout's honor." She starts to pace with my phone, and I watch her as she moves, looking at her feet, listening intently.

"Absolutely. And thanks so much, Greg, so sorry to bother you." Her head pops up and she stares at me with a wide smile. "Oh, definitely. I'd love to give you my number just in case you need it."

Jesus fucking Christ.

She rattles off her number with a laugh and then says a warm goodbye, like my boss is an old friend, before tapping to end the call and handing it over to me.

"You're stuck with me, big guy. Turns out, your assignment is to chaperone me to everything." I close my eyes and take in a deep breath. "Don't worry, I won't make you do anything crazy, but I'm not being some crazy woman who has her security stand in the corner, watching everyone like they're going to attack me at any moment."

"You never know—"

"And you'll be at my side, so if something *does* happen, you're close by, right? Seems like a win-win all around."

I want to argue.

I want to call Greg and ask why the fuck he gave in to her.

But something tells me that even though she's all pink princess energy, she's a rottweiler when she wants something.

And for some reason, this is what she wants.

So, instead of arguing, I sigh and nod, pulling a wide, wide smile for her. She jumps and then claps her hands three times excitedly before stepping closer and looping her arm around mine.

"All right, buddy. Let's go to dinner."

FOURTEEN
JAIME

It's been a full week on tour with Ava, and everything has been going as smoothly as could be expected. It seems we've come to some kind of truce where she doesn't try to drive me up a fucking wall at every opportunity, and I try to quell my urge to be a standoffish dick at all times.

The system isn't perfect, but she hasn't given me that annoyed face in a while—the one where she puts her hands on her hips and glares at me—so I'm calling it a win.

Each event goes as smoothly as I can expect, with Ava staying on her best behavior and not running off to talk to any random stranger or behaving in some crazy way that would shine a poor light on the organization. As an additional bonus, even though she's insisted on having me take part in the entire event, including the pottery painting in Rhode Island and rock climbing in Massachusetts, she's cut back on the flirting.

Maybe she just needed to get more comfortable with me; maybe it was just a defense mechanism since I was being such an ass and making her think I hated her.

Whatever it is, I'm grateful, and it's going to make this assignment much easier.

"I need to use the bathroom," I say, leaning down to say the words quietly. "Stay here. There's a guard right there, one of the Five Star men, if you need anything at all," I say, tipping my chin at the man standing near a door at a non-profit fundraiser Willa Stone, another client of Five Star, is also attending in New Hampshire.

Ava salutes, the smile on her lips doing something to me. "Sir, yes, sir," she says.

Instead of responding, I turn and walk away, knowing better by now than to encourage her.

When I come back to the room, the number of people has greatly reduced, despite my only being gone for a few moments. Unfortunately, when I scan the room, I don't see pink and feathers.

"Where the fuck is she?" I grumble, moving toward Miss New Hampshire, the last person I saw her speaking with. "Hey, have you seen Ava?" I ask.

Her head swivels around the room. "I haven't. I was talking with her a few minutes ago, then she looked out the front door and said she'd be right back."

Something in my gut churns, a panic building at losing Ava. Where the fuck was the other guard? When I look around, I see him in a corner, flirting with some chick, and my hands ball up into fists.

"You've got to be fucking kidding me," I say to myself, then give a smile to the pageant queen, thanking her for her help before moving toward the large glass double doors with a street and sidewalk visible.

I'm going to fucking kill her.

Stepping out to the front of the restaurant, I look around and see...nothing.

There are a few people wandering, but none look like they're from the event, much less Ava. I move, jogging down the street with my eyes scanning and a million thoughts of what could have happened to her running through my mind.

Someone kidnapped her.

Someone hurt her.

Someone has her cornered, and she's in trouble.

She's scared.

Something about that one makes my stomach drop—the idea of sweet Ava with her wide smiles and her sweet flirting scared.

As I run, every worst-case scenario pounds through my mind, but I see nothing. After a few minutes, I turn, run in the other direction, and stop in the restaurant again.

"Jake!" I shout at the other security guard, who is still fucking flirting. His head moves my way, and he slowly walks toward me, not a care in the world.

"Hey man, what's—" he starts with a smile, stopping when he sees my face. "What's wrong?"

"What the fuck's wrong? I told you to watch my mark for two fucking minutes, and now Ava's missing."

"Ava?" It takes everything in me not to hit him, but I don't have time for that, so I don't. "Miss Americana. Jesus Christ."

A bit of color drains from his face, and he looks over his shoulder, checking to see if his mark, Willa Stone, is still in the building. He relaxes when it's confirmed.

How the fuck is Greg threatening my job when he's employing assholes like this?

"Have you done a search?" he asks like I'm a fucking moron. He can't be older than twenty-five, and again, I have to wonder what kind of idiots my new boss is hiring because I know he wasn't someone Hank hired before he sold the company.

"Jogged a quarter mile that way," I say with a tip of my head. "Going the opposite way next. Can you just do a search of the immediate area?"

"Of course, of course. On it," he says.

Without another word, I leave the building, heading the way I haven't checked yet. I'm trying to think of the next steps, who I need to call, and what to tell the police when I hear it.

"You're a good girl, aren't you?" a voice says quiet and sweet, and my feet stop moving altogether, looking 360 degrees to find where the voice is coming from, but there's nothing. No one.

For a moment, I think I imagined it in my panic before I hear her voice again.

"Oh my goodness, you're just so sweet!"

I turn to my left, spotting a small alleyway three buildings down from the restaurant.

"Come on, let's go find the big guy," Ava's voice says, and then suddenly, golden blonde hair catches the light, a pink bow holding it back. I move quicker, closing the gap between us.

"Where the fuck were you?" I say, stepping closer to her and grabbing her elbow, moving her with a little force, though I want to absolutely shake the woman.

I guide her toward the restaurant, seeing Jake, the dipshit, on the sidewalk, hands on his hips, looking around as if he's going to find Ava that way.

"I got her," I say, and he nods.

"Sorry, man, I—"

"Not a word," I say.

"Please don't tell Greg, man," he starts.

"Get your shit together. Go find your assignment and make sure she's safe. And for the love of fuck, stop flirting with chicks while you're on the clock," I say, and he nods, panic in his eyes, but he doesn't move. "Now. We're leaving."

"Of course, see ya, man. Sorry," he says, then runs back into the restaurant where I can see Willa chatting with someone through the window.

Sighing, I once again guide Ava to the parking lot.

"Hey, what the hell? I wanted to say goodbye to everyone!" she pouts, holding her big bag close to her body.

"Everyone thinks you're fucking missing because you couldn't follow one fucking instruction."

"Oops," she says through a cringe of a smile. "My bad." It's clear she doesn't think this is a big deal, that she often gets out of trouble with a cute smile and a faux apology.

Unfortunately for her, I don't find this or her disappearing act cute.

"This is why we listen when I say to stay in place. You got your shit?" I ask. She looks at the giant bag over her shoulder with hesitation, then nods before I navigate her in silence until we reach the SUV. Unlocking the door, I open it to let her inside.

That's when I see it.

A tiny pair of...ears pop up in her bag.

I stare at the ears, then at Ava, then back to the ears, a dull orangey color, then back at Ava before closing my eyes, rubbing a hand down my face, and taking a deep breath.

"What the fuck is that?" I ask, my body exhausted to the bone as I stare at the bag over her shoulder where the head of a tiny cat with bent ears is poking out, big eyes wide, looking around like this isn't weird at all.

A cat.

In her bag.

"The reason I went missing?" she asks in question with a nervous smile. "My new mascot?" Instantly, I shake my head. "Oh, absolutely the fuck not."

Ava's eyes go as wide as the cat's as she pouts. "Come on, she's so cute! And she was all alone. I couldn't just leave her!"

"You absolutely could have. You should have. Now we need to find a shelter—" I say, pulling out my phone again. The woman is going to be the end of me, that much is for sure.

"No!" she says, tugging the bag closer and, in turn, the kitten. "No. I'm keeping her."

My head moves to look at her again. "The fuck you are."

"Just look at her!" She lifts the grimy, dirty kitten out of her bag, holding it like it's a baby rather than a grimy cat she found on the street. "She's just a baby! She needs a mom!"

"Her mom was probably in the fucking alleyway where you kidnapped her from."

Suddenly, she goes from eager to annoyed in the blink of an eye.

"I did not kidnap her, thank you very much. She came right up to me, walked into my hand, and jumped into my bag. Clearly, she wanted to be with me."

"How did you find her?"

"I saw her scurry across the sidewalk," she says with a cringe. "I know, I know you told me to stay, but just look at her. She's so sweet."

"We have to call a shelter," I say.

Her eyes go wide and pleading, a hand reaching out as she grabs me, stopping my hand from moving anymore. "No, Jaime. No! Please. I love her. I need her. She was meant to be mine! She fits the entire aesthetic."

I take a deep breath. "You can't just keep a stray cat because she fits your aesthetic."

"Why not?"

"Because...you can't. And what if she's someone else's cat, Ava?" I ask, my voice a bit softer because she's getting upset now, eyes going wide and watering, and I don't need a crying woman on my hands.

It's absolutely not because she's endearing and I don't like that sad look on her face.

"I'll bring her to a vet tonight! We're off anyway, we don't have a rush. You said we won't leave for the next stop until tomorrow afternoon. I'll bring her to a vet, and they'll scan her for a chip or whatever. But just look at her, Jaime. Do you really think this is someone's house pet?"

The kitten is underfed, dirty, and has a cut on her ear. It's clear, at the very least, she's been out on the streets for a good part of her short life.

"Please, Jaime?" Somehow, her big blue eyes go wider, her pout getting bigger, and it's like she's putting a spell on me.

I sigh, my entire body going loose. "Are you fucking kidding me?" I ask, but this time I ask it to the sky.

God doesn't answer.

I tip my head back down and look at Ava for long moments, trying to weigh my options before I sigh again and speak. "Find a vet."

"Really!?" she says, excitement filling her face.

"We're on the road by 4 p.m. tomorrow," I say with a glare, my attempt at being stern that I'm sure goes right over this woman's head. "If you can't get that...thing situated by then, she goes to a shelter."

"Jaime, I can't just give her up. Look how much she loves me."

"And she'll love whoever gets her from the shelter if you can't ensure she doesn't have any kind of fucking disease."

One hand goes to her hip, the other holds the cat, and she stares me down. "But if she doesn't, you're saying I can keep her?"

I feel as if she's a little kid who found a stray and is begging her parents to let her keep it, but I guess that's what's happening. I stare at her, her eyes wide with pleading, then to the kitten, somehow already asleep in her hands.

"Jesus fucking Christ." I shift my gaze back at her once more, her face full of excitement and hope.

I can't crush her.

And really, how much work could a kitten be?

"Yeah. You can keep her if she's healthy," I say with a begrudging sigh.

She jumps, waking the cat in her arms, squealing and looping one arm over my neck, holding me close. The smell of brown sugar and vanilla swirls around me as she presses her body to mine, then her lips to my cheek.

"Thank you, Jaime."

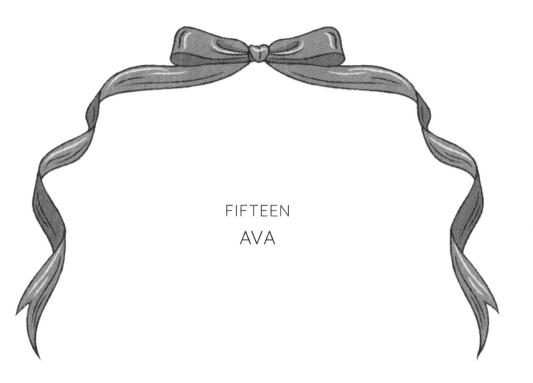

FIFTEEN
AVA

By some kind of magic, I get a vet appointment that night. Jaime drives us both to the office, where I'm told to leave her overnight for some tests and to get a few cuts cleaned and stitched up. Some of the tests won't be in for a few days, but the vet agreed to expedite any she could, promising she'd let me know if it was safe to take Princess Peach on tour with us by noon.

Luckily, she gets cleared for our big adventure. It turns out she's actually a very sweet, very undernourished six-month-old kitten who was probably born on the streets but, to her trained eye, seems relatively healthy otherwise.

When we walk out of the vet smiling (me) and purring (Peach), Jaime glares as he opens the door for me.

"So she's all clear? Nothing crazy or contagious?" Jaime asks as I put the soft-sided cat carrier the vet gave me on the floor of the SUV.

I bite my lip and turn, smiling at him, cat in hand. With my eyes in wide puppy-dog mode and Peach's sweet little face, he can't be *that* mad, right?

"I mean, she doesn't have rabies or fleas or ringworm or anything," I say.

"Ava..." he starts, voice low and rumbling.

"Okay, okay, she has worms! It's no big deal, really, and since she's one hundred percent my responsibility, you wouldn't even *know* if I didn't tell you. She's got medicine that's gonna get her all fixed up in no time."

He stares at me unimpressed before speaking. "I thought we had a deal: no illnesses and she can come."

I wave my hand at him like he's overreacting. "Even the vet said it's no big deal, and she's cleared to come with us. She even congratulated me on being such good person, rescuing this poor little baby."

"Ava, the thing has *worms*."

"She's not a thing, she's a kitten. And it's just some tummy troubles," I say. "Like mother, like daughter." I lift her so her sweet little head is next to mine. "All the best girls have tummy issues, Jaime." He continues to look at me deadpan, a glaring match in progress, before Peaches lets out a tiny meow, and it happens.

His face softens the tiniest bit, his mouth going less firm and angry before he sighs, checks to make sure nothing is hanging out of the door, then slams the door shut before walking around to the driver's side, and all I can do is smile.

When Jaime slides in, he starts the car before he tips his head to the backseat. "I got a few things to get you through until tomorrow." His cheeks are a bit pink, and I wonder if the sun has heated him, but when I look back, I gasp in delight at three filled-to-the-brim bags from a chain pet store.

"Oh my god," I whisper, then turn to look at him with a small smile on my lips. "You knew we were keeping Peach from the start. You weren't going to let me leave her behind, were you?"

His blush deepens. "No, I just figured if she *was* cleared to come with us, we'd need things, and the pet store might close before we hit our next stop." He looks at me for a split second before looking forward again. "It really wasn't a big deal. Kind of part of my job. The guy in the store said that litter box should work for travel, and we can just dump it as needed, and I wasn't sure what kind of food she would need…"

I might have been able to agree if he'd gone and got the bare minimum. I'd be able to believe that this man was just doing his job by getting whatever I needed to get me on the road and to keep our schedule in tact.

But these are *not* the bare essentials.

This is not a couple of cans of cat food and a litter box.

This is…half of the store.

Shifting to look better at the haul, there are at least four or five brands of food, two litter types, a litter box, and the most entertaining part: an overflowing bag filled with toys.

Pink toys, purple toys, mouse-looking toys, balls and laser pointers, and a fish on a stick to dangle in front of her.

"Did you leave anything?

"What?" he asks, eyes diligently on the road as he pulls out of the vet's parking lot.

"At the pet store. Did you leave anything, or did you buy it all?"

The blush creeps down his cheeks to his neck.

"Shut up," he grumbles, and I lift Peach to my face until we're eye to eye.

"Oh, he so likes us, Peach," I say with a smile, and Jaime just groans. I put her back into my lap to settle in the blanket there, but as soon as I let go, she stands, walking on unsteady legs across the console.

"Stay here," I say, picking her up and putting her on my lap again. Again, she stands and walks across the console, this time meowing as she does.

"Peach, no," I say, grabbing her. Unfortunately, as soon as she's in my lap, she tries to move to get to Jaime again. I sigh. "Maybe I should put her in the—"

Before I can finish my sentence, a big hand moves, his eyes never leaving the road as he grabs the small kitten out of my lap and places her in his. Instantly, she stops meowing and settles in his lap.

"Sorry," I say, reaching over to try and grab her, but his hand moves up, blocking me.

"It's fine," he says, his hand scratching Peach's head. It's comical how big his hand looks next to the cat, and I have to roll my lips between my teeth to stop the laugh bubbling in my chest. "You're a sweet girl, aren't you Peachy girl?" he murmurs low.

I stare at him for long moments, watching him drive with one hand and pet my kitten with the other, completely at peace, before I sit back with a smile.

After our next rest stop, where we successfully get Peach to use the litter box and eat before she falls asleep in Jaime's lap again, I'm reading when he speaks. "If we play twenty questions, do I get any?"

I put down my book, confused, before looking at him. His gaze is fixed on the road, avoiding looking at me. "What?"

"The other day, you wanted to play twenty questions, and I shot you down. If we play now, do I get to ask any?"

I fight a smile, trying to act casually like he's a wild animal I'm afraid to scare off.

"Uh, yeah. Sure."

"All right. Let's do it."

We filter through a few easy questions, where I learn he doesn't have a favorite color (shocker), and just like me, he didn't go to college after high school. I tell him about how, even when I was a kid, I couldn't pinpoint what I wanted to be when I grew up, waffling from an astronaut to a makeup artist to a marine biologist to an actress.

"Why are you doing this?" he asks eventually.

"Doing what?"

"The pageant. I get that you never did one before, but people don't really stumble into this kind of thing. What made you try?"

"What, you didn't look me up before we got on the road?" I ask with a smile.

"I've seen the press' version of why you got into this, but they all have an angle they're working. I want to hear *your* version."

I like that.

I like that he wants to hear what *I* have to say on the topic rather than trusting journalists and whatever story best suits their readership, some making me a villain, others making me into some martyr out to change the industry, when really it's none of those.

"Well, I applied because I'm impulsive and I wanted to help my friends," I start. "My best friends own businesses, and they were struggling. We were hanging out and venting, and I decided to find a way to promote them. I stumbled on an ad for the pageant, and....I don't know. It kind of spiraled from there."

My mind moves back to that night, lying on my bed and drinking wine while Harper and Jules complained about not knowing how to promote their businesses.

"I just...I just need one person to collaborate with to get my name out there. It seems like that's the key these days. You need some social media clout, and then you're gold." Harper sighs, flopping back onto the white lace duvet on my bed before rolling onto her belly and propping her chin in her hands. "And I'm just so...bad at it."

She is. Not because she's not the sweetest, kindest human on this planet, but because Harper has absolutely crippling social anxiety, making owning her own business where she needs to hype herself up a near impossibility.

"I get it," Jules says with a sigh, swirling her glass filled with some sweet concoction meant to continue the buzz we've been stoking for hours. "The studio is doing okay, but I'm barely filling two classes a day."

For as long as I've known Jules, she's wanted to use the small inheritance her grandmother left her to open a dance studio. Last year, she found the cutest location and jumped on it. She teaches kids lessons and runs adult fitness classes, but it isn't growing the way she hoped it would.

I sigh, hating to watch my friends struggle.

"You guys need some kind of...in," I say, scrolling on a social media app mindlessly. "A celebrity or some influencer. Someone in the area you can do posts with and tag all the time."

"Yeah, I'll just go into my phone now and call one right up," Jules says sarcastically, and I roll my eyes.

"I know it's easier said than done, but I just meant one person could be the answer for the both of you." My mind keeps moving, trying to put pieces that are just out of reach together. Tapping on the search bar, I type in a few keywords—New Jersey dance influencer— and press go before scrolling. A few of the names and faces look familiar from one of the many reality shows they tried to make in the state.

"What about the C-listers that post incessantly? Like local celebrities?" I ask, an idea starting to form in my mind. We could easily get a list together and send out some feelers for collaborations. I'd even be happy to do it for Harper and Jules, since they either don't have the time or energy to do it themselves.

"What about them?" Harper asks, confusion written on her face.

"If you could design some pieces for one to wear to events or something, it would be a perfect fit. They'd be tagging you for wearing your dresses. Since their fan base is usually hyperlocal, meaning if one of them has a birthday or a wedding or just a special occasion, they'd have your name in their mind for who to hire." I turn to Jules. "And you, you could mention so and so trains at your studio or are taking classes there. Angle it as a trendy new way to work out, which is what you're going for anyway, right?"

If I was interesting at all, I'd put all of my energy into being an influencer myself just so I could promote my friends' businesses, but no one really finds much interest in a bartender with little to no real social life.

And then I see it.

Miss Americana Pageant—now accepting applications!

It can't be that easy, can it? Fill out an application and then you're in?

I click the ad, and upon reading more, I find it is pretty much that simple, so long as your application is accepted. But if there's one thing I'm great at, it's making a killer application. I start putting in my name and address, answering the questions about life goals and ambitions with renewed vigor. This could be the perfect way to help out my friends.

Pageant queens need fancy dresses and a talent.

Best case scenario, I make it to the New Jersey pageant, and I get to tag Harper and Jules as they make a dress and help train me in whatever dance Jules decides would be best to showcase her talent. Worst case scenario, it's a funny story of the time I tried to enter a beauty pageant.

"What are you doing over there?" Harper asks, and I realize the room has gone quiet, my friends watching me intently.

"Applying for Miss Americana."

There's a pause before Jules asks, "Do I even want to know?"

"Probably not," I say as I finish filling out the form, hit submit, and promptly forget about it until a week later when an email hits my inbox.

You're invited: Miss Americana New Jersey Auditions.

And the rest was kind of history.

"Did it work?" Jaime asks, knocking me out of my memories.

"What?"

"Did it work? Helping your friends?"

"Oh, yeah for sure. Jules has all of her classes booked, and she even hired a second instructor to help out. Harper is booked out on custom gowns for almost a year. It's amazing," I say with pride.

"And you?"

"What about me?"

"What did you get from this? It seems like it's taken over your life."

I don't tell him that's another question when it should be my turn, instead I shrug.

"I don't know. The joy of seeing my friends thrive?" He quickly looks at me with a glare that screams bullshit, and I change my answer with a smile. "It's been a grand adventure and I love adventures. And I've always wanted to travel but never had the money or time. So it's an opportunity I couldn't refuse."

"But?"

"But...it's rough when you're faced with an entire organization that wants to change you, who doesn't like who you are. The pressure the organization puts on these women is insane. And Regina wants me to be...this perfect little doll who just does what she's told and keeps her mouth shut."

"Then she clearly doesn't know you." The words come quickly and with a bite of surety and a hint of irritation.

"What?"

"They clearly don't know you at all. Because they'd know how stubborn you are," he says with a tip of his lips, and I smile too. Then, his hand moves from Peach's head to squeeze my knee. Even through my thick sweats, I can feel it like a burn, his hand on my body. "And because if they knew you, they wouldn't be trying to change you, Ava. You're perfect the way you are."

SIXTEEN
AVA

"Are you ready?" His voice is gruff and annoyed from outside my room and I can't help but smile. I've been done getting ready for nearly five minutes now, just sitting here scrolling on my phone.

We're on the third week of our tour and I've learned quite a bit about my new, temporary best friend.

One, he absolutely hates when I tell him he's my new bestie, hence why I've started to sprinkle the term of endearment into my conversations even more.

Two, he has a thing about being aggressively early for everything, so sometimes, I like to spend a little extra time getting ready just to push it. He usually gets to my room about an hour before he tells me I have to be ready, at which point I let him in and lock myself in the bathroom until I'm done. We're at least a good twenty minutes early for everything, but not being *forty minutes* early annoys him just enough to bring me joy.

Three, he finds my primping completely unnecessary and much too timely, not that I care at all. I like getting pretty. Some people meditate, some workout, some journal—I spend time in the bathroom alone, listening to my favorite music and getting dolled up.

"Just about!" I say, moving around some things on the counter to make noise and smiling as I do.

"I know you're just fucking with me, Ava, you're not even doing anything." Finally, I open the door and smile at him.

"You got me." Walking to the table, I grab the small bag I packed earlier with the essentials, then turn to look at him. "Let's hit it." He doesn't move; instead, he gives me a top-to-toe look that heats my body. I force myself to move from where I stand, smiling and moving toward the door, but I eventually pause when he doesn't follow.

"Is that what you're wearing?" he asks.

"Yeah, you like?" I twirl to make my short pink tennis skirt flare out, revealing the barely-there shorts underneath, then adjusting the white sports top. There's a good three-inch gap between the waist of the skirt and my top, leaving a swatch of bare skin, and the pads in the bra make my boobs look fantastic, if I do say so myself. Add a pair of cute little bows to the ties of my low pigtails and some gold jewelry, and the outfit is *perfection*.

"There isn't much to it," he says, crossing his arms on his chest.

I roll my eyes at him and close the gap between us. "That's why I like it."

"Not safe, going out like that when you don't know what kind of creep you'll run into." I give him a soft, chiding smile.

"Isn't that your job? To protect me or whatever? You know, some of us like to look cute and don't feel the need to wear black everything all the time."

"We're going on a hike up a mountain."

"Yeah, and?" I ask, slightly confused, even though I absolutely know where he's going with this. "I go hiking in this all the time."

"You? Hiking?"

I cross my arms on my chest and roll my eyes. This is not a new refrain, and when I get to a trail in my cutesy little outfits, there's almost always at least one man who looks at me and attempts to give me some kind of macho 'this trail isn't for little girls, sweetie,' talk, but I just smile and flutter my lashes and thank them for their concern. Then I smile wide as I pass their panting asses an hour or two later.

"Yes, Jaime, I go hiking. It's my favorite form of exercise. Fresh air, seeing the mountains, nature? Nothing like it." His brow furrows in confusion.

"I thought you danced?"

I laugh, shake my head, and walk toward the door to leave, waving at Peach curled up on the bed as I do. "Bye, Peach!" I call to her, then turn back to Jaime. "God, no. I learned three dances for the pageant, but I'm far from a dancer. I told you, I joined on a whim, won by accident."

"I don't think you won by accident. Saw your routine, some clips. You tried, worked hard, earned it." He closes the door behind us, and I gasp, putting a hand to my chest.

"So you're saying you looked me up," I say with a smile, skipping ahead of him in the hallway. "I don't think that's part of the job description."

"I have one job, Ava. It's to keep you safe. Part of that is looking into you."

"You so like me, Wilde," I say over my shoulder.

He doesn't respond, but, then again, he doesn't have to.

A couple hours later, we're hiking up a trail with Miss Maine, Sarah, the owner of the guided hiking tour business we're highlighting, Anne, Tina, the PR manager for the organization, and a press crew. The weather is perfect, and Jaime and I are trailing toward the end of the pack. I'm pretty sure Tina would rather I be up front where the press is, talking up the pageant and my mission, but Anne is already there keeping them more than enough company.

In my opinion, the point of this tour is to highlight women-owned businesses in the states we visit, so I'd much rather Sarah spend some time promoting herself instead. Plus, being in the back means I get to walk next to Jaime who has kept his eyes diligently ahead, pointing out any rocks or tree roots I might trip on, just in case.

"You know, I think this way there's a cliff with a lookout point," I say conspiratorially, tipping my head to the left where there's a small sign reading *Lookout* with an arrow.

"Mm," Jaime says, his sunglasses covering his face and guarding his expression. I'd scouted out the trail ahead of time, noting that the location we were headed toward was gorgeous overlooking a ravine, but there was another, smaller area with gorgeous views not on the itinerary.

What a perfect coincidence we're passing it now.

"We should sneak away," I say. "They won't even notice. I could get a cute little pic at the lookout and—"

"No."

"What?"

"No, you're not leaving this trail. We're sticking to the schedule. Plus, the lookout trail is taped off." He says it like I'm an idiot and missed the yellow caution tape. But unless it's on a crime scene, I always see that kind of thing as a suggestion. Like, *use caution when you go down this trail.*

"It's just a suggestion," I say with a roll of my eyes.

"It's not, and you're not going. Recent storms have degraded the lookout point, making the area smaller to stand on." I saw that as well while searching, but it didn't say it was impossible to stand on, just that crowds were discouraged.

"Have you always been this boring?"

"Yes," he replies instantly, and I roll my eyes.

"Come on. It would be a quick little diversion. Please?" I give him best puppy dog eyes, but they fail because he's not even deigning to look at me. "Fine. I'm just going to go on my own then." I speed up and move a bit toward the turn-off up ahead.

"Absolutely not," he says, voice firm. I turn around, walking backward, and smiling at him as I do.

"A quick little detour. Nothing crazy."

"Stay on the trail, Ava," Jaime says through gritted teeth.

"Or what?" I ask, with a small smile on my lips.

"Or what?"

"Stay on the trail or what, Jaime?" Even through his sunglasses, a million answers cross his face, as if he can't decide how to answer. I wish he'd give me his first thoughts rather than working them through seventeen filters before letting one through. I think things would get a whole lot more interesting if he did.

"Empty threats," I whisper before I look behind him, then turn to look forward to where the other girls are distracting the media.

The perfect chance for space. Freedom.

I smile wide at Jaime, and then I *run*.

SEVENTEEN
JAIME

One moment, Ava is walking backward in front of me, smiling wide and teasing me as seems to be her way, and the next, she's gone, her pink skirt drifting up on the breeze as she speeds down a smaller trail.

"Ava!" I say, trying not to catch the attention of the paparazzi in front of us but also trying to stop her. All I need is for Greg to find out I let my assignment run off on my watch and for a newspaper to splash it everywhere.

Lookout implies a cliff, and the way Ava is, I wouldn't be surprised if her impulsivity got her hurt one day. My luck, it would happen on my watch.

I can see the headlines now: *Miss Americana Sweetheart Dies a Gruesome Death After Fleeing Bodyguard.*

With that image in mind, I make a split decision and run after her.

I move quickly, pivoting off the trail and toward her, but she's faster than I would have thought. She weaves between trees, the little bows in her hair bouncing with each graceful step she takes over rocks and dodging low-hanging branches. She keeps looking over her shoulder at me, smiling as she does, and each time, it both angers me and turns me on in a way it *absolutely* should not.

The trees open up ten feet ahead of her, and beyond that, it looks open, sending my heart thundering as she continues to look over at me instead of forward.

"Ava, stop!" I say louder this time, not worried about anyone hearing. "Slow down!"

"Catch up, old man!" She breaks past the trees, and there's fifty, maybe one hundred feet of stone before it ends, leaving open air.

Something snaps in me, my legs pumping faster as I bolt toward her. I'm no longer thinking about a headline, my job, or Greg's disappointment if something happens. I'm just thinking about Ava, gorgeous, pretty, sweet Ava, getting hurt.

If she won't worry about her well-being, I'll have to do it enough for the both of us.

She slows as I near, jumping and twirling and twisting like she's doing one of the dances her friend taught her on a stage instead of at the edge of a cliff, and each move, each turn of her sneaker in loose stones has me panicking. One wrong slip, and—

Finally, I reach her right as her foot slips beneath a rock, my arm going around her waist and catching her, then stumbling back until I right my footing. Her eyes are wide, her face pale, and small rocks fall down the cliff into some body of water that is definitely not deep enough to survive a thirty-foot drop.

"What the *fuck* are you doing!?" I shout, birds flying off as I stand tall, pulling her body to mine, my arm still on her waist.

She gives me a small cringe before answering. "Having fun?"

"Can you have fun without giving me a fucking heart attack?"

"I mean, I *guess* I could, but it sounds substantially less fun."

"Sacrifice some of your fun for my heart health," I say in a gravelly voice I barely recognize.

"You *are* pretty old," she teases with a smile.

My pulse is pounding from nearly watching her fall to her death, and *definitely* not because her body is plastered to mine. "Jesus, you could have died, Ava."

"So you were worried about me?" she asks, a smile on her lips.

"It's my job, Ava."

"Mm-hmm, I guess. Or it's because you like me," she teases with a smile and the line that seems to be her most common refrain—the line crafted with breaking my sanity in mind and not much else.

"I definitely don't like you, Princess. I've never met a single person in my life who drives me crazy the way you do."

There's a pause as she smiles at me, lifting a hand to brush back hair before saying all breathy and low, "Then why are you still holding me, Jaime? You could have let go a while ago."

Instantly, I realize my mistake, dropping my arm and taking three big steps backward. Her smile is wide and teasing like she finds this entertaining, but all I can think is she's too fucking close to the edge still, so I reach forward, grab her hand, and tug, taking a step back as I do and pulling her from the cliff's edge.

"Oh, you *so* like me, Jaime," she says, her pink lips encasing a huge smile.

"I—" I start to argue, but she shakes her head, her little bows and pigtails swaying as she does.

God, she's fucking gorgeous, all blonde and curves and pink bows I want to tug on. Every shift of her body is a temptation I can't seem to ignore, and the worst part of it?

She fucking knows it.

"If I admit I like you, will you behave for me?" Her lips tip up, and a part of my brain tells me I'm treading thin ice and could fall to a freezing death at any moment.

"Probably not," she whispers with a smile, so quiet I almost don't hear it, but my eyes are locked on her lips just inches from mine. It wouldn't take much at all to lean forward and kiss her. A moment passes and I wonder what would happen if I just said, *fuck it.*

"We should go back to the group before they wonder where we went," I say, stepping away.

I expect her to argue, to tell me I'm no fun, something along those lines, but instead, she nods and waves a hand before her.

"Lead the way, big guy."

I understand the allure of this form of exercise when we hit the top of the mountain and look out over the valley. I was never a hiking guy or even much of an *outdoors* kind of guy. I'd much rather get my physical activity at a gym studio with plenty of air conditioning and no bugs. But this view is worth it.

Then I watch Ava taking in the mountains and the lush green trees with childlike excitement, and I know that's what she sees. I get why she likes hiking, why she apparently chooses this as her workout of choice. Even more, I'm forced to come to terms with the fact that, once again, I judged her too soon, thinking she wasn't the kind of person who hiked when she barely even broke a sweat at the steeper inclines.

And with the backdrop, in her little outfit with the bows and the pink shoes, she fits. A work of art surrounded by more beauty. I reach in my pocket for my phone, tapping the screen the way she showed me.

"I'll take your picture," I say, starting to snap before she even poses and catching a look of pure shock and joy.

"You're going to take my picture?"

"You need them for your social media," I say, lifting the phone from different angles, again like she showed me. I've also been watching everyone else do the same, realizing it's not just her neuroses.

"I mean, yeah. I just never thought you'd offer," she says, but shifts her body so I can catch different angles and expressions—some silly, some sexy—within a matter of a few moments.

"That should be good," she says, then reaches for my phone as I continue to take shots. She's smiling, like this is some joke she's in on, and for some reason, that last photo—her hand out, her smile wide—is my favorite of them all. She grabs it, instantly finding my photos and scrolling through them. "You're not bad at this, big guy," she says with a smile, looking up at me. "We'll make a social media boyfriend of you yet."

"I'm not—"

"Trust me, I know. You can barely tolerate me," she says with a wink, tapping a few of the photos and then opening a new message to send them to herself.

"I just meant I don't even have social media," I explain, and she smiles once more before handing me my phone back and opening her mouth. But she doesn't get the chance to say whatever quip she's brewing up because someone is calling out Ava's name.

"You two want a picture?" Miss Maine says, and I shake my head as Ava nods.

"Yes! I'd love that, thank you so much!" She hands her phone to the woman, then grabs my hand, tugging it. I don't let myself think about how well her small hands fit so well in my larger ones.

"I'm just the bodyguard," I say low. "You don't need photos with me."

"You're on this adventure with me whether you like it or not, Jaime," she says with a smile as she leads me a few feet back to where she was standing before then turning to look at Miss Maine, who already has Ava's phone lifted.

"Smile, Jaime. You're already coming along for the ride. Might as well enjoy it while you're there."

I sigh as Miss Maine takes a few photos before forcing myself to smile for the last few, feeling uncomfortable. But when Ava gets her phone back and swipes through them, her excitement at the shots makes any hint of discomfort worth it.

While Ava does a few interviews up at the top of the mountain, I snap a few photos of the scenery, sending them to Riggins Greene from Atlas Oaks, knowing Maine is one of his favorite places. I have to admit, now I see why. When we all make our way back down, Ava doesn't veer off trail, making the hike back down much less heart attack-inducing.

It isn't until long after we had a casual dinner with the group and we're back at the hotel that I get a text from a number I don't have saved, but I've sent photos to.

Night, big guy, the text reads, with a photo of the two of us attached.

For some reason I can't explain, I save the shot and apply it to her new contact.

> It's barely seven.

Unfortunately, I have this crazy, protective, boring bodyguard who would never let me do anything fun, so it's an early night for me.

> We have to be up early.

I know. I'm just fucking with you. I'm tired from the hike anyway. Just going to listen to a book and play my silly little game.

> The fairy one?

Faerie, but yeah.

I wait long moments before I type out my last text, then delete it, then type it again, each time telling myself it's a dumb idea.

And then I send it.

> To make a pink flower, you have to plant a white one, then leave a space, then a red one.

What?

I don't answer.

> Jaime, did you look up how to play my game?
>
> Oh, my god. You did. I tried it, and it worked. I can't believe it.

I can almost picture her face, the smile there, the excitement, but I still don't respond, setting my phone to Do Not Disturb before setting it on the nightstand and getting ready for bed.

In the morning, when my alarm goes off for my workout before we have to get on the road, I see it.

> You so like me, Jaime Wilde.

And I'm starting to think she might not be completely wrong.

EIGHTEEN
JAIME

Our next stop is Virginia, where we go to a flower shop to make bouquets. Ava brings the cat, which I end up holding half of the time. As much as it kills me to admit, the cat is sweet, willing to be held almost every moment, and has fallen asleep in my arms more often than I can count.

I never had a pet as a kid, and with my career, I never got one as an adult. I always thought once I retired I'd get a dog like Riggins' German Shepherd, but this cat is pretty great. Not that I'd ever admit that to Ava, since she'd never let me live it down.

Now I'm walking off the elevator of the hotel in front of Ava, the cat on a fucking leash while she carries it.

The woman bought her tiny fucking cat a *bedazzled leash* to take her on, and I quote, "silly goofy kitty walks." I drew the line at holding that fucking leash.

As we walk toward the hall our rooms are in, she continues to ramble on about God only knows what. When we approach the hall, her words become even more of a static noise as I notice something is...off.

"What the—" I mumble as she continues to talk, light spilling into the hallway as we approach her hotel room door. Ava, not realizing I'm suddenly on alert, walks right into my back. Her body presses into mine, and my arm moves behind me to wrap around her until she steadies herself, but not turning, keeping my eyes locked on that door.

"Jaime, what's—" she starts, but I use my arm on her back to squeeze and put a finger to my lips.

My arm drops, and I reach for my back pocket, touching the phone there and pulling it out before taking another step closer. Common sense wants to believe it's just housekeeping, nothing nefarious, but my gut...my gut thinks it's something more.

Unfortunately, my gut is very rarely wrong, something that's confirmed when I get close enough to lean forward and peek in the door.

Destroyed.

That's what her hotel room is.

Quickly, I run through my options, balancing my all-consuming need to keep Ava safe, to keep her by my side, and to keep her from seeing what's in front of us. She puts on a strong front, playing the tough, doesn't give a fuck chick, but even though I haven't been around her that long, I know it's just that: an act.

The Ava *I* know is soft and sweet.

Looking down the short hallway, I note there's only one other room in this hall, and it's the one I've been staying in right across from her. I make a decision, reaching into my pocket for the key and opening the door to my room before tugging her inside and closing it behind me. It seems quiet and untouched, but still, I walk through the room, checking closets and under beds, until I confirm there's no one in here.

Moving back to Ava, I put a hand on her shoulder, squatting a bit until we're face-to-face, and I'm looking into her big blue eyes. "Stay here, don't move," I say. "Do you understand?"

"Jaime, what—"

"Two minutes, stay here."

"You're freaking me out, Jaime."

I lift a hand and press it to her cheek, those big, beautiful eyes of hers widening. "I know. Listen to me. You have your phone, yeah?" She nods. "Good girl. I'm going to go check the room. Any noise, anything seems off, call 911."

"Jaime—"

"I know you need details to feel comfortable, so I'm going to give them to you. Your hotel room has been ransacked. I'm going to leave you in this room while I make sure there's no one in your room still. I'm going to check your room while you stay in here with Peach, okay?"

"Jaime—"

"It's probably nothing," I lie. "But I don't play with safety."

"Safety?" The word is whisper soft, and I wonder if finally, the severity of her reality has finally cut through her mind, the need to have me with her, to listen to the rules I give her, finally sink in.

I step closer to her, crowding her space, ignoring the way it feels so good to be this close every single time, like some kind of invisible string usually stretched tight finally goes lax with her proximity.

"Ava. Please. If you're only going to listen to me one time, let it be this one. Call 911. Stay in this room with Peach. Once you get someone on the line, tell them where we are, that your room was broken into, and your security is checking. If they hang up before I'm back out, call the hotel next. If anyone—and I mean anyone, Ava: a kid, an old lady, a guy dressed in a fuckin' clown suit—comes to the door, you scream. You do not open it at all. Do you understand?" Reality seems to wash over her, her mouth opening slightly as she stares at me, and I lower my voice. "Hey, Princess, do you get me? I need to go check the room, but I can't leave you here unless I know you're good."

She blinks once, twice, three times before she nods. "Got it. Call 911, and if anyone comes, scream and sick Peach on them," she says with a small smile.

I stare at her, her eyes shining while fighting a laugh, and not for the first time, I wonder if she's insane. This is not how a normal person responds when they realize their hotel room was broken into.

But then again, this is Ava.

I nod at her once more, squeezing her arms. Without thinking about the pros and cons or anything beyond her being in front of me, I press my lips against her hair. Then I step back, graze my fingers over the top of the orange cat's head in her arm, and move into the hall. I check the door once it clicks behind me, making sure it's locked, and hear Ava put the chain on.

As I walk through to Ava's room, I curse under my breath seeing the destruction—her things, thankfully, seem to be intact, though thrown everywhere, but everything else in the small hotel room is turned over, not like they were looking for something but just to make a statement.

They wanted us to know they were here.

I walk around for a few minutes, looking for any kind of clue but finding none, nor do I find some kind of culprit.

"Is there a note or anything?" a voice asks, and I jump, turning to see Ava behind me.

"What the fuck, Ava? I told you to stay in the room and call 911 and the hotel!"

"I did! Then I came in here when it was pretty clear no one was going to pop out and jump you. You needed backup."

"Is it *that* impossible for you to listen to one instruction *one fucking time*?"

"No, but when the instruction is to stand in a mildly sketchy hotel room with clearly terrible security versus in this destroyed but seemingly empty room where my bodyguard is, I choose the one with my bodyguard."

I glare at her, wanting to argue but knowing I can't because, unfortunately, there's some logic in her statement. "You could have at least said something."

"And miss catching you off guard? Hell no."

"What if I thought you were the intruder and I attacked you?"

She rolls her eyes like that's insane and huffs. "As if you would ever make a mistake like that." She waves a hand over me, saying a lot without saying much, then she looks around, letting out a low whistle as she does.

"Wow. This is kind of crazy, huh?" She moves in a circle, looking around, checking the destruction before starting to walk around, moving a coffee table on its side with the toe of her shoe, and then looking over her things. "Weird, they didn't touch my shit, right? That's weird?"

"I mean..." I hesitate to say anything, but I decide we're long past playing games. "Yes, it's strange. And there's no note, not that I could see at least. Don't touch anything though, okay?"

"I've seen enough CSI to know the rules." She lifts Peach to her face, rubbing her cheek against the sleepy kitten before pressing pink lips to orange fur.

"Why aren't you freaking out about this?" I ask, suddenly concerned because this isn't a typical response to finding your room ransacked.

"Oh, I'm sure I'll panic a bit once the adrenaline wears off. But right now, I'm just happy we were lucky enough no one was here, and Peach was with us," she says, lifting the kitten. "Right now, I'm being delusional and telling myself it's kind of funny, exciting, and interesting."

I stare at her and shake my head.

"That's not normal, you know that, right?"

"I enjoy living a life of delusion, thank you very much." She pauses like she's contemplating something. "Maybe that will be my next hyperfixation. I'll become one of those true crime girlies, listening to podcasts and researching serial killers."

"Well, maybe we don't commit to that just yet. Plus, who said this is a serial killer, Ava? How did you even get from a ransacked room to a serial killer?"

"I mean, this is clearly not the work of a stable human being, Jaime."

"But a *serial killer?*"

She shrugs then opens her mouth, probably to continue to argue her point, but a knock on the door frame comes, a hotel employee standing in the doorway with an officer behind him, and my attention is refocused.

NINETEEN
AVA

It's long past dark when we pull up to the new hotel the pageant booked for us after it took almost two hours after the police let us leave, promising to keep Jaime up to date on any news. The previous hotel offered a new room for me, and I would have accepted because, honestly, once the humor of it all wore out, I realized I was exhausted and headed for a crash of monumental proportions.

Unfortunately, Jaime refused, calling his boss, filling him in, and getting a new location he approved of to spend the night at. Then Jaime helped me pack up my things. I've never been more grateful I only brought one of the suitcases into the room, but I'm sure Jaime saw a good number of underwear and bras regardless.

That I will be wiping from memory, thank you very much.

We walk to the front desk of a new hotel, where they quickly check us in and hand Jaime two key cards, unlike the past few stops where he was given four, two for each room.

Which means...

One room.

Me and Jaime in the same room.

My mind moves to when his hands were on my shoulders, the

way he looked at me, the way he calmed me down, the way he called me Princess, the way he kissed the top of my head before going to check my room out.

When we're in the elevator, I finally speak, attempting to ease the tension that is near suffocating. "One room?"

"Greg and I decided it's better for us to stay together if someone is after you."

I roll my eyes and sigh. "Isn't that a bit much?" Jaime taps the button for the top floor, and slowly, the elevator rises. "No one is *looking into me.*"

"Your room was broken into and destroyed, this after you've had multiple threats and messages sent to you on multiple platforms. If it were up to me, this would be the bare minimum of what we do." His jaw goes tight, and I try to parse out what he means. Then I decide I don't really want to know what drastic steps his crazy ass would take.

The police and the hotel staff agreed that, although there was no camera in the hallway my room was in—a budget hotel the pageant picked—it was probably a group of kids screwing around. According to the police chief who came to personally reassure Jaime, there was no imminent threat to my life. It's something that's been happening a lot in the area. With nothing to keep the high school kids entertained on weekends, they resort to being little fucks, causing enough trouble to be a headache but not enough to be a real issue.

Instead, I return to the subject at hand.

"So, one hotel room," I start, a wide smile spreading on my lips and bumping him with my hip. "Are we going to have some fun on the bed trope shenanigans?"

"What?" he asks, staring at me with the kind of exhaustion a parent gives an unruly child.

A pretty good analogy, if you ask me. If Jaime is the responsible parent, I am absolutely the overactive kid.

"You know where we're supposed to have two twin beds, but there's only one king, and you try to put up a pillow wall between us, but then I wake up with you spooning me." I smile at him, and he stares at me before taking a deep breath.

"What the fuck?" he asks, confused and a bit annoyed, I think. I just smile and continue.

"Or maybe I have a horrible nightmare, and you wake up thinking I'm being hurt, then hold me until I fall back asleep." His brows come together now seeming concerned.

"Do you have nightmares often?"

"I don't think more often than the average human." I smile and pat his shoulder. "Don't worry, you're not going to have to cuddle with me because of my bad dreams."

He shakes his head at me, both in exhaustion and confusion. "Where do you come up with this shit?"

"I read a lot," I say.

"Read what? Horror books?"

I roll my eyes at him and scoff. "No, you doofus. Romance. The one-bed trope is a *classic* in romance books." There's a pause where I think he'll make some snide remark about reading romance, at which point I'll have to get all self-righteous, which is a shame because it's been a long day, but instead, he just gives me a somehow more annoyed look.

"Did you just call me a doofus?" The elevator dings, the doors slide open, and I step out before he can first, turning to face his glaring face.

God, he's so fun to tease. And so easy to rile.

"Sure did. Now which room is ours, *doofus?*"

"Wow, this is nice," I say, stepping into what seems to be a two-bedroom apartment with a very small kitchen.

"The only thing in the area that had a suite and allowed cats. Full disclosure, after what happened, we're getting a two-bedroom suite at each stop from now on instead of two separate rooms," he says.

"There goes my snuggling hopes and dreams," I say with a sigh as he grabs my overnight bag and glares at me.

"Which room do you want?"

"I don't care," I say with a shake of my head, because I really don't. We'll only be here one night before we pack up, do our event, and drive to North Carolina for the next event.

He just walks off, puts my bag in one room, and then walks back out to me. "I'm going to shower. You okay here?"

I nod, pulling out my book and cuddling on the couch with Peach as if the entire chaotic night didn't even happen.

"Yup, all good."

He stares at me for long moments until I feel uncomfortable under his glare. "You're really okay?"

I sigh and roll my eyes, setting my book aside and standing, moving toward him.

"Yes, Jaime."

"It's okay to be shaken up," he says, his voice soft and kind. I move until I'm standing in front of him in the pajamas I put on before we got back in the car, looking up at him and putting a hand on his chest.

"I probably would be if I had anyone else with me. Lucky for me, I've got a Jaime, so I know you'd never let anything happen to me."

He opens his mouth like he wants to say something, then closes it before opening it again. Then he nods and steps back, my hand dropping.

"Gonna go shower," he says, his face turning red as he does.

I don't have to say it out loud. Instead, I just think about it with a smile.

God, he really fucking likes me.

I'm sitting for a total of five minutes reading my book before Peach comes, rubbing on my ankles and yelling at me.

"Hold on, Princess Peach, give me a minute. I'm at a good part," I mutter, lifting her as I read and putting her on my lap for a cuddle. She doesn't seem to be in the *cuddling mood* and instead nips my wrist, clearly saying something along the lines of *feed me now, you bitch, or I'm going to make your life a living hell*. With a sigh, I put my book down and lift her up until we're face-to-face.

"You know, if you weren't so cute, we'd have much bigger issues," I say in a cloyingly sweet voice that's annoying even to my ears. She must agree when she nips at my nose.

I sigh, putting her down and getting to work, getting her bowl set with water and food before taking a deep sigh and trying to regulate myself.

Even though I'd never admit it to Jaime, I'm a bit shaken after everything that happened. It's too real, too close to me. Messages and comments, I can put on the back burner of my mind because they're just that—words on a phone from some random stranger who knows where.

But someone breaking into my hotel room?

That's real.

That's why, instead of reading in my bed like I'd normally do, I chose to read on the couch because it felt safer, or, at the very least, closer to the safety that is quickly becoming what Jaime gives me.

When I walk back into the main living area, Peach content as she stuffs her face with the most vile cat food on this planet in the small kitchen, my reading spot is taken. In its place sits Jaime in a white tee and gray sweatpants, an utter dream, sitting in my vacated spot on the couch, reading my book.

An utter nightmare.

"You better not have lost my spot," I say with a smile, trying to play off what he could be reading.

He jumps a bit, like I caught him off guard, before he looks up at me, shaking his head. "Is this what you're always reading in the car?" he asks, lifting the book back up.

"I mean, not that specifically. Sometimes, it's vampires or faeries or hockey players. Cowboys is kind of new to me." I lean over his shoulder to see what he's looking at and fight the embarrassment at him reading about a cowboy tying a single mom to her bed.

I reach to grab it, but he moves at the last minute to keep it out of my reach before standing. I walk around the couch and reach to grab it once again, but he's much too big and reading at an angle he knows I can't reach. When I almost get it, he stands, making it impossible to reach my book now.

"Jesus, Princess, you like this kind of stuff?"

I can't see my face, but I can feel my cheeks burning violently as I move to try and grab my book back. I should have started reading on an e-reader, but I've always liked the permanence of books most of all, and I like being able to tab and annotate the physical version.

"I don't know," I say, jumping to grab the book again, but he's too tall when I'm barefoot, not that five-inch heels could have really helped here.

"You don't know? How do you not know?"

"I've never done any of it, Jaime. I just read it." I stand up straighter, crossing my arms on my chest.

"Why?"

Fine. He wants to play this game, I'll play too.

"Because have you *met* men these days? I barely trust them to take me to dinner, much less choke me while they fuck me."

He stands there, his face gaping at my words, and I smile, happy I've evened the playing field once again.

"Now, you? I bet you know how to choke a woman and make sure she likes it." I smile wide then wink before turning toward the small kitchen again to refill my water bottle even though it's half full. I just need some space to breathe when he's looking at me like that.

"Can you stop that?" Jaime finally says, standing in the entryway of the kitchen.

"Stop what?" I ask over my shoulder.

"Stop..." He stutters a few times, trying to find the right way to say whatever it is he's trying to say, and I fight the rush of satisfaction, knowing I've got him so flustered. "Flirting with me."

"Why?" I ask, but then something else comes to mind, horror taking over me as a new thought hits. "Does it make you uncomfortable?" I ask, turning toward him. Flirting with him because it flusters him is one thing, but making him uncomfortable when he's just trying to do his job is another.

He answers quickly and concisely. "No." A blush comes over his cheeks like that one word alone was more of a confession than he would want to make. "It's just unprofessional."

"Unprofessional?"

"My job is to protect you, Ava. Not flirt with you."

Funny that he said *flirt with me* rather than me flirting with *him*, which is intriguing.

Has this been his brand of flirting?

If so, he is *really* bad at it.

Something about that makes me smile, knowing that Jaime Wilde is actually bad at something.

I let a smile spread over my lips. "Then it's settled."

"What's settled?" he asks hesitantly as if he isn't sure he really wants my answer.

"You like me. That's why my flirting with you gets you all flustered." I caught him right as he was taking a sip of his water, and he chokes on it. I have to fight the urge to laugh as Jaime coughs a few times before, finally, I come over and pat him on the back. "You good there, big guy?"

He turns toward me, leaving barely a foot between us before he glares at me. "I'm fine. You just caught me off guard."

"I'm really good at that," I say with a smile.

He takes me in, his discerning gaze taking in my features, my eyes, my face, my lips...then he stops on my lips, his eyes lingering there too long for someone who wouldn't want to kiss me.

"I don't like you," he says, his voice growly and going places it absolutely should *not* go.

"Yeah, you do. That's okay. A little crush never hurt anyone," I say with a smile, then step back, grab my water bottle off the coffee table, and walk off.

TWENTY

AVA

"Do you know the address for the next hotel?" Jaime asks when we're about two hours from our next stop in Tennessee. Our plan once there is to go to the hotel, get ready (in his words, *quickly, Ava—none of this fucking around bullshit),* and then go to dinner with Miss Tennessee and a few members of the press.

"No." He sighs, and I smile. "Haven't you realized I have no idea what is going on on this tour? I'm the *talent.* I don't bother myself with petty things like *addresses.* I barely know what state we're going to next."

"We're going to Tennessee."

"Yes, I got that, big guy. But I don't know the name of the hotel, much less the address for it." Another sigh before he gestures at his phone and then the screen of the SUV.

"It's on my phone. Can you grab it and then put the address in?" I nod, reaching to the center console and grabbing his phone, lifting it to his face to unlock it before scrolling to his apps. "It's in my email, should be from Greg at Five Star."

"Got it," I say, but then I freeze at a familiar, vibrant-colored app.

A social media app.

"You big liar," I say with a smile, pushing his shoulder.

"Jesus, Ava, I'm driving."

Peach, from her spot in his lap, lifts her head and glares at me.

"You're driving, and you're a *liar*!"

"What am I lying about now?"

I lift the phone and show him the screen even though his eyes barely leave the windshield as I do. "You have social media!"

"Ava, no, I—" he starts, but I cut him off.

"What's your handle so I can follow you?" I ask, tapping the icon because I'm nosy.

"Ava, I don't—" he starts.

"Oh," I say, looking at the phone. He stops attempting to stop me, instead sighing. "*Oh*."

I say *oh*, because, when I open the phone, there's a Jaime0914 username with no followers and...one account he's following.

Me.

The man follows me.

"Ava—"

"When did you start this account?" I ask, but when he doesn't answer, I look up at him, seeing a deep red flush and a tight jaw. I think I know why when I navigate to his liked posts, trying to see what he's liked recently.

My content.

The man only likes *my content*.

"You got social media," I say, an accusation of sorts.

He sighs, then nods. "Yeah," he admits reluctantly.

"Because of me," I say.

Again, he lets out a deep sigh. "I didn't get it for my health."

I let a moment pass before I speak again. "Are you going to admit it yet?" I ask, opening my phone and finding his handle, making sure to follow him.

"Admit what?"

There's exasperation in his tone as I pick his phone back up, tap on his emails, find the location of the next hotel and type it into the navigation before handing him back his phone and sitting back in my seat with what I'm sure is a smug smile.

"That you're in love with me."

A long beat passes, during which I assume he won't say anything, so I pick my book back up and start to read. But a few long minutes later, under his breath, I hear him.

"You know, Peach, your mom might be cute, but she's a real pain in the ass."

And honestly?

I'll call that one a win.

"So those books...they're all romance?" he asks an hour or so later once I close my book for a short break, stretching my neck and pulling Peach from him into my lap for some snuggles.

"Yup."

"What's your favorite kind?"

"What?"

"There are different kinds, right? Like funny ones, sad ones..."

I put a hand to my chest and gasp. "Are you asking my favorite tropes?"

"I have no clue. Maybe?"

"Well, since you asked." I turn to him. "I like rom-coms most, romantic comedies. They're a little funny and goofy, and kind of outrageous, but that's the fun of them. I love grumpy sunshine, forced proximity, opposites attract." I pause, then smile. "We fit a lot of my favorite tropes," I say, thinking about it. "Even big, big man, small, small girl."

He closes his eyes and takes a deep breath before looking at me. "Do I even want to know what that means?"

"You know, she's small and short and dainty. He's a big, tall, muscled man. It's hot, but I always wonder about the logistics. Just look at you and me. You're a giant. We'd never be able to do doggy, you know?" I expect him to blush, to stutter, even to groan, the way he does when I say anything like that.

"It would work, trust me," he says instead, shocking me and causing me to sit there, blinking at him. I don't miss the tiny tip of his lips.

Silence fills the car as I try and process that bomb he just dropped before he speaks.

"Why only romance?"

"Because I like them and I don't like other genres as much. I don't believe in doing things in life just because it's what other people think you should be doing."

"Hmm," he says.

"Plus, who doesn't love the idea of love? Of falling in love and falling in lust. It's the most beautiful thing in the world. When you read romance, you get to watch it over and over in different ways—what's there not to love?"

There's another pause, and I think that's it for the conversation before he breaks the silence again.

"But you...you don't have a man?" he asks, seeming confused.

"Nope."

"Why not?"

I shrug. "Haven't found anyone I like enough to spend more than a couple weeks with. Life is too short for that. I've seen friends date men who are all kinds of wrong for them just because it was comfortable or he checked just enough boxes to make sense. I don't want someone who *makes sense*. I want someone I'm crazy for." I shrug again, feeling much too under the microscope for comfort. "When I find him, I'll know, and that will be that. Could be next week, could be in forty years. I'm not putting my life on hold just because I'm waiting for some man."

Jaime looks at me quickly before returning his eyes to the road. "That's pretty wise, coming from a self-centered beauty queen, you know?"

There's a small smile on his lips, and I gape at him before laughing and slapping his arm.

"I can't believe you actually just told a *joke*. And that it was kind of funny."

"It was plenty funny," he grumbles, and I reach over again to rub his arm.

"All right, all right, big guy. You're right. It was plenty funny."

We drive in silence for a bit, the navigation the only sound to be heard, before I get up the courage to break the silence.

"So what about you? Do you date?" I ask, suddenly shy to even ask that, which is so out of my nature. "It sounds like your job is pretty unpredictable, and you're always *on*. It must be hard to date or have a relationship." I look over to catch him shaking his head, eyes stoically on the road.

"This job can't have distractions." It sounds like a line he's told himself many times before, and for a moment, I wonder if he means it.

"Distractions? Like, say, pretty passenger princesses whose ass you can't stop staring at?" I ask with a smile.

"Exactly."

"I bet we could be a fun distraction, you know." It's my normal MO to flirt just to watch him blush, but I didn't get the blush this time.

Instead, I just get his honesty.

"Ava, you're a distraction of the worst variety."

"Doesn't sound like too much of a bad thing."

He finally looks at me for just a moment and gives me a smile, shaking his head, before diverting his attention back to the road.

"I've been in this game a long time, Ava. I've seen guards come and go, men and women who think this job is easy, think it's just watching over entitled people and playing cops and robbers. Distractions are what get people hurt."

That makes sense, even if it makes the tiniest of disappointed rocks settle in my tummy. I ignore it.

"Do you like it?"

"What?"

"What you do. Bodyguarding."

He hesitates a moment longer than acceptable, indicating the answer isn't fully *yes, but also not fully no. He's...conflicted.*

"It's a fun job. I get to travel the world and get paid to do so. When I'm assigned to Atlas Oaks, when they're on tour, I get to hang out with a bunch of guys who have become my friends. That's pretty awesome."

"Not a bad gig, I'm learning." I'm shocked when he smiles *again*, like he maybe, possibly finds me endearing.

"But..." I say, carrying out the word and waiting for him to fill in the gaps.

He sighs. "But this job isn't forever." For a moment, he looks shocked to have said it out loud, like he didn't mean to admit it. Then he continues, I'm assuming because he's already halfway there. "My boss—my old boss—he sold the company almost a year ago, and he had some really great benefits that would set in in about three years, which is when I could retire early. The new boss gave me this assignment and implied that if things didn't go how he wanted, with it ending in securing a contract with the organization, I might not be around to see those benefits."

My mouth drops open. "Oh, my god, he threatened to kill you!?"

"Jesus, no. Just potentially letting me go, I guess?" Well, that's less dire, I suppose.

"So this is like...a trial run?"

"I guess that's what you could call it."

I cringe, turning to look at him, suddenly apologetic. "And I'm making that harder?"

"I mean...not specifically."

"But I'm not making it *easier*," I say, scrunching my face up. He doesn't answer, so I ask him a new question. "What do you want to do when you retire?"

"Absolutely nothing," he says with a grin, and it makes me smile, too.

"I don't think you would do well sitting around for any period of time."

"Maybe, but I'm willing to give it the old college try."

That makes me laugh before I sit silently, thinking of Jaime sitting around doing nothing. It would never last. The man is always alert, always busy. He'd die of boredom.

"What about you? What's next for you after all of this?"

I shrug. "Not sure."

His brows furrow at my answer. "Not sure?"

"Nope," I say with a smile.

His frown deepens. "What does that mean?"

"I kind of always just...go with the flow. Life is short, you know? Why spend it doing things you don't like?"

"Hmm," he says, but it doesn't sound like he's buying it.

"I have always just gone with whatever opportunity falls into my lap. Before the pageant and influencer stuff, I was a bartender. Right now, I've got prize money from the pageant that I'm not really spending on anything, and every day I'm getting requests for sponsorships on social media. So we'll see. Eventually, I'll fall into something and realize it's what I want to do forever. Until then, I'm just living my life."

Time passes as we drive, Jaime contemplating my words before, finally, he speaks.

"You know, for a self-centered princess, you're pretty damn smart."

'And don't you forget it, big guy," I say with a smile, picking my book back up.

TWENTY-ONE
JAIME

"What are you reading?" I ask without meaning to when Ava is silent for a long time. When her head perks up as she takes off the big pink headphones with white ribbons tied to the frame and a broad smile on her lips, I instantly regret it.

"What?"

"What are you reading? You keep giggling."

Her smile spreads on her face, and she shifts in the seat to look at me, tucking her feet beneath her. Peach moves in my lap, stretching an arm out to Ava, and she returns the move, scratching behind her ear.

"An omegaverse."

With my eyes on the road, I take a deep breath. The way she said the simple, nonsensical word, I know she's excited for my response. Still, something tells me I probably don't need to know whatever she says, much less *want* to know.

"Do I even want to know what an omegaverse is?"

"Oh, absolutely," she says, then proceeds to move into a long , drawn-out conversation about alphas and omegas and betas, designations, and mates. Then she gives me a very in-depth explanation of what a fucking *knot* is using a straw and wrapper, and I was right.

I did *not* want to know.

"Get it?" she asks. I continue to stare at the road, but when we hit a red light, I turn to her, her smile wide and her eyes wider.

God, she's fucking cute.

"I miss who I was before this," I say, and her head tips back with a twinkling laugh, the blonde of her long ponytail grazing her arm as she does. The light turns green, and I start to drive before confessing, "You know, I thought I'd spend time with you—"

"Under duress, of course." She rolls her eyes, and I smile because I cannot help it.

"Of course. But I thought I'd spend time with you, and you'd turn it off."

"What?"

"Your pageant girl. The happy-go-lucky, friendly-to-everyone, ball-buster version. That you'd be a bitch or uptight or something." I turn my head when she doesn't respond, looking quickly as I'm driving to catch her turned to look at me, a wide smile spread across her lips.

"But...?" she says, almost jumping with joy.

"God, you're a fucking pain in the ass."

"Hey, hey, no, finish! What did you expect?!"

"I expected it was an act, that it wasn't really you. But I've never met a person in my life who doesn't put on airs for anyone. You're the same in the car with me as you were on that stage, as you were talking to that kid on the boardwalk, as you were at the top of a mountain being interviewed. The same person each time." I pause, trying to think of how to explain it. "It's impressive. Not many people are like that."

"You know, Jaime, I think that was *almost* a compliment," she says with a smile, and I have to fight one of my own. After a bit of silence, she breaks it, her voice lower and almost nervous. "I am, you know. Sometimes."

"What?"

"Fake. I don't think anyone can be completely *real* all the time. But it's normal, I think." In my peripheral vision, she shrugs, a bit of her sunshine smile dimmed and something in me wants to go after every person who ever made her feel like she has to be *on* all the time, like who she is at any given moment is utter perfection. "I think everyone puts on a face for the rest of the world. No one is exactly the same behind closed doors and out in the public, especially not when cameras and careers are involved. Everyone's a little fake sometimes."

"I don't," I say.

Liar, my mind says. *What a fucking liar.*

Because I'm just a little fake when I'm pretending Ava doesn't get to me, that she's not shifting something in me. I'm fake when I see her flirting with anyone else, and I have to act like it doesn't bother me, or when she flirts with *me,* and I have to pretend I don't care.

"No, no, you're not."

"What does that mean?"

"You're on much higher alert in public, for one," she says, which is valid. "And you definitely aren't letting kittens sit on your lap and scratching behind their ears or buying pageant queens a dozen types of ice cream because you feel bad out in the world."

"I guess...I guess that's fair."

"It's much more exhausting than I thought it would be, being on all the time. Sometimes, I wish I could be normal out there, too. Drop an f-bomb or sit with a slouch, or just be in a bad mood."

"Why can't you?"

"Well, for one, the internet is forever," she says with a laugh. "And I don't need a photo of me sitting with horrible posture and resting bitch face while someone talks to me to follow me for the rest of my life."

"I guess that's fair," I say, holding my instinct to tell her she's gorgeous no matter what.

Goddammit, Wilde, get it together. She's a client.

"And people come to see *pageant* me. They drive a long while and take time out of their busy lives, rearranging schedules and finding babysitters or taking time off work, the whole nine, because somehow, I inspired them or made them feel good about something or got them interested in pageants." She sighs, a soul-deep sound, and it hits me dead in the gut.

"They'd love the real version of you too, Ava," I say, even though I should keep my mouth shut. "If you let her out more."

What am I saying? That real version she hides away is for a reason, because if she did, Regina would lose her mind and find a reason to cancel her contract. My job is to keep her in line, not encourage her to toe it more than she already does.

"Yeah, maybe," she says.

"Not maybe, Ava. Definitely." And then I reach over, one hand on the wheel, and grab her hand, squeezing it once.

"Thanks, Jaime," she whispers, and I know the two words mean more than just *thanks for the pep talk.*

I don't respond.

I also don't let go of her hand, twining my fingers with hers.

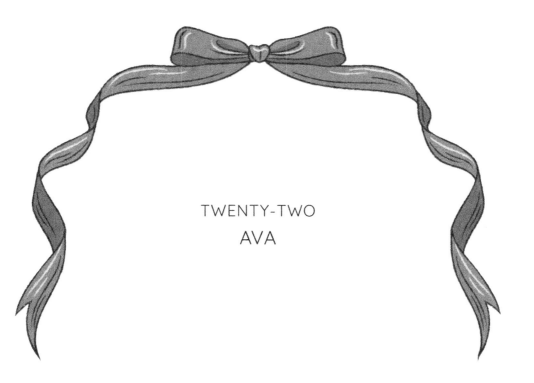

TWENTY-TWO
AVA

"We're so excited to have you here in Florida!" the instructor for the snorkeling business we're highlighting for this stop says. We're all on a large charter boat, part of a locally owned snorkeling business. With us are a few members of the press, Miss Florida, Anne (unfortunately), Jaime, and me.

"Today, we're going to be snorkeling, one of the most popular tourist attractions for coastal Florida. We're going to see some gorgeous fish and coral today. There should be a few sharks out there, but they're a docile variety and shouldn't give us any issue."

Jaime's body goes still briefly, and for a split second, I stop watching the instructor and instead turn to look at him, a furrow on my brow.

His face is stoic and on the speaker, not shifting at all, even as I obviously stare at him. The instructor starts to go through measures for what to do if and when you see a shark, how to stay safe, but I'm too busy watching Jaime to pay much attention. His jaw has gone tight, and some of the color has gone from his face.

I lean in and whisper to him. "You okay? You look like you saw a ghost. Or a threat." A chill runs through me at the thought of a threat being nearby and Jaime being freaked out by it.

"I don't like sharks," he whispers, and it takes everything in me not to scoff out a laugh.

"*You?* You don't like sharks?" I whisper.

"They're a threat I know nothing about and can't control other than staying out of the water. What's there to like about them?"

One thing I've learned about Jaime is his undeniable love for all things predictable. I think it's why I drive him so crazy, why I rub him so wrong most of the time, considering I am the *opposite* of predictable. I love spontaneity and chaos and flying by the seat of my pants.

I also love fucking with Jaime.

"They're pretty," I say with a smile, knowing it's going to annoy him. The rush of a win runs through me when he looks at me with a droll expression, though entertainment lies beneath it.

"Pretty things can be dangerous," he says pointedly and I smile.

"Like me? Am I dangerous to you, Jaime?"

Before he can respond, the instructor claps loudly, a wide, jovial smile on his lips. "Okay, so who wants to be fitted for a lifejacket first?"

I raise my hand instantly. "Me!"

Jaime's jaw gets somehow tighter, and I wink as I turn back to the instructor before pulling off the cover-up and revealing a one-piece bathing suit with no back and a super low front.

"Can you take this big guy?" I ask, handing him the gauzy fabric, then, under my breath, whisper, "You should really stop grinding your teeth. Really bad for your teeth."

When I move to the instructor, I notice he's a cute-enough-looking guy, but compared to Jaime, he looks small. Normally, he'd probably be my type: flirty, with a good smile and longish, sun-bleached hair, but suddenly, his surfer boy look doesn't do it for me.

He smiles wide at me before digging through a bin for the right-sized life jacket, and I joke about how they don't have a pretty one. It's clear he uses smiles and boyish looks to land tourists, but I'm not falling for it, not as his fingers glide over my arm as he slides the life jacket on or as he buckles it, trying to look into my eyes.

The entire time, I can't help but look over his shoulder at Jaime, his jaw still tight and arms crossed over his chest. He's in a pair of olive board shorts and a tight-fitting black tee, his skin already tan, reminding me I didn't see him put on sunscreen.

"All right, who's next?" the instructor asks, smiling at Anne, clearly coming to terms that his charm is not working on me.

Her hand lifts, and I move, walking on the gently rocking boat back toward Jaime. I slip my flip-flops into my bag, digging for the sunscreen to try and bug him into wearing some, but then a strong tug comes on one of the loose straps of my life jacket, making me stand straight.

"What—"

"He did a shit job. I'm tightening these," Jaime mumbles under his breath, and then mine catches as he moves to his knees before me, pulling himself face-to-face with my chest. His eyes are locked on the buckles of my life jacket, undoing them and then tugging and manipulating the loose straps so they'll be more secure. My hands move to his shoulders as I nearly lose my footing when a finger grazes the side of my breast.

"Sorry."

I don't reply because my breath is inexplicably caught in my throat at the mere, slight touch. I joke that Jaime likes me, mostly because I find it hilarious to push his buttons and his definition of "professionalism," but he's a handsome man. I'd be lying if I said I wasn't into him, and I didn't have more than the occasional inappropriate thought drift through my mind.

"Is this also you not liking me?" I whisper for his ears only.

He shakes his head but doesn't look at me, just keeps his eyes on the straps of the life jacket, untwisting them and making sure it's secure.

"It's my job to keep you safe; that's all I'm doing," he says in a low growl. "That fucker was too busy staring at your tits to make sure you were strapped into this right."

"Mm-hmm," I say unconvincingly. "Because you don't like me, right?"

"Right," he growls, then stands abruptly, moving to the bin where the life vests are and grabbing one his size.

"What are you doing?" I ask as he comes back, vest in hand.

He tosses it to the seat next to my bag, then reaches behind his back, grabbing his T-shirt and tugging it over his head. My mouth goes dry, seeing the lines and muscle definition *everywhere*. Jesus Christ, no wonder he has to wake up so early to work out—it must take a century to maintain that. He's broad, which I knew, but now I see it's because of muscled shoulders and a strong back, his front dotted with the perfect amount of chest hair.

"If you're snorkeling, so am I."

"Jaime, you don't have to—"

"My only job here is to take care of you and keep you safe, Ava," he says, cutting me off. "I *do* have to."

"But you're afraid of sharks."

His eyes shift to the sky, a move he often does when he's with me, as if I'm constantly pushing him to a point where he needs a higher power to step in. "I'm not afraid of sharks, Ava. I just don't like unpredictability."

"You must hate me, then," I say with a small smile.

He stares at me, not even a tilt of his lips, as he reads my face behind dark sunglasses. "I'm the furthest thing from hating you, Princess, for better or worse. I think it's pretty clear."

It knocks me off my game, confusing and shocking me with his surety and the way it's the opposite of everything I ever thought about Jaime.

Sure, I fuck with him by telling him he likes me, and sure, I never thought he actually hated me, *but* it wasn't like I was under the impression that this was his ideal assignment, driving a beauty queen around the country while she constantly almost gets herself into trouble.

I continue staring at him as the instructor says something I don't hear, lost in Jaime and what he said, until his thick arm raises, eyes aimed at the instructor behind me.

"We'll go first," he says, slipping on his life jacket quickly and efficiently before putting a hand on my lower back to turn and guide me to the back of the boat.

The next thing I know, Jaime is standing at the edge of the back of the boat after the instructor gives us each goggles, a snorkel, and a list of instructions. I barely hear, my mind still racing, but Jaime is glued to him as he speaks, taking in everything.

"All right, you two," he says finally. "You can either get in gently or jump on in." His smile is genuine as he looks at us, and suddenly I remember where I am, the fact that there are cameras, and that we're about to cross off one of my bucket list items.

"Jump!" I shout, and everyone on the boat laughs like it was expected of me to want the more fun version.

Jaime huffs but nods.

"Whenever you're ready," the tour guide says with a chin tip to Jaime.

"You first," he says under his breath, but I shake my head, my braid grazing my shoulders as I do.

"Together."

He looks at me, a slight irritation in his look before he rolls his eyes. "Fine." Then he looks forward like he's waiting for my countdown.

I lean infinitesimally to my left toward him. "You gotta hold my hand," I whisper.

"What?"

"Before we jump in. You have to hold my hand."

He looks at the water and then at me. "Why?"

"I don't know, it's what everyone does when they jump off boats."

He glares at me, and I laugh. "You know, holding my hand won't ruin your professionalism, big guy," I tell him.

"I think I've already fucked the professionalism beyond repair," he grumbles under his breath. I laugh loudly, and his lips part in a smile he can't fight.

"Well, then hold my hand and jump in."

And he does.

TWENTY-THREE
AVA

"What is that?" Jaime asks when I step out of my bedroom four days later to head out for the day's excursion.

"A bag," I say with a smile, lifting the small cream-colored lace clutch.

"You know what I mean," he says, and I do, of course.

I went with a pink corset-esque top with bows at the shoulders and a short, cream skirt that's fitted until mid-thigh before it flares out in a short ruffle. Although the top has an underwire to hold me in and give me much-needed support, my breasts nearly spill out the top, and although I'm wearing nude boy shorts under to cover my ass, the skirt is definitely short.

Jaime looks irritated.

"Oh, this little old thing?" I ask with a wide smile, twisting so the ruffles on my skirt flare just a bit.

"Emphasis on little," he says with a frown. I can almost see the gears in his mind working.

"Hush, it's more coverage than half of the outfits I wore for the pageant. The bathing suit they made all of us wear barely covered anything," I say, referencing the required swimsuit I wore for the Miss Americana pageant.

"Yeah, trust me, I know."

"You watched the pageant?" I ask, suddenly interested.

"Part of my job is knowing who I'm watching. Your photos are plastered all over the internet. Those swimsuit photos are pretty hard to avoid."

"Don't sound too happy about that, now."

"Trust me, I'm not."

"Let me guess, you're one of those guys who thinks a woman should only wear skirted one-pieces at the beach."

"No, but it would make my life a bit easier if you covered more of your ass."

I take a step closer to him and smile. "So you've been watching my ass?"

Something flares in his eyes, but it's gone as soon as it comes.

"I think the entire country has seen your ass at this point."

"Maybe it's a good thing you don't like me then," I say with an eye roll.

"You can say that again," he says.

"Why, because if I was yours, you'd go all caveman on me, put me in a nun habit at all times?" Something in him seems to snap as his jaw goes tight. He steps closer with a shake of his head, and my heart begins to race.

"No, Princess."

"So you'd just never let me leave the house?" My voice is a breathy whisper, barely two feet between us.

"No, sweetheart. If you were mine, I'd take you everywhere. Anywhere. Show you off any chance I got. A woman like you, you don't tell her what to do, what to wear. You let her do it, then prepare to watch her ass as she moves, stay alert while she lives her life, ensuring no harm comes to her. You make it so she never has to realize there's a world outside of her bubble that isn't sunshine and rainbows."

His words stop my breath in my lungs, stop the blood in my veins, my heart skipping a beat.

"Sounds pretty close to what we're doing right now, doesn't it?" I ask, and even to my own ears, my voice sounds breathy and seductive, a Marilyn Monroe quality to it. "Me wearing whatever I want, doing whatever I want, you watching my ass so nothing bad happens to me?"

He shakes his head, a bit of regret in the look. "But you're not mine, Ava."

"I could be," I say, taking a small step forward and smiling up at him. He's so fucking tall, and I haven't put my shoes on, making me even smaller than normal around him.

"I'm your bodyguard," he says as if he doesn't want to say it but is forcing the words out all the same.

"But if you weren't," I clarify. "If I wasn't a client, if I wasn't someone you were paid to protect, you'd want me?" One more step, and I'm almost chest-to-chest with him. I feel exposed like this, in a tiny outfit, him dressed in a black tee and black pants.

"Ava..."

"For science, Jaime." I put a hand on his chest and feel his heart beating there, pounding against my palm.

He must see something on my face or maybe he's as tired of the games as I am, because he finally makes what feels like a confession. "Yeah, Princess, if you weren't a client, I'd kiss you."

That's what I need to hear. I won't throw myself at a man who doesn't want me, who never wanted me or never *would* want me, but this? This I can work with.

Slowly, giving him time to say no, to push me off—a move I would respect even if I'm constantly pushing at his buttons—my free hand moves up until it's on the side of his neck. Then I move, lifting to the tips of my toes, rising to try and meet him, using light pressure on my hand to urge him to bend his head a bit, which he does before he wraps an arm around my waist, pasting my body to his in the most delicious way.

And then my lips are on his, a gentle press, a lingering of lips on lips that has my heart racing and butterflies erupting in my stomach.

It's over much sooner than I would like as I lower back to my flat feet with a gentle, easy smile on my lips. My eyes slowly float open to look at him, his head tipping down to look at me, eyes discerning and reading me.

"You kissed me," he says simply, and I feel every syllable as it moves through his chest against my nipples in the absolute best way possible.

"I did," I say with a smile.

"You kissed me," he clarifies like he finds the concept absolutely baffling.

"Sure did," I repeat, with a smile.

"That's not how that works, Ava."

I lift an eyebrow and tip my lips up. "I think it's exactly how it worked," I say with a laugh.

"No, not with me."

I tip my head to the side and roll my eyes. "Then how's it supposed to work, Jaime?" I say with challenge in my words, waiting for his stupid man-explanation where he will probably tell me I shouldn't have done that because of work or blurring lines or who the fuck knows.

Instead, as seems to be his way, he surprises me by doing neither of those.

"Like this."

TWENTY-FOUR
JAIME

My knees bend a bit, and my free hand moves under Ava's ass before I stand up straight, lifting her off the ground and moving toward the wall behind her. Instantly, her legs wrap around my waist on instinct, as if even her body knows this is how it's supposed to be.

I thought I was in my head.

I thought she was just gorgeous, and we were around each other too much, because there is no way this all-consuming attraction I feel for Ava is anything more than convenience or in my head.

Then she kissed me, and that theory was thrown out the window.

Now, I need more.

I am so fucked.

But I can worry about that another time. *Any* other time.

Right now, I press her back against the wall, her face right in front of mine now that we're on more even footing, her lips brushing against mine as I whisper, "This is how it works, Ava. I kiss you. Every time, *I* kiss *you*, and I do it in a way that you can never forget what it's like to be kissed by a man wholly and completely obsessed with you."

It's a confession of sorts; the answer to all of her prompts about whether I like her and her constant teasing that I'm learning is just her way. Each time she asks me, bugging me about liking her, I have to force myself not to say, *Yes, I like you, Ava. I more than like you—I'm fucking obsessed with you, and I can't seem to do a single thing without you on my mind.*

Ava Bordeaux is the first thing I think about the moment I wake up and the last thing I think about as I'm falling asleep, and it has nothing to do with my need to protect her. Not even a little.

My hand on her jaw tips up her face to better angle it, and I dip my head down, letting my lips graze hers gently. She sighs into the kiss, a sound that goes straight to my dick, and I use it to open her lips, slide my tongue into her mouth, and taste her.

Bubblegum. She tastes like fucking bubblegum. My pink princess, who drives me up a fucking wall, *tastes* like bubblegum, and for a moment, I wonder how she tastes everywhere else.

When her tongue comes to touch mine, dancing with it, battling for dominance, it's like our everyday interactions but in a kiss: sugary sweet with a hit of fire.

It makes me hard, makes me want—no, *need*—more, so I move closer, pinning her more fully between the wall and my chest, my cock grinding into her center at this angle.

"Oh, god," she whispers into the kiss, and what I would fucking give to hear her make that sound naked beneath me as I fuck into her.

"You're fucking perfect," I groan against her lips, my teeth nipping and then sucking to soothe the bruised skin. Then I trail my lips down her neck, sucking and tasting her gently as I do. She's an addiction—the sweetest dessert, the most potent liquor—and I'm already drunk on her.

"Fucking weeks, teasing me in your sweet little outfits." I nip at her neck and she moans again, bucking against me, tipping her head to the side to give me more room to work with.

"Teasing me and telling me I'm into you when all I want to do is do my fucking job and try to forget how *much* I want you. You know how much I want you, though, Ava, don't you? You've known since that first day. I'm shit at hiding it." My tongue runs up the skin of her neck before I bite her earlobe. Her hips are moving now, a gentle rocking against my hard cock.

"I want you too," she whispers, a plea.

"I know, Princess. Fuck, do I know. I don't know how much longer I can resist you." I suck at her neck, moving and nipping, being sure not to stay too long in one spot, because even in my heightened state, I know not to leave a hickey on the pageant queen.

My hand slips down her side, then back up until I cup her breast, my thumb swiping over the raised spot of her nipple before pushing the cup down. "Oh, god," she groans into my ear, and I grind my hard cock into her again, living for how she continues to rock on me, attempting to get some kind of friction. "More, please."

My mouth moves back to hers, tasting her before I pinch her nipple, rolling it, and drowning in the yelp she lets out as I do. Her breasts are perfect, filling my palm with tight pink nipples I'd give anything to suck on right now, her body responsive as I play. I start contemplating ways to get her to the bed, what I'll do next, how—

Then my phone beeps with a text, probably the coordinators asking if we're heading downstairs or if there's an issue, and I come back to myself.

We shouldn't be doing this.

We have places to be, people counting on us. We both have a job to do.

Still, I slow the kiss instead of pulling back, unable to end it completely.

No matter if this was a good idea or not, I don't regret kissing Ava.

Not even a little.

My hand grips her ass one last time, squeezing the perfect globes I've been watching much too often for someone simply protecting her before I loosen my grip, letting her slide down my body, fighting the groan as I do.

Looking down at her, her lips all swollen, lipstick nearly gone, I almost change my mind. I almost send a text to the coordinator saying

Ava has food poisoning and we won't be able to come today, instead choosing to make Ava come in my bed all day long. But I know more than anything, Ava is hardworking and doesn't like to disappoint people.

Even though she'd enjoy herself, she'd regret not doing what she's here to do. So I press my lips to hers once more, whispering, "*That* is how this works, Ava." Then I step back, holding her waist until she finds her footing, fighting a smile as I watch her waver a bit. Once she does, I step back again, fighting back a groan as I catch the pink nipple of her full breast out of her top. Reaching over, I gently grip the cream fabric of the bra top and tug until she's covered again.

She lets out a low mewl as I do, like the feel of my fingers barely grazing her skin is bliss in and of itself, and I realize I need to leave this hotel room before things get out of hand.

Stepping back, I take her in one last time—face flushed, lips swollen, eyes wide—and commit it to memory before I reach out and wipe the side of my thumb along her lower lip. "Go fix your lipstick, Princess. I'll wait for you in the hall."

I could barely focus on anything for the rest of the afternoon, not after Jaime pressed me up against a wall and kissed me as if I were his. It took me a full five minutes to float back down from whatever planet that kiss took me to, fix my lipstick, and step into the hallway. When I did, he put a light hand to my lower back, guided me toward the elevator, and acted as if nothing at all happened.

The afternoon event is simple, exploring the cute Main Street of Augusta, Miss Georgia's hometown, and then going to a fundraising dinner with a meet and greet where fans donated extra to say hi to me and Miss Georgia, a sweet woman named Vanessa, and, unfortunately, Anne.

When we walk into the room, it's super cute. There are two high-top tables with headshots and markers on top and a big cream backdrop with tiny pink bows all over it. Two men dressed in black, with additional security from the hotel where the dinner is being hosted, are chatting with each other,.

"I'm going to be in that corner," Jaime says as we walk in, pointing to a corner of the room as we walk to the high-top table I'll be standing at. "Don't throw a fit because I'm not right at your side; I don't want to be in your pictures."

I fight a smile before shaking my head at him. "It's all right, big guy. I think this is a solid exception."

"Why is he even here?" Anne asks, coming over to us, all drama and attitude. I give Vanessa a *here we go,* look, and she smiles with wide eyes. "What kind of trouble could you possibly get into at a meet and greet?"

With a sigh, I turn to Anne, trying to make my voice as calm and friendly as possible. "Despite what you seem to think, Jaime isn't here just to keep tabs on me and report my every twitch to Regina, but because I've got some weirdos with just a bit too much interest in me."

Anne huffs before rolling her eyes at me and putting her hands on her hips. "You know, we all have weirdos in our messages, Ava. I don't know what makes you so special to need a bodyguard."

I lift my hands, attempting to appease her. "Look, talk to Regina. I never said I needed a bodyguard—you were at the meeting where I said it wasn't necessary. They just stuck me with this guy," I say, hitching a thumb at Jaime, even though I've been increasingly happy he has been by my side over the past three weeks.

"Well, you're just going to be here shaking hands and taking pictures. There's security at the hotel. I'm going to be in the main room where there's *no* security." She tips her chin up and puts her hands on her hips. The stance and her face make her look like a small child who isn't getting her way, like she's about to stomp her foot or lie on the floor, tantruming until she gets her way. "I want him to come with me."

Jaime's body tightens next to mine, and a wave of jealousy and panic overwhelms me, but I keep my snotty smile on.

"Come with you? For what, Anne? To protect you from the millions of people who voted for you to win?" Vanessa lets out a small snort, but I keep speaking. "If you feel so threatened by them that you want Jaime to assist you, you have to talk to Regina. Or Jaime, but good luck with that."

"Good luck? What's that supposed to mean?" she asks.

"It just means he isn't really into all of." I wave my hand around the room. "This."

"Well, maybe it's just *you* he's not into," she replies in a way that kind of makes me want to rip her hair out.

My mind goes directly to the kiss this morning, the way he held me, the way he looked at me, the groan he let out when I ground on him...

Oh, he's *definitely* into me.

But I won't be letting Anne know that, of course. "You're so right," I say with wide eyes. "That must be it. Maybe you can fix him, you know?" Jaime snorts before coughing to disguise the laugh as she looks at me, assessing before rolling her eyes and walking off.

As she does, Vanessa leans into me. "God, she's insufferable," she says. "How are you doing it?"

"Doing what?"

"How many stops has Anne been on with you? And how have you not absolutely *lost* it on her yet?"

"Oh, that. Yeah, too many, if I'm being honest. But on the bright side, she hates my guts so much that she mostly stays away from me."

Vanessa lets out a laugh and gives me a genuine smile.

"God, that must be nice. I've spent so long playing nice with her since we've been on the same circuit; I think she thinks we're friends."

"Ah, yes, well, unfortunately, or, maybe, fortunately, for me, I don't think we'll ever get to that final state of acceptance."

"Definitely fortunate," she says before her voice drops a bit lower. "Wicked witch and her monkey incoming."

"Wha—" I start, but Regina is walking my way on a mission, Anne trailing behind with a smug smile, and I understand.

"Mr. Wilde, today I need you to go with Anne to her signing," Regina says without any sort of hello to anyone.

"What?" he asks. "No, I'm assigned to Ava."

Her posture goes straighter, and her chin juts out, and something tells me this woman is *not* used to not getting her way. "Well, actually, you're assigned to the Miss Americana pageant. We've just asked you to follow Ava."

Jaime's jaw goes tight. "We've had active security threats on Ava. Have there been any threats on Miss Utah?"

Something about him calling me *Ava* and Anne by her pageant name makes warmth bloom in my belly, but I don't have time for *that* because she continues on her tirade.

"I get weird messages just like Ava *does*. We *all* do, right, Vanessa?" She turns to Vanessa, who lifts her hands in an *I'm staying out of this* way before Anne crosses her arms on her chest. "She's nothing special."

The words bring back what Jaime said that first night I met him, when he thought I was some drunk birthday girl trying to cute my way into a VIP section.

The acid churns but doesn't last for long when Jaime speaks. "Ava is incredibly special." My entire body stills as I watch a faint blush creep over his cheeks. "And she's also at a higher risk, given her hotel room was broken into barely a week ago."

"We have standard security at the event; they can keep an eye on Ava while she's doing her meet and greet. And the hotel issue was explained to me as some local kids messing around, nothing actually related to Ava herself."

Jaime's jaw goes tight. "Why can't that security go with Anne, and I'll be in this room with Ava and Miss Georgia?"

"She's going to be doing some meet and greets in the main dining area to break things up a bit. There's hotel security here, but nothing upfront. I'm asking you to do the job I contracted you to do, Mr. Wilde." The way she says it is a clear threat.

"I just don't understand why we can't—"

"It's fine," I say without thinking. "Borrow him for the afternoon."

"What?" Regina and Jaime say at the same time.

"This room is small, so they're only going to let, like, five people in at a time, plus press, and there's the event security. It would be really hard for something bad to happen here," I say, looking directly at Jaime as I do.

"Absolutely not," he says.

"I don't understand why you're having such difficulty following a simple order. I suppose I'll have to make a note to tell Five Star how —" Regina starts, and I know the path she's headed down, threatening Jaime's job.

I don't want him to leave me, the idea of it already building my anxiety, removing the security blanket I didn't realize he'd wrapped around me with his presence, but I won't let this dumb argument hurt his career.

"Give us a few minutes, okay?" I say to Regina and Anne before grabbing Jaime's hand and tugging him into an empty room.

"Absolutely not," he says with a glare, arms crossing on his chest like he wants to strangle me as soon as the door shuts us in.

"Absolutely, *yes.*"

"Ava—"

"There's security in there. There's very little that could happen. Is it worth Regina reporting to your boss you're not doing your job? Is it worth losing your retirement?"

"Your safety is worth that and more."

My belly goes warm with that, but I can't let him do this.

"And I *will* be safe, Jaime. But I won't be able to sleep if something happens and fucks up your shit," I say. When he opens his mouth, I cut him off. "And that might mean they take you off my case, and who else is going to hold Peach while I be pretty?" His mouth closes, and his jaw gets hard, but I think I've won.

"So I'm just here to hold Peach?" he asks, his voice somehow lower, huskier.

"Oh, definitely. That's the only thing you're good for," I say with a smile, even though I don't feel any kind of humor. We spend a long stretch of time staring at each other in silence.

"I don't like this," Jaime says, finally.

"Why, because you're so in love with me, you can't bear not being by my side every second of every day?" He rolls his eyes.

"No, because I know you, and even when you're not trying, which you usually are, Ava, you find trouble at every turn."

"I'll be fine, Jaime. I'll have other security there; it's not like it will be a free-for-all. It's our only option, and you know it." I close the gap between us, putting a hand on his chest and looking up at him, all brooding eyes and clenched teeth before pressing a kiss to the underside of his jaw.

With that, he lets out a sigh before finally, he nods. "Fine. Only if you're on your best behavior, though, Ava. I mean it."

"You're the best! Thank you!" I say, stepping back and clapping my hands. "Okay, let's get back before—oof!" I shout, nearly twisting my ankle as I trip on a small piece of the carpet that's pulled up. I'm headed for a faceplant on the carpet, but his arm wraps around my waist, tugging me into his chest and saving me from my inevitable demise. My heart pounds, his thumb brushing the bare skin between where my top stops and my skirt starts.

"See the benefits of having you within arms reach?" he asks, his voice a low rumble against my chest. I look at him over my shoulder and smile.

"Yeah, I can see the benefit of having you close," I whisper. I don't miss the way his eyes flash, the way they drop to my lips, the way they move back to my eyes just a hair darker, the thoughts I wish he'd just act on playing there.

And then he leans down, placing a quick peck to my lips like he can't resist himself before he moves to let me go. His hand gently moves as his fingers linger like he doesn't want to let go. Once he knows I won't fall on myself once more, he crosses his arms on his chest and nods, then tips his head toward the other room.

"Fine, I'll go with Anne, but not because Regina wants me to. Because you asked me to. But I'll be having a talk with the security here, warning them about how you are."

I smile because how could I not?

"Thanks, big guy."

TWENTY-SIX
AVA

The fan meet and greet was fun for the first two hours, but I'm ready to have the spotlight off me.

I'm smiling so much my jaw is starting to get tired, but when I look at the clock above the door, we've only got about five more minutes before we'll be out and headed to dinner, where I can eat, and then sneak out quietly and head back to the hotel for the night.

"Big fan, Ava," a man says after a group of young girls walks off, giggling. He puts his hand out to shake, and I accept it with my gracious pageant smile plastered across my face, but it slips just a bit when he uses the handshake to tug me into him, forcing me into a hug. His cheap cologne envelopes me, and when I step back, it clings to me. I don't say no to hugs since I usually don't mind it, especially with young fans, but now I'm contemplating adding it to the rules.

In this moment, when my eyes drift to the corner Jaime was going to stand in, I regret not pushing Regina to let me keep him at my side.

This man makes me feel uneasy.

"You're gorgeous, which you know, of course. I'd love to take you out tonight and help you get a more intimate feel for the city of Augusta."

Absolutely the fuck not.

I give him a kind but closed-lip smile, the type women give just to appease creeps, and shake my head. "Unfortunately, I've got so much going on, I don't have time for anything else. Thank you so much for the offer, though," I say apologetically. The door to the room closes, indicating that this man and the three groups behind him are the last of the meet and greet.

He reaches into his pocket, grabs his wallet, and pulls out a card. "My number, in case you change your mind." He hands it to me with a wink, and I grab it with as small of a smile as I can manage with the cameras still on me before setting it on the small table next to me we used for holding the small gifts or letters people have given me or signing things.

I shift back to the creep, facing the assistant who is holding his phone, and turn for a photo. As I do, his hand moves behind me, landing on my lower back, and even though I want to tell him to fuck off, I grin and bear it, ready to do whatever it takes for his turn to be done. Cameras click all around as I smile, tilting my head a bit, and then it happens.

His hand moves down and then out, and he slaps my ass.

It's not hard, the angle strange, but he does it all the same, and I step back, shocked. I don't register anything other than the wide, proud grin on his lips.

"Did you just slap my ass?" I ask, still in shock. The side door opens and closes as I do, but I don't move my gaze, continuing to stare at this man.

"Oh, come on, it was just a love tap," he says with a chuckle and that same self-satisfied dude-bro look on his face.

"A love tap? A *love tap?*"

"Don't make it a bigger deal than it was," he says, hands raised in that way asshole men do when they feel like a woman is overreacting.

He wants overreacting? I'll give it to him.

I pull my hand back and slap him across his cheek, staggering a bit as I do, my heels putting off my center of gravity.

"What the fuc—" he says, then stops when someone comes behind him, grabbing his arms and pinning them behind him. I barely even registered that the man had started to lift his hand to strike me.

And holding him back is Jaime.

I don't even know when he came back or when he walked into the room, but for the first time in a long time, I feel safe.

Relieved.

Jaime's eyes are on mine as he holds the man's arms back behind his back with ease, regardless of how much he fights, jerking against the hold.

"What the fuck, man?" the man spews.

And in that flash of time, I see it all. Regret and fear and anger in his eyes, and I know—I *know*—it's my fault for insisting he go with Anne just so I make less waves. None of this would have happened if I'd just listened to him and let him insist on not going with her.

Right on its heels, another thought knocks through me, reminding me it's *not* my fault. This wasn't supposed to happen. It *wouldn't* have happened if this fuckwad knew boundaries.

It's *this* asshole's fault.

With that thought, my hand pulls back, and I slap the man across his face. Again.

"How do you like it, huh? A little love tap?" I ask, slapping him again as Jaime holds him back, adrenaline rushing through my veins as I do. "Not so fun, is it? A love tap, *my ass!*"

I don't let myself wonder what would have happened if Jaime wasn't here and didn't grab him when he did. Instead, I meet Jaime's eyes as he shifts the man out of my striking range, and somehow, I settle myself, coming back to reality.

"Ava! Ava!" reporters call, and my skin heats, the adrenaline coming down as I realize what just happened: I slapped a man, and every moment was caught on camera.

This is going to be everywhere in ten minutes, max.

"Ava! How does this reflect on the Miss Americana organization?" a reporter from the American Star I've seen a few times asks.

"What?" I ask, stilling. I look over my shoulder as Jaime hands over the douche who smacked my ass to the hotel's security.

"The Miss Americana pageant. How do you think this reflects on them, considering you're here on their behalf? You assaulted a man repeatedly." Preston Smith, I remember what the reporter's name is. He's fond of writing disapproving and speculative articles about me.

Lovely.

For a split second, panic fills me. Does this break my contract? I remember there being a line about being the spokesperson for the pageant and how my actions reflect upon them and being liable for damages if my actions reflect poorly on them.

And then I remember I don't fucking care.

If defending myself after someone *assaults me* reflects poorly on them in their eyes, they can fuck themselves.

That's one time I'd be willing to lose the crown to Anne for sticking up for myself.

So I straighten my shoulders and look at one of the cameras dead on.

"I slapped a man back after he, a complete stranger, slapped my ass without my permission." I smile sweetly at the reporter, putting my curated pageant girl in place, the real version that won me the social vote and, ultimately, the pageant. "Payback's a bitch, you know?"

"I just mean, the ideal for the Miss Americana contestants are docile caretakers, not someone who seeks retribution and violence. As you know, young girls are watching your every move. You've become a role model."

My head moves back as if the reporter slapped *me*. In my peripheral vision, Jaime's head snaps up as well, not because he's shocked by the question like I am, but because he knows. We might not have been working together that long, but he already knows me well enough to know that question is going to piss me off.

"You're right. Girls *are* watching; they're watching women in the spotlight and using what they see to shape how they believe they deserve to be treated and how they should act at any given moment. They're watching how we do or don't stand up for ourselves when assholes like that—" I jab my finger in the direction of where the man was. "Take advantage of us. And I hope they're taking notes on how they must stand up for themselves. When I was growing up, much of the media I saw told me to grin and bear it, to let it happen because, chances are, that woman did something to deserve it. She didn't dress right, or she said the wrong thing or encouraged some entitled man. But that's fucked. Why should I live my life any differently simply because *men exist?*" My chest is heaving now, and everyone around me is silent. "So yeah. I hope girls are watching. And you can take that quote and twist it however you want, but when I say it, I mean I hope girls are watching women stand up for themselves, and I hope they are taking notes. That's what the real Miss Americana should be, and that's the Miss Americana *I'm* going to be."

Finally, I'm out of words—or, at least, I'm out of words and bravado—and I'm staring at the small crowd of fans and reporters when it happens.

I hear a single set of claps from my left, where Miss Georgia is standing, a wide smile on her lips. I smile back, and more claps start from another woman I don't know but recognize as a popular social media influencer. Her phone is up as if she's been recording my entire tirade.

God.

I totally am fucking this whole thing up.

More claps start around the room, fifteen or twenty people here to witness everything, then some cheering. I start to panic because what am I supposed to do with this? Encourage it? Try some form of damage control. I'm not completely sure.

Of course, he sees it. Jaime sees the panic taking over.

"All right, shows over," Jaime says, voice booming through the small room. "Everyone out."

"There's still—" the PR manager squeaks out.

"No, there's not. Ava will sign some things for whoever we didn't get to, but we have a police report to file, and Ava needs to rest after all of this." I blink at Jaime, whose face is as hard as stone, something the reporters definitely see because, without any argument, they start to leak out. And I'm grateful because adrenaline is suddenly gone from my veins, leaving an uneasy panic in its wake.

"Come on, Princess," Jaime says a few moments later, his arm going to my waist and guiding me towards a chair. "Let's get you in a seat."

"I've got it, big guy," I say, fighting his arm around my waist. "I can walk, and I won't run off to go slap another asshole who absolutely deserves it."

"I know. Trust me, I know. You're a tough, capable woman. But please, give me this."

I don't have it in me to argue, not with Jaime, so I just let him lead me to the chair, sit me down, and manage the rest of the evening with gratitude.

TWENTY-SEVEN
JAIME

Tension fills the car as we drive back to the hotel after filing a report and picking Peach up from the pet sitter. All I can think about is how I should have been there the entire time, regardless of what anyone insisted on, how I should never have agreed to be in the other room, and what would have happened if I had been just another minute longer.

"Okay, so next meet and greet, you're in every picture," Ava says with a small, self-deprecating laugh. "Attached at the hip for a while, okay?"

I look at her quickly, seeing her holding the cat tightly to her chest like a security blanket.

"If it were up to me, you wouldn't *have* another meet and greet." Unfortunately, it's *not* up to me.

"What? Stop, Jaime, you're insane." I can hear the eye roll in her voice.

"You were almost hit today, Ava. Someone assaulted you. We're lucky it wasn't worse. Why are you acting like this isn't a big deal?"

"Because it's not, Jaime."

"You've got to be kidding me," I murmur.

"I just...this kind of shit, it's going to happen. I signed up for it knowing what I was doing, putting myself on this stupid pedestal, and then I got on social media doing the same. I got into this...job, knowing I would basically be a doll for people to look at and pick apart. I'm okay with it. Sometimes, people think that means I'd be okay with more, which sucks, but that's why I have you, right?" Her smile is uneasy, but not because of the man. It's because of me and what my face must look like. I want to change it, to shift my expression, but I just...can't.

"That's fucked, Ava."

She shrugs. "That's life, Jaime," she says in a counterargument.

"Not for you," I say, shaking my head and pulling into the hotel parking lot.

"What?"

Everything I was thinking about in the two hours I was away from her came crashing into me: the possession, the need, the want. Followed by everything I felt as I watched that man lunge for her, watched her hit him, and watched her sit silently and in shock as she filed a report with the police.

It's all clashing in my chest, and I need air.

I need air, and I'm realizing I need Ava as if she *were* air, and we need to get out of here before I do something stupid.

After putting the SUV in park, I turn it off and step out, slamming the door as I walk around the front. I take a deep breath to steady myself. When I reach her door, I open it, reach over to unbuckle her, then grab the cat and place her in the carrier.

Ava steps out of the car, and I hold Peach's carrier in one hand while I place my hand on her lower back, moving us both toward the hotel entrance without a word.

"Jaime," she says, but I keep walking through the quiet hotel lobby until we're at the bank of elevators, pressing the up button and stepping in when the doors slide open.

"What is going on?" she asks as the doors close us in, her scent filling the small area and making it impossible for me to breathe again. "You're freaking me out."

I hit the button for the top floor and wait for the doors to shut, turning to her. "The fact that you're not freaked by what happened is freaking me out even more, Ava."

She rolls her eyes before she steps back and crosses her arms over her chest, pushing her tits up a bit. "It's just some weirdo, it's fine."

I shake my head and take a step closer to her. "No, it's not." My voice is low, even to my ears.

"It's just part of this gig. It happens to all the girls. We have things in place—like *you*, Jaime—to make it less dangerous." She takes a step back, her back hitting the metal of the elevator.

"This shit should not happen to you or *anyone*, Ava."

She rolls her eyes, her signature move toward me at this point. "It's fine. All's well, that ends well."

I look at her, shake my head, and let that irritation and fury win. Not irritation at her, but at the world, at this pageant, for making her feel like she has to just accept *this, that* she would think this is normal —a man getting into her personal space and expecting...anything from her.

But mostly, there's fury at myself.

This is *exactly* why I've shut down any *thought* of Ava, regardless of the fact that I've felt a pull to her since that first night in the club: it leads to distractions. This morning I was weak, and I let her kiss me, then I kissed her and held her and touched her and it twisted every single thought and action thereafter. It made it so when she asked me to go with Anne, I wanted to do whatever would make her happy, rather than whatever I needed to do to make sure she was *protected*.

"This morning should have never happened." It feels wrong to say it, considering every moment of having her in my arms, my lips on hers felt more right than anything I'd ever experienced. I don't turn to her when her head snaps to look at me, but I feel the burn of her glare all the same.

"What are you talking about?"

"I shouldn't have kissed you this morning," I say, then the elevator doors open and I step out, waiting for her to follow.

She steps out of the elevator and crosses her arms on her chest, glaring at me. "I kissed you," she says, and I sigh deeply.

"Ava, you know what I mean. We shouldn't have kissed this morning."

"Why not? We're two consenting adults, Jaime."

"Because I'm here to keep you safe, Ava, and today you weren't. In this job, you can't have distractions, and you are the biggest distraction known to man. My being distracted led to this afternoon, and I won't let that happen again."

She stares at me for long moments, assessing, before she shakes her head. "I never thought you'd be the type to get scared off too easily," she whispers.

"I was terrified," I reply quickly, my voice just as low.

"What?"

"I was *terrified*, Ava. I've never been as scared in my entire life than when I saw that man reach for you, and I've seen some fucked-up shit. I was terrified, and it's all my fault. If I were there the entire time, it wouldn't have happened. If I wasn't so twisted up in the idea of you, I would have used my head and known I needed to be there for you. But I wasn't, and it was because I was too worried about keeping you happy than I was keeping you safe, and look how that ended." Her eyes go a bit soft, her shoulder relaxing as she reaches out to touch me, but I step back out of reach.

"Jaime," she says.

"I'm serious. It was a bad idea. I never want to feel again how I felt in that room, and I especially never want to see the look of panic in your eyes. You want to hate me because I won't give into whatever there is between us? Then hate me. But at least you'll be safe," I say, staring at her, letting her see everything behind my walls.

Everything I feel.

Everything I *can't* feel.

"So you're saying there's something," she whispers, and I sigh for what feels like the hundredth time.

But before I can say anything to further dissuade her, the elevator dings once more, sliding open, someone standing there and stepping off, breaking the moment. With that, I step forward, grab Ava's hand in mine, and lead her to our room.

The entire time, all I can think is *you are so fucked.*

TWENTY-EIGHT
JAIME

"What the fuck happened yesterday?" The voice booms through the line early the next morning. It's seven a.m., and Ava is still asleep as I try to get out onto the balcony without her waking.

"Greg—" I start, sliding the door closed behind me. I've already worked out in an effort to quiet my mind after the chaos that was yesterday and gotten coffee, so two hours of peace without dealing with my asshole of a boss has to be a win.

"What the *fuck* happened, Wilde?" he shouts.

"Look—"

"This is *not* what we need happening right now," he says, continuing to steamroll over me.

"I get that, but—"

"Where were you?"

I snap. "If you would let me fucking answer, I could tell you everything."

Finally, silence rolls through the line, and I close my eyes, taking a deep breath before explaining.

"Yesterday, before the meet and greet, Regina insisted I take one of the other contestants to their meet and greet because, in her opinion, there would be sufficient security at the hotel ballroom where Ava was. She insisted I was not on assignment for *Ava* but for the Miss Americana organization."

A low curse comes through the line, which I take as a good sign I'm not totally screwed before I continue.

"Ava wants to make as little waves as she can, so she asked me to go. Thankfully, the other event ended quickly, or there could have been a real issue: I'd barely just walked in before the man assaulted Ms. Bordeaux. If I hadn't grabbed him..." My voice trails off, thinking about the force in his arm and how he was more than willing to let that punch land. "I swear, I was under the impression she'd be safe. That's how it was explained to me, and I didn't feel I was given an option."

"Well, she wasn't safe," he snaps.

"Yeah, I get that, but I—"

"And then she ran her mouth to the press," he says, and my back goes straight.

Last night, Ava told me Regina texted her to ask her to *refrain from speaking with the press off-handedly in the future to protect the image of the Miss Americana organization,* not even an, *are you okay?* text to preface it. It made my hands ball up into fists, and that feeling is even stronger now with Greg spewing his bullshit.

"Your job is to keep that chick in line."

My jaw tightens.

"My job is to keep her safe."

"Regina and the Miss Americana organization are tired of her bullshit. She doesn't want to make waves? That's all she fucking does. Keep her shit in line, Jaime."

I take a deep breath, running a hand over my face and nodding before speaking, remembering he can't hear me. "Got it."

"Remember what's on the line," he reminds me as if I could fucking forget his not-so-subtle threats. But for the first time, I wonder if it's worth it, if sticking this out for three more years in complete misery is worth it.

"Yeah, Greg. I got it."

Then the line goes dead.

Motherfucker.

I take a minute or two to control my breathing, to get my shit in check before my phone rings in my hand, a familiar name on the screen.

"Yeah," I say in greeting.

"You're up early," Hank says. "Anything to do with what happened yesterday?" He's laughing out the words like this is some kind of funny joke.

"You mean my assignment getting assaulted after the pageant runner insisted I essentially run some pointless errand with another contestant? Yeah, I'm up because of that."

That takes the humor right out of his words.

"What happened? Where were you?" he asks, not with the same accusation Greg laid down, but in a confused way, like he knows it wouldn't happen on my watch.

I fill him in, leaving out the ongoing threat of getting fired and losing my benefits. I don't need him stressed about that. "I swear to God, Hank, if I had known..." My voice trails off, my mind forever stuck on the *what-ifs*.

"I trust you, kid. Just happy she didn't get hurt."

I sigh, rubbing my hand over my face. "I'm toeing the line to keep the organization happy, as well as keep *her* safe. And I'm failing. I don't know how to handle this." I've never had an assignment like Ava, and I mean that in so many ways.

One who is so fucking mouthy.

One who doesn't listen to a thing I ask of her.

One with a penchant for trouble.

One so gorgeous, it's distracting.

One who is *so goddamn* tempting.

"You did exactly what I trained you to do, son. You got her safe, but let her live her life. Not a single word that girl said that I don't agree with. I've got daughters, you know that. When they were little,

I'd want them looking up to a Miss Americana like Ava, not like those pageant girls who are shy and let people walk over them. That's not what the world needs these days."

I roll my eyes even though I agree. "She's a pain in my ass."

"The best women always are." I don't respond to that, knowing it would be gasoline to a fire I don't want to stoke, seeing as I can *hear* the smile in Hank's voice. "I've seen pictures with you and that girl, you know," he says and I freeze.

Pictures?

"What?"

"She's got paparazzi following her like she's a lifelong pop star rather than a first-time pageant queen. Lots of pictures."

I relax just a bit when he doesn't mean some kind of photo of us in a compromising position. Of course, he isn't wrong. Every outing with the organization is absolutely *flooded* with reporters, more and more at each stop, all trying to get just a minute with Ava to get some headline-worthy quotes. When I took the job, I thought it was going to be simple, but sometimes it feels like she gets the same treatment as pop star Willa Stone.

"Yeah, I'm uniquely acquainted with that fact," I joke, deadpan.

"Just saying, occasionally, the two of you are in shots and you look good together."

I groan. "Hank—"

"You know I met my Janine on an assignment. If you met a pretty little thing while doing the job, I'd never—" I cut him off to nip that.

"Half of my job is to make sure she stays within her contract." I say the first thing that comes to mind. "Part of that contract says she has to stay single until the end of her reign."

When I read that clause in Ava's contract, I was shocked, so I did some research. Most of the clauses under the morality section that would instantly void Ava's win and, in turn, the prize money she doesn't receive until the end of her three-month tour were pretty obvious and, I can almost guarantee, were added after an issue with a previous constant. No sex tapes, no cyberbullying, no in-person bullying, no speaking poorly about the organization, that kind of thing.

But not dating required me to dig a bit into the history of the pageant on a Reddit forum—always an interesting mix of truth and speculation, but this time, it made sense to me.

The current Miss Americana contestant is contracted to exemplify the basic, in my opinion, outdated ideals of the all-American woman, including her ability to be snapped up by some good ol' boy. If Miss Americana stays single, it's as if any man in the country still has a chance with her.

"Yeah, but we all know that's not enforceable," Hank says like it's no big deal.

"Hank—"

"Tell me there's a judge in this country who would look at that and agree it makes sense in this context, in this decade?" I can't, of course. "All I'm saying is, if something happened, I wouldn't give you shit." There's a pause, and then, with a smile in his words, he adds, "Fine. I wouldn't give you *as much* shit, at least."

I roll my eyes and flip him off even though he can't see me. I decide I need to get Hank off the call before he gets into my head too much. I made up my mind yesterday that, despite my brief lapse in judgment, I need to maintain the professionalism between Ava and me. Nothing more.

"Anyway, the reason for my call," he says as if he can sense I'm about to sign off.

"So it wasn't just to give me a hard time?"

"I was, but also...she's been getting notes, right?"

"Notes?" I shake my head. "No, just messages. Threatening ones on social media, creepy photos. That kind of thing."

"So you haven't heard anything about any physical threats?"

I take a deep breath and try to calm my pounding panic, knowing I'm not going to like where this is headed. "Yes."

"Okay, well, I happen to know they got at least one letter."

A beat passes before I speak. "A letter?"

"A letter. Yeah. A physical letter was sent to the Miss Americana offices. My name must be on a contact form somewhere because some kid from the Miss Americana Organization called me to let me know."

"And?"

"And he told me he works in the mailroom; Ava got a threatening letter. His boss told him to call the security company. I told them to contact Regina and have her report it to Five Star. Not going to step into Greg's business."

"What kind of letter?"

"It could be nothing," he says, not answering the question.

"*What kind of letter?*" I repeat through gritted teeth, my hand tightening on the railing.

There's a deep sigh before my mentor speaks. "It's probably not anything to worry about."

"But?" I ask, hearing the words he didn't say.

"It's a letter telling Ava to step down or something bad will happen. It has her name on it, addressed to her, sent to the offices, but it mentions a lot of personal details. Where she's been, where she's worked, her friends..." I'm silent through the line, trying to assemble pieces before he speaks again. "Look, Jaime, it's probably nothing to worry about. I just wanted you to know."

"Nothing to worry about? She might have a much too invested fan, best-case scenario, and worst-case, a stalker. And why is no one telling me about this?" My mind is swirling through all the options and worse-case scenarios.

"Look, all we can do is make sure she's safe, right? Things aren't adding up, and we can see that, but there's only so much we can do. You keep that girl safe; I'll do what I can. Unfortunately, your hands are tied, son."

"I think she's waking up," I say, hearing the bathroom click shut. "We gotta get on the road, so I should start packing up for the road."

"All right, son. You take care of that girl, yeah? I'll see if I can dig anything up; call a few friends."

I sigh in relief. "I owe you, Hank," I say, relieved that I have *someone* on my side right now.

"When you're in California, bring her to me. I want to meet this beauty queen who has you so flustered."

"She doesn't have me—"

But then I realize the line has gone silent, Hank having hung up before I can argue.

The *ass.*

Walking back into the hotel suite, Ava walks out of the bathroom, her hair a mess, a crease in the side of her face, her pajamas one giant oversized men's T-shirt that spawns some kind of jealousy I refuse to put a voice to, thinking of her getting it from some random asshole.

"Mornin'," she says, squinting and staring at me. She's like this in the morning, I've learned. It's not that she's not a morning person—not like she's grumpy or irritated when she wakes—just that she's not all there like part of her is still curled up in her bed.

Stop thinking about her curled in bed, I tell myself when my mind wanders to what she'd look like, blonde hair spread over a pillow, curled up on herself, that tee riding up.

"Iced coffee's in the fridge," I say, tipping my chin toward the hotel's little kitchenette.

"You're a lifesaver," she groans, then scuffles there, pulling the cup I grabbed earlier this morning and taking a long sip before she leans back to the counter.

I watch her, my arms on my chest, before speaking. "Do you know self-defense?" I ask.

"What?" Her voice is less scratchy as if she's slowly coming back to the land of the living, and I fight the smile.

"Self-defense. Do you know it?"

Her head lifts, and a small, sleepy smile curves on her lips. "No, why would I need to?"

"You're a public figure, Ava. You're a gorgeous woman. You're alive. You were just attacked yesterday. How many reasons do you need to want to know how to protect yourself?"

She shrugs. "Don't know. Never really thought about it. But..."

I see the flash. I know she was thinking about that man last night and how things could have gone much worse. My mind is thinking of a dozen or so other situations that could have gone bad, the letter Hank told me she's receiving...and I come to a decision.

"I'm gonna teach you."

"What?"

"I'm going to teach you some basic moves of self-defense."

"You're going to teach me?"

"Yeah." At the very least, it will make me feel better, her knowing how to protect herself if the worst comes true—to know that if I'm not around, she can protect herself. "Yeah," I repeat, the idea taking form in my mind. "We'll rent a space at the next stop." I start calculating where that would be, pulling up the calendar in my mind and taking mental notes to scout out a location.

"We should get to Alabama by the end of the day unless we hit traffic, and we have nothing on the schedule tomorrow. I'll find a studio and rent it out." I'll use my own money if I have to.

"All right, big guy. But know I'm not going easy on you," she says, her smile wide, and it's clear she's finally awake.

"Yeah, yeah. Pack up and get dressed. The sooner we get on the road, the sooner we get to the next stop."

She salutes, then turns toward her room, coffee in hand. When Peach walks over to her, rubbing on her ankles, she bends to pick her up and fuck me; the shirt rides up, revealing the lower half of her ass.

I am so fucked.

TWENTY-NINE
AVA

"All right, next, we'll work on releases. There are three main versions: a wrist release, a bear hug release, and a hair release," Jaime says the next day, his eyes meeting mine in a mirror.

Upon waking this morning, he informed me he'd already found a dance studio to rent twenty miles away for my first official self-defense lesson. When we walked in, I felt at ease. The familiarity of a dance studio hit me with a wave of homesickness for my friends that I quickly brushed off.

Once we arrived, he wasted little time, first teaching me about different strikes and the correct way to do them, then moving on to how to be situationally aware in any situation. It's been eye-opening and a bit frightening to realize just *how* unprotected I am at any given moment and how unprepared I am if something *were* to happen, God forbid. I won't admit it to Jaime in this lifetime, but to some degree, he's right: I don't value my own safety nearly enough.

"A bear hug sounds fun. Let's do that first," I say with a smile.

For the millionth time, Jaime closes his eyes and sighs before his lips start to move quietly—a prayer of sorts.

"Fun?"

"Bears are cute and cuddly. It has a fun name," I say with a smile. I'm only saying it to irritate him, but clearly, it's working.

"Fine," he says with a shake of his head, then moves to stand behind me and stares at me in the mirror's reflection. "Okay, a man comes up behind you and grabs you; what do you do?"

I shrug casually. "Where's he grabbing me?"

"Does it matter?" Jaime asks, confused.

"Well, yeah. There's a huge difference between him grabbing my hand and grabbing a handful of my boobs."

With that, he closes his eyes, taking a deep breath like he needs to find some inner zen.

I don't think he succeeds.

"Fine," he says, arms wrapping me up in a big hug, pinning my arms to my sides. "He grabs you like this. What do you do?"

"I yell for help."

He shakes his head at me. "No, you don't yell help, you—" he starts, and I cut him off.

"Oh, yeah, you yell *fire!*"

He nods at me. "Exactly. People are more likely to come if you yell fire. Yelling for help has proven people don't think they'll be able to help or assume someone else will come. But let's say there's no one around. What do you do?"

"Uh... kick him?" I say, moving a foot back toward his knees.

"Maybe that could work in some situations, but you're pretty small, Ava."

I purse my lips, annoyed even though he's not wrong; in a panic, I don't think I'd have enough height to kick a man behind me where I'd need to in order to make any real impact.

"Ideally, if your hands are below the attacker's, you try and slide out," he says. When I try, basically lifting my feet and using my body weight and gravity, I'm able to wiggle out, even with his arms tight on me.

Jaime proceeds to show me then how to slow and injure the attacker and flee once I'm out, what to do if my arms are locked above the attacker's hands, and how to escape to safety before we try something new.

Next, he's in front of me, an arm's width away, staring down at me, his chest rising and falling with the slight effort he's been expending. In contrast, I'm already slick with sweat. Then his hand, calloused and rough and huge, wraps around my throat.

"A man gets you here; what do you do?"

I smile. It's not that I'm not taking this seriously that makes me smile. It's more that taking it *too* seriously will be a complete system overload for me and send me into a panicked spiral I might never crawl out of. And, of course, the way he looks *so freaking serious* makes me want to be the complete opposite.

"Call him daddy?"

He shakes his head at me, and my smile grows.

"Jesus fucking Christ, Ava, please try and take this seriously."

"I'm sorry, I'm sorry! It was too perfect of an opening!" He glares, and I give in. "Okay, okay, no more choke me daddy jokes, promise."

His eyes close, and he curses under his breath.

Maybe I *shouldn't* have said, *choke me, daddy*. Now, way, *way* too many ideas are running through my mind.

"Are you into that shit?" he asks, and instantly his face goes a bit pink like he didn't mean to say it aloud.

"Calling men daddy? It's not for me. Choking? I'm not sure yet. I've never tried it."

His eyes go wider. "But you've called someone daddy?" The words come so quickly, I have to assume they're an impulse.

"Once. It wasn't for me. I ended up laughing the entire time, which didn't do much for his ego." His jaw goes tight, and I smile. "Okay, fine. Choke me, *Jaime*."

Something snaps in his eyes, and heat floods my belly, but all the same, without a word, he lifts his hand, wrapping my throat and staring at me.

"If someone attacks you like this, the goal is to get their fingers off you as soon as possible. First, grab my wrist with your left hand," he says.

"Like this?" I ask, wrapping my hand around his wrist.

"Yeah, Higher is better. With your other hand, grab my fingers that are on your throat.

"Grab your fingers?"

"Yes."

I grab them with my free hand, feeling a bit silly. If someone is choking me, shouldn't I try and push him away?

"Good, good. Pushing away fucks with angles and weight distribution, so you have to go a bit against instinct," he explains. "Now you want to grab those fingers tight, squeeze them together. It'll hurt him and mess with his grip." I squeeze a bit, feeling the fingers lifting as I do. "You grab it like that, peel back, and push. Yeah, yeah," he says, as I remove his fingers from my neck. "Then push, shove my elbow into my side." I do it slowly, a bit confused by the instructions, making sure I get it right. "Then push those fingers back toward his wrist. Ideally, you do it fast, but we're just practicing."

"Got it,"

"Then you're going to push back and break my fingers." My eyes go wide. "Not literally, not right now, at least. Now, if you do this, with the elbow moving back, the fingers breaking, he's going to go down. Then you knee him in the face, and you *run*, Ava. Run and scream."

"Got it. That I can do," I say.

"All right, again," he says before he makes me run through it a few more times until I feel like I understand the move and all of the variations of it.

"Okay, now we're going to run through some scenarios," Jaime says an hour or so later.

"What?"

But instead of responding, Jaime goes right into it, grabbing me by my ponytail, which he told me is the most dangerous hairstyle for a woman, and expecting me to get out of it. We fight, and I use the moves he taught me, but this time, it's clear he's not playing or in teaching mode—this time, I have to actually fight to make the moves he showed me before he approves, and we move into a wrist release and then a bear hug. I'm panting and sweating by the time I get out of his second bear hug move, and then I trip, falling to the ground and catching myself on my hands.

And then he's on top of me, rolling me over until I'm pinned beneath his body.

This, attached to the panicky adrenaline from trying to escape this "attacker" over and over, should spike something in me: fear and panic.

But it does the exact opposite, flooding me with lust that I can't tamp down. My chest is heaving, and so is his as he looms over me.

I wait for his instruction, but it doesn't come, instead, he just continues to hover over me, eyes assessing, dozens of thoughts moving behind those eyes.

And with every other heartbeat, his gaze stops on my lips like he's weighing the pros and cons of leaning down. It wouldn't take much at all for his lips to be on mine, to once more experience the momentary bliss that was Jaime kissing me.

He said it was a mistake, that we shouldn't have kissed, that it caused distractions...but I don't *care*. I don't care if it makes me lose the crown or fucks up this entire tour.

I want Jaime Wilde in a way that supersedes every bit of logic.

"Kiss me," I whisper without really thinking.

"What?"

"Kiss me," I repeat.

"Ava—"

"Say fuck it and kiss me, Jaime. I'm so into you, I can barely breathe even though I know you're the *one person* I shouldn't be thinking about."

"Ava—"

"I know it's crazy, but you know there's something there. Why else would you spend your entire day off renting out a studio to teach me this? Touching me all day, driving me insane." His pupils flare with lust, and I see it there: a silent confession. "That kiss wasn't a mistake, and you know it. Admit you like me." Time passes like molasses as I wait for his response.

"I like you enough to not want something bad to happen to you. I like you enough to want to keep you safe beyond it being my job. But I also like you enough to not want to fuck this opportunity up for you and to know we can't act on whatever chemistry is between us."

Hope and excitement bloom in my chest. "We could, you know," I whisper, holding his eyes in the mirror. I expect him to play dumb, but instead, he shakes his head, holding my gaze all the same.

"The other day proved we can't. You're my charge, and I need to stay focused. And you're supposed to stay single."

"Oh, sweet boy," I say, reaching up and patting him on the cheek, then leaving it there, letting my thumb brush his full bottom lip. It should be illegal for a man to have such perfect lips.

"What are they going to do, take my crown? The best part about me and about this entire gig is I'm not in it for the crown or the title. I was in it to help my friends, and now I'm sticking it out for the adventure and because I'm stubborn." I let time pass—moments or maybe hours. I'm unsure how long before I whisper it. "Kiss me, Jaime."

"Ava," he whispers, but he doesn't say no and doesn't back away.

"You said you're the one who kisses me every single time. So do it."

He seems to contemplate my words, then slowly, so fucking slowly I think I'm hallucinating it, one hand moves, rough calluses scraping up the delicate skin of my neck until he's cupping my jaw and moving down toward me, his lips barely grazing mine.

Then a knock comes on the door, his head jerking up. The moment is broken before he moves. He stands quickly and offers me a hand to help me up.

"Time's up," he says.

THIRTY
JAIME

My cock is hard when I wake up an hour before my five a.m. alarm.

The self-defense lesson fucked with my head, touching her all day, sweating with her, and hovering over her in a way I'd really fucking like to do without clothes on.

It's what has me in such a state right now, the mere *thought* of having Ava spread out in a bed before me while I'm braced above her, sliding in deep.

Just the thought of it was utter bliss.

It was completely inappropriate, even in a dream.

The woman is fucking with me, burrowing deep under my skin with her smiles and her flirting and her sweet laughs and teasing. I sure as fuck should not have clicked the link Wes sent me last night, a social media clip of Ava during the swimsuit portion of her pageant.

Not that it was the first time I've seen it, nor will it probably be the last. I'm a glutton for punishment, it seems, dying to torture myself with what I can't have.

Because no matter what she keeps saying, I can't have Ava Bordeaux.

With a quiet groan, I roll out of bed and trudge to the large bathroom. The countertop is littered with Ava's things in a way I don't hate, another thought I file away in a vault I'll never allow myself to investigate too much.

I should turn the water to cold and shock my system into normalcy, but instead, I make it warm before grabbing her stupid fucking body wash and using it to make my hand slick, then my hard cock slippery.

A glutton for punishment, remember?

Her smell fills the steamy room as I stroke myself, picturing Ava's wet cunt as my eyes close and I rest one hand on the wall, letting the water run over me as her sweet scent envelopes me.

My mind returns to the dream as my hand continues to pump at my cock.

She's naked, full tits on display, sprawled on the bed, her hair a waterfall around her. Her fingers move to her nipples, pinching and rolling, her lips swollen from kisses. She mewls as my fingers dance over her, down her stomach to her pussy that's already soaking wet. Sliding a finger in, I groan at just how wet she is and at the way she clamps down on me.

"I need more," she groans, her hips moving up.

"What do you need, Princess?"

"You, please." Taking myself in hand, I rub the head of my cock down her wet slit, and she moans again. "Yes, fuck me."

"Is that what you want, baby?" I ask, notching myself at her entrance and bucking my hips just a bit until the head of my cock sits barely inside of her. She pulses around me, clamping down to try and get more.

"Yes, yeah. Please. I need you," she whispers, then shifts, taking me another inch.

"Fuck," I groan before shifting, grabbing her legs, and draping them over my shoulders before slowly, torturously slowly, sliding inside until I'm planted deep, hovering over her with a hand on either side of the bed next to her head.

"I'm so full," she moans, and I smile before sliding out, then back in, continuing the slow torture, savoring it.

"God, you look so pretty like this," I moan, watching my cock disappear in her, watching her take me. "You take my cock like you were made for it. Born to be mine, to be fucked by me." My balls slap against her ass as I pound into her as she tightens around me. My fingers grip her hips, digging into the soft skin there, and she moans louder like she likes the hit of pain.

"Jaime, oh god," she moans, her voice soft and needy, deeper than usual, huskier. Her big blue eyes lock on me, her pussy tightening around me as her hands move to her pink nipples, pinching and rolling. My head turns to the side, pressing a kiss to her ankle, one of her high heels still on her foot. I think I'd like that most of all, pressing kisses to her soft skin whenever I want, everywhere I want.

I continue to fuck her, her hips lifting to take me deep before I move us so I'm on my back, Ava full of me as she sits on my hips. My hands rest on hers before gently guiding her and showing her what to do.

It doesn't take long for her hips to start shifting. "Ride my cock. Take what you need, baby."

Her hand moves to her nipples, and she leans back just a bit, changing the angle as she shouts, tightening on me.

She looks fucking gorgeous like this, her hair tumbling down her back, face tipped to the ceiling, hands holding her breasts, filled with me, and dripping down my cock.

"You feel so good," she moans, pinching my nipples and riding me, her other tit bouncing with the movement. She's beautiful like this—a goddess taking what she wants, using me for her pleasure. "You're going to make me come." Her free hand moves down her belly to her clit, rubbing and making her moan loud. I slap her hand away, then slap her inner thigh, her pussy tightening on me as I do.

"That's mine, baby," I murmur, using my hand to soothe where I just slapped her, then moving to her clit to rub her there, pulling a deep moan from her. "Whose pussy is this, Ava?"

"It's yours," she whispers, and my pulse pounds more. "It's yours, Jaime. Fuck!" She starts to move more now, taking me deeper and deeper, fucking me, and using me for her pleasure.

I'm close and want her to tumble over the edge with me. My thumb moves to her clit, rubbing in small, rough circles, her hips rocking as she rides me. My orgasm creeps closer, the edges of my vision dimming as she fucks me, and I start to rub her clit faster.

"I'm going to come," she moans.

"Come on, Ava. Come on my cock and take me with you, let me fill your cunt." Then my free hand moves to the back of her neck, pulling her close and pressing my lips to hers as it builds.

My hand pumps faster as the Ava in my head arches her back, shouting my name before I come.

As I come, one hand propped on the wall of the shower, the scent of Ava hanging in the air around me, and unable to remember if I made a noise as I did, I think the same thing I do every fucking time I do this.

I am so fucked.

THIRTY-ONE
AVA

"Ava," the voice says, a low rumble in my ear as I shift out of my dreamless sleep. "Wake up, Princess. I let you sleep in as much as I could, but we gotta get on the road."

Cracking open one eye, I see Jaime's face not far from mine before he stands straight, crossing his arms on his chest casually like he wasn't just inches from me moments before.

"Mmm," I grumble, closing my eyes again and rolling over.

You know I'm tired when I'm too exhausted to even pick on Jaime when the perfect opportunity is in front of me, but after the past few days, I'm fully drained.

"Uh-uh," he says, his voice suddenly firm. "No, we have to get on the road. We're already cutting it close if we want to get to the next hotel before the sun gets down."

I groan again but don't move. I packed last night, and all I'll have to do this morning to get ready for the next leg is pack up my last-minute things, put some clothes on, and try and convince Jaime to take me to a coffee shop for much-needed caffeine. Maybe a snack stop, too, because I've already eaten through my stash, and it's a nearly a six-hour drive this time.

"Ava, we have to get going, or we're going to hit traffic."

I let out some kind of inhuman sound, this time grabbing the edge of the blanket and rolling with it, curling in on myself and the warmth of the bed.

And suddenly, the warmth is gone, air conditioning taking over my body and forcing my eyes open. "Wha—?" I say, rolling back to my back and looking around, propped on my elbows. In front of me stands Jaime, eyes wide as he stares at me, hands holding the white hotel blanket in his hands, frozen in place.

Except for his big hazel eyes that graze over my body.

He's lucky I made the decision that I had to wear pajamas to maintain a bit of common decency on this trip, but even *I* know these pajamas are barely decent. A pair of silky shorts and the world's tiniest silk cami provide nearly no coverage, leaving a large swatch of my stomach exposed. No bra and the cool air conditioning cause the nipples on my full breasts to pucker, but I don't cross my arms over them to hide it. My hair is crazed, over my shoulders, and probably a total mess, but I smirk at him through my tired eyes.

Gotta fake it till you make you.

"Like what you see, big guy?" I ask, pushing my shoulders back and my tits out.

"I-I-I—" he stutters, and my smile grows more, then he throws the blanket back on me. "We have to go." Then he's out of the room.

I give him the courtesy of not laughing until the door is closed behind him, though he definitely hears it if the groan that comes from the other side means anything.

But Jaime wins the next round of *who can shock the other more* when we walk into the parking lot, with him holding my bag over his shoulder even though I told him I could. He's stiffer than usual, hyperalert like something is going to happen, but it's six in the morning and the lot, while there is a scattering of cars, is mostly empty.

After opening the back door of the black SUV and tossing in my bag, Jaime makes his way to the passenger seat door and opens it for me, but I hesitate getting in.

My brows furrow in confusion as I ask, "What....?".

There's a big iced coffee already in the cupholder, a fluffy white blanket on the seat, a book I have never read or owned, and my headphones on the seat. In the footwell, there's a bag, and sticking out is the recognizable top of my favorite kind of chips. Through the thin plastic, I think there are the gummy bears I like—the ones I definitely told him in passing were my favorite, but not more than once or twice.

I turn to my bodyguard and driver to see he has a hand behind his neck, gripping it there, the other on the door of the car.

"What is this, Jaime?"

"It's...nothing. Really."

"It's definitely not nothing, Jaime. It's...is that a new blanket?"

"It was at the store, and it looked comfy. You need comfy; this leg is a bit longer."

"At the store. What store? When? When did you go to the store?" I turn fully to him and cross my arms on my chest. It's clear on his face he wants me to drop this, to just get in that car and pretend I didn't notice a thing, but I will never. I smile wide, waiting for his answer.

"Jesus, Ava, can't you just get in the fucking car?"

"Once you tell me when you went to the store and why."

Finally, he sighs, giving in after staring me down for a minute. He realized he wasn't going to win, I guess.

"I woke up early and worked out. I realized you were still out like a light, which, considering yesterday, makes sense. You were wrung dry, burnt out. I'm not doing my job if you collapse from exhaustion, so I ran out to a twenty-four-hour store and grabbed a few things so you could sleep in the car." There's a pause like he realizes his next addition might help his case, even if it's a total fucking lie. "If you sleep, I'll get some peace and quiet for a bit."

I shake my head at him, flabbergasted. "You're so full of shit."

His head tips up to the sky like he's looking for divine intervention that never comes.

"The book? Where'd you get that?"

"There was a girl there who worked there. She was stocking the shelves. I named some of the books I've seen you reading; she said this one just came out, so I thought it was a safe bet." Again, he pauses, almost biting his lip before stopping as if he were catching himself. "Have you? Read that one?"

God, he's *nervous*. Jaime Wilde, the giant bodyguard who gets paid to protect people, is *nervous* because he isn't sure how I'm going to take this utterly sweet act of kindness. I take a step closer, closing the gap between us a bit, then put my hand on his chest.

"I haven't, big guy. Thanks." I pause, looking into his eyes, which, for the first time, have the heavy guard down, like it's too early or he forgot to put it up. "Why did you do this, Jaime?" I ask quietly. "You didn't have to," I remind him.

A long beat passes when I think he won't answer, but then he shifts, and intentionally or not, our bodies are closer now, almost touching. I'm wearing a white oversized hoodie and a pair of bike shorts, my hair slicked into a low bun since there won't be any appearances, and I'm focused on comfort. In any other situation, I'd feel weird not having my face done, not having my armor on.

But Jaime always sees through it anyway.

He sighs before finally answering. "I just... I wanted to make sure you were comfortable so you could relax. You had a rough couple of days." He shrugs, his big shoulders seeming gigantic on him when he looks shy and nervous like this. There's a light blush across his cheeks, and he *refuses* to make eye contact with me.

I should just say thank you and hop in the car.

But god, this is too perfect. I can't do it—I think if I could make a career of it, I'd be CEO of Making Jaime Wilde Blush.

Honestly, it has a pretty good ring to it.

But since I can't actually make that my career, I'll just settle with doing it as a hobby.

"Oh, you like me," I say with a smile, looking at the little space he's carved out for me, then back at him, his head shaking vehemently and that blush growing.

Jesus, for such a big, tough guy, the man sure does blush a lot around me.

He so totally likes me.

"What? No, no, I don't. Just doing my job."

"Your job is to wake up early so you can set up my seat for me because you know how tired I was last night and want to make sure I could relax? Bullshit." He stares at me for a moment and I think, just maybe, he'll explain himself.

He doesn't. "Get in the car, Ava," he says instead.

I shift so my back is to the car and cross my arms on my chest, smiling at him. "Not until you admit it."

"You're such a fucking pain in my ass, you know that?"

"A pain in the ass that you like."

He stares at me, thoughts moving behind his eyes, but I continue to smile because, slowly but surely, I'm winning him over.

"You're tolerable, is that enough?"

I'll take it, I think. It feels like a colossal win, all things considered.

"Now get in the car, Princess," he says lower.

And I do as he asks, but I do it with the world's biggest smile on my lips.

THIRTY-TWO
AVA

Jaime has been nothing but a professional gentleman.

He has been perfectly attentive and kind, but he hasn't touched me, not even a gentle guiding hand on my lower back, which I hadn't realized I'd gotten used to.

Some sick part of my mind can't help but think he was proving a point and nothing else. I kissed him, and he wanted me to know in his stupid *alpha male world*, men make the first move. Men kiss women, not the other way around.

Something about that, about him using that moment that I've hung in my mind in a gilded frame as some perfect moment in time to one-up me, makes my tummy hurt every time I think about it.

I've given it a week. A week where I sat on the emotions of kissing Jaime, of being kissed *by* Jaime, of letting it simmer and see where it was going, only to get more and more disappointed with each passing hour.

Finally, though, I have some alone time. One glorious hour locked in this hotel room, the deadbolt and chain up, and some crazy pole Jaime has taught me to put across the door, keeping me in and everyone else out while he goes for a run and I get ready for the fundraising ball we're going to tonight.

Once I shower at lightning speed and sit in the bathroom to get ready, I don't waste a moment of time calling my best friends to see if they can help me make some sense of my life.

"Hey—" Jules says when she answers the FaceTime request.

"Don't talk. I'm waiting for Harper, and I'm not telling this story more than once," I say, stopping Jules before she can even say anything.

"What?"

"I—"

"Hey, girl. Ooh, look at the tan! Are you making sure to put something in your hair before you go in the water? Even natural blondes—" Harper starts as she pops on, but I have no bandwidth for her, even though it's really, *really* good to see her face.

"I kissed him," I blurt.

Silence takes over the line.

"What?" Jules says cautiously

"I kissed Jaime. And then he kissed me. And then some, I—"

"Wait, wait, wait," Harper starts. "Back up. Go back to the beginning. Didn't he hate you, like, a week ago?"

Jules shakes her head, disagreeing. "That man never hated her. Even at the bar, he didn't hate her. He was annoyed with her, probably because she was the tenth woman to come and try to use her girlish whims to say hi to the band, but he didn't hate her. He was *intrigued* by her."

"What?" I ask, suddenly thrown off because where was this intel weeks ago?

"Oh, for sure," Harper agrees. "I didn't mean he actually hated her," she says to Jules as if I'm not even on the line. "I just mean—"

"Can we pause your personal dissecting of my non-relationship and whether he's been into me all along or not until I'm *not* on the phone because I'm actively having a meltdown?"

"What? Why?"

"Because some crazy shit went down with a weird fan right after and he thinks being distracted put me in danger, so now he's insisting we keep things *professional* even though it was the absolute best kiss of my life."

"Of your life?" Harper asks, and I nod.

"Okay, but like...why is that giving you a meltdown? You had a good kiss, and now he's being an idiot. His loss, right?" Jules asks, and I sigh. Normally, I'd agree. If it was anyone *but* Jaime, I'd agree. But...

"Because..." I start, then pause because suddenly, I'm nervous about admitting everything.

If I admit this, it becomes real. If I admit it to my best friends in the whole world, I can't play things off like it's just a silly little crush.

"Because...?" Harper asks.

I mumble an answer and watch a look pass between them, the split second making me so homesick that I can barely focus.

"What?" Harper asks.

"I like him," I whisper under my breath.

"What was that?" Jules asks, a small smile playing on her lips now.

"I like him," I repeat through gritted teeth.

She grins now, and I know what's coming.

"I'm sorry, one more time? I can't seem to hear yo—"

"I like him, okay? I like a boy," I say, putting down my curling iron that I was pretending to use and putting my head in my hands.

"That is *not* a boy, Ava. That's a *man*," Jules says, and I roll my eyes and look at my phone again.

"Fine, I like a man. But like...I really like him."

She lets out a whistle and leans back, and finally, I let it all spill, a dam breaking after having *no one* to girl talk with for the past month or so.

"He's kind, even though he pretends he's not. I like how he's sweet with Peach and that he puts up with my bullshit. I like that he lets me flirt with him and that he really, really wants to keep me safe and not just because it's his job. I like that he wants to find a way to let me be *me*. And I like that he knows I'm going to be crazy and wild and a little cringey, and he doesn't care. I don't know." I pause, staring at the ceiling. "I just like him."

Silence fills the line, and with each second, my stomach gets more and more anxious, waiting for my friends to tell me how stupid this crush is, how I need to use my head and think about the real world.

"Wow, I never thought I'd see the day when Ava Bordeaux admits she likes someone for real."

"I *have* liked people," I say with a roll of my eyes, exasperated.

"I mean, yeah, but not like...for real. Not like...this. This is different."

"Is it?" I ask, a strange mix of nerves and excitement filling me.

Maybe it's not just me. Maybe it's not all in my head, and I'm not just blowing things out of proportion because he's a hot man attached to my hip.

"It so is," Harper says.

"Yeah," Jules agrees. "So what's the problem? You like him; you kissed him, it sounds like it was a good kiss..."

It *so* was, and I'm about to confirm that when Harper speaks.

"She has to stay single," she says, and I groan aloud at the stupid fucking contract. It's *ruining my life,* and I mean that in the most melodramatic way possibly. "Or else she could lose the crown and the tour, and that dumb bitch would win."

I, of course, had filled my friends in more than a few times about Anne and the bullshit she's been dishing me, and they hate her potentially more than I do at this point, as all good friends do.

Are your friends really friends if they don't hate who you hate with a fiery passion?

"I mean, am I breaking my contract if I'm just *imagining* him touching me? Because if so, I'm fucked." I can hear rather than see Harper's eye roll.

"No, Ava, you aren't going to get sued by thinking about fucking your bodyguard. In fact, I don't think you'll get sued for fucking him at all, just if you have a boyfriend, obviously ruining the *idea* of the perfect Miss Americana, the effervescent, single, unattainable, pure woman men can fantasize about."

I gag a little at that.

"But in my opinion, you'd be even more of a badass if you said fuck it and stopped caring about what that stupid contract says about how you act and who you can or cannot date. Imagine the press firestorm you could start if you just *leaked* something about how they're expecting you to act," Jules says.

"Absolutely not. Don't even *give* her that idea. Something tells me if the Miss Americana organization is fine with putting a clause about remaining single, they definitely put in something about not openly talking about the contract they made her sign," Harper says.

"I could read it, figure out if there's some kind of NDA in there."

"Jules, you're a dance instructor, not a lawyer."

"I could figure it out, I'm a wiz with Google," she says. I shake my head, remembering why I *actually* called and my limited time before Jaime returns.

"It doesn't even matter," I say loudly to stop their arguing.

"What?"

"That's why I called you. Ever since we kissed, he's been ignoring me."

"Excuse me?"

"Not ignoring me, that's not fair. He's ignoring *us*. And everything that happened that morning." I fill them in on how, for the last three days, he's been absolutely nothing but professional. How, before when we had a few free hours in a hotel room at night, he'd hang with me, joke with me...*flirt* with me in a very Jaime way that I still considered flirting, and how now, every night he locks himself in his room, and I don't see him until morning.

"So what are you going to do about it?" Jules says when I finish.

"What?"

"What are you going to do about it, Ava?"

"I don't know, I just wanted to call you guys and complain. I—"

Harper shakes her head, cutting me off. "I have never known you, Ava Bordeaux, to just sit back and let the chips fall as they may."

"I don't—"

"You always have a plan. You need a plan, Ava. Something that will put his shit into gear. Something he *can't* ignore," Jules says.

"You guys, I—" I start, but Harper sits up straighter, an idea forming on her face.

"The pink feather dress," Harper says.

"What?

"No, no. Floor-length champagne," she says. "Yes, that one's perfect. The slit is high, the back is non-existent, and your boobs look phenomenal in it."

Jules nods like she sees where she's going. "Oh, yes, definitely that one. Pink lip, classic cat eye. Highest heels you packed."

Slowly, I pick up what they were saying. "Okay," I say with a nod.

"And be you. Gloves off, babe, no more playing nice. Be flirty, sexy Ava. Remind him that, if he doesn't want you, that's fine. There will be at least a dozen men there who would *love* to be with you."

And as I continue to get ready with my friends on the phone, I start to feel good again, reminded of just who I am.

THIRTY-THREE
AVA

The dress works.

Okay, it doesn't work in the sense that he grabs my hand and drags me back into a room, fucking me until we both can't see straight, but when I step out of my room in the floor-length champagne dress covered in sparkles with its nonexistent back and plunging neck, meaning I can't wear a real bra with it and the slit that nearly goes to my hip, I do catch Jaime closing his eyes and taking a deep breath as if praying to some unseen god.

I won't deny that I also prayed to whatever god was watching over Jaime's outfit choices, thanking her for putting him in the perfectly fitted suit, black on black with dark dress shoes, every inch of him a dream.

When we walk into the ballroom, Jaime leads us to a large round table with familiar faces seated at it. Atlas Oaks as well as Stella and Willa Stone are all seated around it, and I smile.

I can't help but turn to Jaime and put a hand on his arm, putting on a mask of faux nerves. "Do you think it's okay if I say hello to them? I know I'm not on their approved list, but..."

He rolls his eyes and groans before putting his hand to my lower back, his hand warm on my bare skin, before pushing me toward them.

"Hey, guys! Look, I made it past security this time without any kind of issue." I turn to Jaime, then to Stella. "Does this mean I've made it?"

"Jesus," Jaime grumbles under his breath.

"Oh, I like you," Wes says, putting an arm around my shoulder and tugging me in for a side hug.

"Well, good, at least someone will. Jaime hates me, so—"

"I don't hate you," Jaime says with a huff.

I look at him with a loving gaze before continuing. "Oh, yes, I forgot. He's in love with me and hates *himself* for it."

"I'm not in love with you," he says through gritted teeth, and I nod solemnly, looking at Wes.

"He's in denial. It's really hard on him."

"Jesus fuck, woman," Jaime groans.

"I wish," I say under my breath, and he looks to the ceiling, praying to another silent god.

"I thought we were over this shit?" he asks.

"All bets are off, big guy."

He looks at me, and it could be in my head, but I see the wheels turning like he's starting to understand what I'm saying and isn't sure how he wants to play it.

Tough luck.

"Oh my god, it's like a TV show," Stella says under her breath, her husband pulling her in close.

"Never thought I'd see the day he met his match," Reed says, watching Jaime and me just a foot apart, me looking up at him and him looking down at me. "Much less a five-foot princess." Finally, I break my stare down with Jaime.

"A queen, thank you very much."

Reed smiles wide before bowing. "I'm so sorry, your highness.

"I'll accept it, I suppose."

"Okay, you're sitting with us," Willa Stone says, coming over to me, putting an arm through mine and tugging me to where Stella is sitting. "And we *must* talk about this dress and how I can get myself one."

And then I spend the next hour sitting with iconic songwriter Stella Greene and pop star Willa Stone talking about dresses and makeup and adventures, and I wonder the entire time how I got here.

And not once do I not feel Jaime's eyes burning on me.

The music and dancing start after dinner, and during that time, I watch people get up and move to the dance floor, but I stay seated, occasionally chatting with the Atlas Oaks boys or Stella and Willa as they go out to mingle and return. This event has been fabulous since it's, for once, not centered around me, meaning I'm just here to make an appearance, not have the spotlight on me.

But when one of my favorite songs comes on and the band plays the opening notes, I gasp and start to sway a bit, watching couples come together on the dance floor.

"What?" Jaime asks, looking around like a threat is going to jump from around the corner.

"I just...I love this song," I mumble, then turn to him, eyes wide, lips pouting. "Can we please dance?"

"Absolutely not," he says instantly, and I deepen my pout at him.

"Come on, Jaime. Please? I'm bored! Everyone is dancing!"

"I'm sitting right here," Beckett, the Atlas Oaks drummer, says from the other side of the table.

"Do *you* want to dance with me?" I ask, turning my attention to him.

He smiles wide and opens his mouth, then stops. Even over the music, I hear the chair scraping as Jaime stands, pushing back his chair and grabbing my hand.

"Fine. One. One dance."

"Yippee!" I say, grabbing his hand and nearly skipping as he leads me onto the dance floor.

"Did you just say *yippee?*"

"Yeah, I'm excited. You should try it, feeling emotion every once in a while." That has him rolling his eyes.

"I feel emotion," he grumbles. "I felt emotion in Georgia."

A chill runs through me that doesn't leave me the least bit cold. I rack my brain for what to say next, but then he stops in a semi-clear spot on the dance floor, taking my hands and putting them on his shoulders and gently placing his hands awkwardly on my waist. A small laugh leaves my lips as I look up at him.

"God, what is this, middle school? Are we leaving room for Jesus?"

"What?"

"I dated a guy in high school who went to Catholic school, and that's what they said at the dances. We needed a foot between us to leave space for Jesus. It was to discourage grinding, though half of the kids were sneaking out to fool with their dates anyway, so it didn't work too well."

"Huh. Well, yeah. Professionalism, remember?"

I roll my eyes, then step closer, moving until my arms wrap around his neck, looking up at him with a sly smile. "Yeah, it was real professional when you pressed me against a wall, your hands on my tits, and kissed me until I saw stars."

"Ava..." he says, starting to let go and shaking his head. "This was a shit idea."

"No, no, come on. I'll be good," I whisper, sincerity lacing in the words. "Just a dance. A real dance that won't look like I'm forcing you into it." I give him big puppy dog eyes, and it only takes a moment before he gives in, before his arm wraps around my waist, pulling me into him tight.

"This is so unprofessional."

"If anyone calls you out on it, I'll be sure to tell the world it was my idea and I forced you into it. I'll tell them all about how you can't stand me and are barely enduring me." He shakes his head, irritation on his face as his arm around my waist loosens. "What? What did I do wrong this time?"

"I think I've made it crystal fucking clear by now that I don't hate you, Ava. I feel the furthest thing from it."

"Well, you always look so annoyed dealing with me," I say as we sway to the song, a crooning voice and slow instruments swirling around me. I've had a single glass of champagne, yet somehow, at this moment, I feel completely inebriated. "Gives a girl a complex, you know."

Time passes as we sway, and then his hand presses on my back, forcing my body to glue tightly to his as he stares into my eyes.

"I'm annoyed with myself most of the time. Annoyed that I let you get to me. I'm obsessed with you, Ava. I've told you as much. You tell me all the time that I'm into you, that I like you. You spend every day fucking with me, flirting with me, telling me I'm in love with you, and then any time I do something marginally nice, you act surprised as fuck."

"Because I'm just fucking with you, Jaime. I don't actually think—"

"Don't lie to me, and don't lie to yourself, Ava." He lifts one hand, brushing my long, loose curls over my shoulder and down my back, rough fingertips grazing my neck as he does.

I don't speak for long moments as we sway, unsure how to respond, especially with his body so close to mine in a way that fits too right.

"You're quiet," he says eventually.

"Hmm," I say, not answering his unspoken question.

"You gonna tell me why?"

I let out a deep soul sigh. This was fun when it was an idea in a hotel room while getting ready, when a small, daydreamy part of me thought he'd see me and make grand confessions of how into me he was, how he wanted to throw away all threads of professionalism and try this thing that's been burning between us since the beginning.

But now that it just seems to be more of the same—the same confusion, the same mixed signals—I'm tired. I'm tired and confused and so scared that I'm going to get hurt.

"Just trying to understand what's going on here."

"What?" Finally, his head tips down to look at me.

"What's going on here, Jaime? Me and you. One minute you're doing everything in your power to avoid me, then you're slow dancing with me and telling me you're obsessed with me. One minute you're kissing me like it's what you need to function, and the next you're telling me I'm just a job to you. I don't mind the flirting because I do it right back, and I don't mind you wanting to keep lines clear because I can respect that. But these mixed signals are getting old."

"Ava, I—"

My body stops swaying, looking up at him, and when his face goes just a bit soft, I know. I know he sees it there, because I *let* him see it. The hurt and the confusion hiding under the mask of confidence I always wear.

I shake my head at him.

"I deserve a man who, when he looks at me, when he says he wants me, he means it. He knows it to his bones. I deserve a man who is decisive. I don't deserve this whiplash you've been giving me. I don't deserve someone who kisses me like he's going to change my life, then ignores me and treats me like any old job. I deserve the world, and if you're not willing to give it to me, I need to know now."

He doesn't answer, but I keep staring at him. His jaw is tight, and he's too fucking handsome for his own good. Right in front of me and somehow miles away,

"So what's it going to be, big guy?"

I wait for an answer.

I wait, and I wait as people sway around us, and with each moment, with each note of the romantic song, my gut falls and falls.

It's in that moment I realize I fucked up.

I fucked up so huge because somehow, someway, I've started to fall for this big stupid idiot.

And I'm just a job to him.

As abrupt as the realization, the song ends, and Jaime steps back like that was the only reason he was holding me in the first place.

"I have to use the bathroom," he says.

"I'm sure you do," I whisper back, turning toward the table where Beckett is still sitting, now with Wes, a glass in hand, one leg kicked out as he watches us intently, a small smile playing on his lips, but I know there's none on mine, not at all.

Jaime leads me back to the table we're seated at with a firm hand at my back, but not in any way other than the touch of a bodyguard on his subject.

"Can you keep an eye on her?" Jaime asks his friend, and without even pausing, he walks off toward the exit.

I watch him even though I don't want to, and I don't miss how he doesn't even look back at me.

"So, has he admitted he's head over heels in love with you yet?" a voice says, snapping my attention to Wes, watching me with a smile.

"What?"

His smile grows with my attention on him. He sits up and turns toward me, puts his forearms on the table, and shakes his head.

"So that's gonna be a no. He's too thick-skulled for his own goddamn good."

THIRTY-FOUR
JAIME

I fucked up by waiting too long to answer.

I also lied when I said I needed to go to the bathroom, which is why I'm pacing outside the entrance to the ballroom, taking deep breaths to try to calm myself down.

I shouldn't have done it, taking her hand and pulling her to the dance floor, not when she's been pushing my buttons since I got back from my run, not when she's wearing that dress that has me fighting a hard-on all night. But I did, some ghost taking over my body when she offered to dance with Beckett.

That same phantom that made me lift her, press her against a wall, and kiss her just days ago. The one that made me buy her ice cream when I should have been doing everything in my power to convince her I wasn't into her. The one that had me buying cat toys and iced coffees before dawn the exact way she likes it, and books for her to read in the car.

I'm losing my fucking mind.

She's right. I can't keep dragging her along, sending mixed messages incessantly when hers are crystal clear.

But the question is, do I have the guts to take her as mine? And if

I don't, do I have the stomach to stand back while she moves on with someone else?

The answer is clear, and it has my feet moving with a new wind back toward the party.

Ava is mine, and it's time she finds out exactly what that means to me. That's when I hear a familiar woman's voice speaking.

"You need to calm down," the woman's voice says.

"I can't calm down because *I'm getting fucked,* Regina!" a woman responds with a shriek. "She's wearing *my crown!* And every day people ask me all these questions, and more articles are calling her the people's princess like she's fucking *Diana!* That's supposed to be me, Regina! If you don't fix this, I'm going to have to tell everyone—"

A slap rings in the hall, followed by a whimper that sounds like Anne. Did Regina just hit her?

"You stop your fucking whining. I'm tired of it. You stirring the pot and making her want to stay to prove you wrong *isn't helping.* You're making things more difficult, Anne. Keep doing what you're doing, and things will be fine. We just need to be patient." A door opens, and the sound of the party fills the space and drowns out the conversation I'm trying to listen to before it closes, leaving it quiet once again. "But right now, you need to go to the bathroom, clean your fucking face, and play the game. You'll be Miss Americana sooner than later, but not if you look like shit." Then heels click away down the hall.

So much just happened, but I can only think of one thing.

Ava.

Ava, Ava, Ava.

I need to get to Ava because something about that is wrong. And because I just need to be by her, talk to her, and fix this mess I made.

Stepping back into the ballroom, my eyes move to our table, and my blood goes cold. Ava is perched on the edge of the white table-cloth, head tipped back, turned toward Wes. His hand is on the table right next to her hip, skin revealed by the dress's high slit, not touching but close enough. Her feet kick as she giggles, and Wes's face is tipped up with a smile playing on his lips.

He's enchanted, the way everyone feels around Ava.

They look like they belong. They look like a couple having a great fucking time like they've been together for some time.

Comfortable.

Too fucking comfortable.

Her hand moves, pushing his shoulder as she laughs, and he grabs her wrist, stopping her from slipping off the edge of the table, and I have no clue what happens.

Something in me snaps, and I'm moving—nearly running—people stepping back as I walk quickly past them with no apologies until I'm at our table, grabbing her hand, putting a hand to her waist, and sliding her off the table.

"Come on," I say once her heels are steady on the floor—those high heels that I've thought about having digging into my back all fucking night.

"Jaime—"

"We're heading out," I say, putting a hand to her elbow and grabbing the small pink bag Wes hands me with a smug smile.

"Jaime—"

"Do not argue with me, Princess," I say under my breath.

"What the fuck was that, Jaime?" she shouts once we're out of the ballroom, following me as I keep a tight hold on her hand, leading her toward the elevators.

"Me? What the fuck was *that*, Ava?"

"What was *what?!*"

"*You and Wes*," I say in hissed tones, punching the button for the elevator.

"He was being *nice!* God forbid, right? We were just talking about the pageant and—"

"That man gave zero fucks about pageants. His eyes were glued to your tits. He wants to *fuck you*, Ava."

She throws my hands in the air in irritation. "At least someone wants to!" With her words, my body goes stiff, but Ava ignores it, continuing on. "At least *someone* wants me, shows interest in me. At least *someone* is fucking going for it."

"Ava," I say, and to my own ears, my voice is low and dangerous as I grab her hand. A chill runs through her, but she shakes her hand out of mine, taking a step closer and poking me in the chest with one white-tipped nail.

"You don't get to kiss me, fuck with me, tell me how bad you want me one morning, then spend the next few days doing everything in your power to not even brush your arms with me. You don't get to get jealous when you've had all the chances in the world to make me yours and never taken them. You don't get to keep me on a string, at your beck and call for when you decide you want to take me out of my box and play with me." She stabs her finger into my chest like she wants it to hurt. "I told you in there you needed to make a decision about what you want from this, from me, and you walked away."

"I needed air," I say.

"And I needed an answer, but just like everything else, you're too much of a fucking coward to do anything about anything."

A bell dings, the elevator arrives, and the doors slide open. She stomps into the elevator, pressing the button to close the doors before I can step in, but I slap my hand to the doors and step in.

She rolls her eyes and turns to face me, arms crossed on her chest. "I'm tired of this, Jaime. Either you want me and you're willing to say fuck it to all of the rules in your head, or we agree to be amicable, platonic friends for the rest of this tour. I'm tired of the games."

She's right.

And because of that, I step into her space until she's backed up against the wall, my hand on her hip, the other on her jaw, tipping her head to look up at me.

"Fuck it," I say.

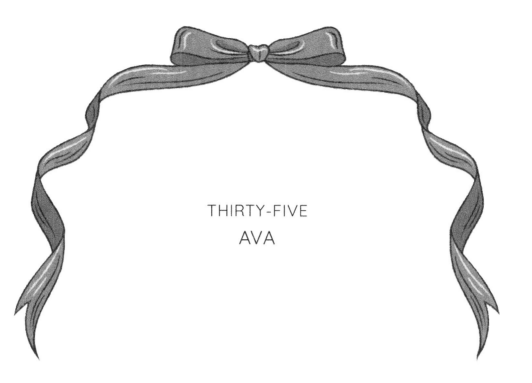

THIRTY-FIVE
AVA

His lips hit mine, and it takes the breath from my lungs. One hand moves to the back of my head, holding me there, tipping my head back, and holding me where he wants it as he devours my mouth.

Instantly, my entire body goes up in flames, any irritation I felt moments before melting away as his tongue slides into my mouth, twining with mine. He presses me so my bare back is against the cool metal of the slow-moving elevator, his hips pressing into my belly so I can feel him growing hard.

I let out a breathy moan at the confirmation that I affect him as much as he affects me as his lips trail down my neck and he dips his knees, a hand going to my ass to lift me. My legs wrap around his hips, the slit in my dress making it possible.

"You drive me fucking crazy, every moment of every day," he says into my neck, kissing and licking my ear and biting the lobe. The hand not holding me shifts to palm my breast, and without thinking, I arch my back into his hand.

"I want you so bad," I moan. "Please."

"You'll have me, Princess," he groans, my nails scraping at the back of his head, moving him to my mouth again so I can kiss him, claim him, and convince myself this isn't some wild dream.

The elevator stops, dinging on our floor, and instead of setting me down, he carries me out of the elevator and down the hall, my lips pressing beneath his jaw as he takes us to the door of our room. He unlocks it, walks in, and then pins me to the wall to grind on him while he locks it.

Finally, his lips are back on mine, claiming and devouring and tasting me like his life depends on it.

"We shouldn't be doing this," I say, breathing heavily as his hand dips beneath the low neck of my dress and cups my breast.

"Give me one good reason not to," he says against my neck, scruff scraping the skin there.

"Your job," I pant into his neck, trying to remember *why* we shouldn't do this, and he shakes his head.

"Who fucking cares?" he groans, his fingers rolling my nipple and pulling another moan from me. "Fucking perfect."

"You should," I say, unable to even form complete sentences, my hand on his neck pulling him close.

"Your contract," he counters, and I see what he's saying.

I don't even care anymore. If it means I can have this man, does anything else matter?

"'So fucking worth it.

"Exactly."

He walks with me, leaving the little entryway to the living area before setting my feet on the ground. His hand pushes one strap of my dress down, and it falls easily with the low back. He then does the same with the other side, the entire front of my dress falling to my waist, revealing my breasts to him.

He groans, a sound that comes deep from his chest, and I watch this giant man fall to his knees, one hand moving to cup my breast and bring it to his mouth, the other moving to the fabric stuck around my waist. His lips suck on my nipple, his tongue rounding the point as he tugs with no patience on my dress.

"Zipper," I say in a moan, my hand moving to the back of his head to hold him at the source of the deep pleasure I'm experiencing. "In the back."

His hand moves, trying to find where it is, his mouth nipping at my nipple. Finally, he grips the zip, tugging until the entirety of my dress is pooling around my feet.

"Even these have little bows for a sweet little princess, don't they?" he says, fingers grazing over the tiny bow at the front of my thong with the back of his hand before grazing down, a phantom of a brush over my already swollen clit through the fabric, then down further, my hips bucking to get more. Then his fingertips trail back up, starting at my center. "God, you're soaked, and I've barely even touched you."

I nod, looking down at him, and somehow, I feel both completely at his mercy and fully in control at this moment, a queen being worshiped by her loyal subject.

Holding my eyes, he dips down, pressing his mouth over my panties, licking over my clit and as he does, he groans loudly, like he's getting more pleasure out of this than I am. My nails scratch at his head, pressing to get more of whatever he'll give me.

His hands move up the sides of my thighs before his thumbs hook into the waistband of my thong. Dragging the panties down my legs, he stops halfway, then moves my legs apart, forcing the underwear to pull tight, a constraint that cuts into my skin and sets my skin ablaze.

Finally, one thick finger slides through my parted sex featherlight.

"Jaime," I breathe, watching his finger circle my clit, knowing he's looking at my face as he does, taking in my every minute reaction.

"Do you know how long I've waited to hear you say my name just like that?" he says low, then slides a finger into me with a low moan, enjoying this just as much as I am. "*Fuck*, Princess." The finger slides out, the low lighting in the hotel bouncing off my wetness before he slides it in again. "How long I've wanted to finger this tight pussy, play with your pretty tits?" His fingers leave me, and I groan at the loss as his hands lift, spreading wetness over my nipples, cupping the weight of my breast in his hands. "How long I've waited to taste you?" He leans in, sucking my nipple into his mouth and licking me off of my skin. The groan that rips through him vibrates along my skin as he laves my nipple, getting every drop before releasing me.

"Yeah, I need to eat that," he says as if to himself, standing before pulling my panties all the way down and lifting my naked body, walking ten feet to the couch with my legs around him as he takes my lips again with his. When his tongue slides in my mouth, I taste myself there, mixed with the distinct taste of Jaime, and it sends a new rush of wetness between my legs.

Setting me on the couch, he shifts to his knees in front of me.

"Spread those pretty legs of yours," he says. And I do as he asks, sitting at the edge of the couch, legs wide as I can. His hands go to the insides of my thighs, pushing to part me further.

"Wider." His voice is a deep growl now. "I need room to play."

And then he does.

His wide tongue runs along me from my entrance to my clit, sucking and forcing me to buck my hips before he looks up at me. "Even better than I imagined, Ava. And I've imagined what you'd taste like a fuck of a lot."

"Oh my god." I look down at him, my jaw slack, and my eyes hooded. "I need more. Your fingers," I moan. "Please. I need to be full."

I don't have to ask a second time as he groans at my words, his eyes locking on mine, and two fingers slide in. He starts to fuck me with them, sliding in and out, curling them exactly how I need, going the perfect speed as his mouth returns to my clit.

I lean back on my hands, looking down my body at him, at this man on his knees for me, eating me like his only wish on this earth is to make me come on his tongue. Never in my life have I felt so powerful or so wanted as I do with this man moaning into my pussy while he eats me out.

My orgasm builds in my stomach, big and hot and growing as he groans into my pussy. My hips move, bucking to get more, to get there faster, before his free hand moves, gripping my thigh and pushing my legs wider like he instructed.

"I'm going to come, Jaime!" I shout as the slight pain of the stretch of my hip tugs me over, feeling it wash over me as my orgasm explodes. His fingers slam deep, stroking me as I come on his tongue, shouting his name.

The orgasm expands, doubling when he moans into me and when I see his hand working his cock through his unbuttoned slacks, like the pleasure of eating my pussy was too much to bear.

As I slowly come back to myself, he licks me clean, kissing my clit and the sides of my thighs before he stands, sliding his pants and underwear down, his long, thick cock bobbing before my face as he does. Then his hands move to his shirt, unbuttoning and sliding both his jacket and button down to the ground as I watch, my body still humming.

"You're always so mouthy with me; let's put it to good use. Open up, baby."

My entire body heats with the command because that's exactly what it is: a command to open my mouth so he can fuck it. When I do, he fists himself, tugging once, twice, and making me mewl at the visual before twining my hair around his fist and using his leverage to guide my mouth to his cock.

I look up at him as he slides in, so I get to see his mouth drop open, his eyes rolling back as he hits the back of my throat, using a tug on my hair to pull me back, then push forward again, drawing a moan from him as he looks down at me.

He's fucking my face.

He's fucking my face, and I fucking *love it*. My eyes begin to water as my hand trails down my body, my legs still spread as I sit on the edge of the couch, finding my dripping pussy and circling my clit, a low hum of lust shooting through me.

"God, look at you playing with yourself, ready for me again just because you're sucking my cock." I watch him watch me, fingering my pussy, my mouth sucking him. His hand on my hair quickens, moving my mouth on him faster, and he's thrusting into my mouth, hitting the back of my throat as I finger fuck myself in the same rhythm. "Jesus," he groans, then pulls back, and I moan in disappointment.

A small smile hits his lips, and he shakes his head. "The perfect woman." And then he's shifting, lifting me and moving us to the arm of the couch while kissing me, the taste of his precum on my tongue mixing with the taste of my pussy on his lips from earlier.

I groan at the taste as he breaks the kiss before placing me on the arm of the couch, shifting me until my knees rest there so I'm kneeling, my hands on the seat of the couch. His finger trails down my slit, and I look over my shoulder at him, one hand on his cock as he watches that finger move.

"I got tested before this assignment, and everything came back normal," he says. "And I know you're on birth control. I'm happy to go grab a condom, but I'd be lying if I said I haven't been dreaming about filling you with my cum, Ava."

I clench at his words, and I know he sees it when he moans and slides a finger inside me.

"I was tested at my last appointment, and I'm all good. Please, god —oh fuck," I moan as he notches the head of his cock with my entrance, one hand resting on my hip.

"Move back, baby," he says, his voice almost sweet.

I do as he asks and a low, guttural moan fills the room.

My moan.

My moan as Jaime's too-thick cock stretches me and fills me deep at the pace I set. His hands hover gently on my ass, but I'm doing the work, filling myself with Jaime. When I look over my shoulder, he's standing, looking down in awe as I take him.

"Jesus, baby, you should fucking see this, how pretty you look taking me. See how gorgeous you look full of me."

My hips move back until I hit his thighs, finally full of him, the stretch just barely tinged with a pain I savor.

I take a deep, shaky breath. *I'm going to explode.*

I'm too full, he's too perfect, and I can't take it.

"I know, baby," he says. "I know." It's as if he feels the all-consuming, thought-melting perfection of being joined like this.

Slowly, he slides himself out and then back into me, a hand moving to my lower back, pressing to guide me until my chest is pressed into the couch, my legs out, widening myself for him. My ass tips back, somehow taking even more of him, feeling him hit a set of nerves no one has ever touched, and my body jolts with it. He slides out again before slamming in hard, repeating the move as I groan at the exquisite feel of him.

Suddenly, it starts, the pleasure is too much, and I need to come.

I need to come, or I might explode.

"Jaime," I say, my hand sliding until I stop at my clit, rubbing hard, trying to ease the all-consuming ache between my legs he's started, that he keeps stoking as he hits that spot deep inside me with each snap of his hips.

"That's it. Rub that pretty clit while I fuck you, Princess. That's it, baby."

My hips buck as the pleasure builds in me as he fucks me, as he slides in deep, both hands on my hips guiding my movement, keeping me where he wants me. One hand leaves, coming back and spanking my ass. I moan with the move, with the burn, and with the way the pleasure floods my clit.

"Fuck, I knew you'd like that, my bad girl." He stops moving, staying planted in me, and I moan my disapproval. The opposite hand from the first time lifts before cracking down on my skin as a scream leaves me, and my clit throbs beneath my fingers.

"Jaime, I need you, please."

"Then take it. Take what you want."

I moan, but I start to move, bucking my hips and doing as he asks, moaning as he slides in then out. I start to move faster, fucking him as my fingers work my clit, as the orgasm to end all orgasms builds in my belly again.

"Look at my bad girl taking what she needs, fucking herself on my cock."

"I'm so close, Jaime."

"I know, baby, keep going, just like that."

"Yes, yes," I breathe. His fingers tighten on my ass, spreading me open for him. A distant sound hits my ears, then wetness hits my ass, his hand moving and his thumb rubbing in the wet on my asshole.

He spit on me.

He spit on me, and...his thumb on his left hand starts to move, pressing in slowly. My eyes drift shut at the feeling of him filling my ass, of being so fucking full of Jaime, at the way my hand is moving on my clit, the way his cock throbs as I fuck myself on it.

"Come for me, Ava." And then his other hand moves, coming down with a loud clap, and I explode.

Too many sensations at once, all-consuming and cracking through me like electricity, and I come, screaming Jaime's name as I shake. Somewhere, I hear Jaime groan as I clamp down on him, seeing stars.

As soon as I come down, he reaches over my back and tugs on my shoulder, so I'm on my hands and knees again. It's a new angle, and he slams in harder than before, fucking me deep, this time for himself. My mouth drops open, but no noise comes out as he fucks me, as the fire burns, as my head goes a bit lightheaded, but the pleasure builds and builds in my belly once more.

I reach for my clit to take me over the edge, but he slaps the hand down before he pauses when his hips pull out until he's barely in me, stopping the orgasm that wants to hit like a freight train in its tracks. I mewl in my throat, tipping my hips to try and get more.

He leans down, his chest pressing to my back. "You only come when I tell you to, Ava. That's what bad girls get," he says low and rough in my ear. "And you're going to be my good girl and hold on until I let you come."

"Jaime," I moan, both because that's the sexiest thing I've ever heard and because I don't think there's any universe where I can hold on much longer. "I can't."

"Yes, you can, and you will. For me, Princess, you'll hold on." His hips move finally, sliding in slow, easy thrusts, endless, dull pleasure crashing through, but not enough—not what I need.

"Jaime, I need—"

"I know exactly what you need, Ava." His right hand moves, wrapping around my hair and pulling my head back. The pinpricks of pain as he tugs transmit right to my pussy as he starts to fuck me hard again, as pleasure twines and twines with the tug on my hair, gasoline for the orgasm of a lifetime. When his hips hit deep and grind into me, it starts to spark and...

And he fucking stops, his hand releasing my hair, his cock sliding half out and stilling.

"Jaime!" I shout, looking over my shoulder at him. "Please."

"You look so pretty begging me, Ava."

"I can't—" I say on a near sob, and the hand on my throat moves gently, skating down my neck, over my chest until he cups a breast gently.

"You can," he repeats, his finger rolling my nipple, and he slides in slowly, filling me to the hilt before sliding out once more. The hand on my breast moves down again to rub my clit, the hand on the couch next to mine holding his weight as he does. My body aches, forcing him to slide in deeper, and I scream, but it's not enough, just featherlight touches against my oversensitive clit.

"Jaime, Jaime. Please." I can barely choose words in my brain, much less conjure full sentences, when all my brain can think about is how good he feels, how much torture this is, and the now constant pulsing in my clit.

"I know, baby, I know," he says, sliding in and out and moving his hand up my body, pinching my nipple again. "I'm gonna fill you, Ava, as soon as you come for me. Fuck, you feel so good," he groans, his body over mine as he bucks into me, fucking me hard, before finally, finally, slamming in deep and holding there, the hand on my nipple moving to my clit and rubbing as I shatter around him.

I come and I come, my entire body bucking into his as he groans my name loudly into my neck, filling me with his cum. He keeps slowly sliding in and out of me, his fingers on my clit, pulling one last orgasm from my body as he whispers hot words in my ear, but the last one is slower, softer, and somehow sweeter.

Silence takes over the hotel room before, finally, still inside me and with smugness in his words, Jaime speaks. "I told you we could make doggy work."

And then I burst into laughter.

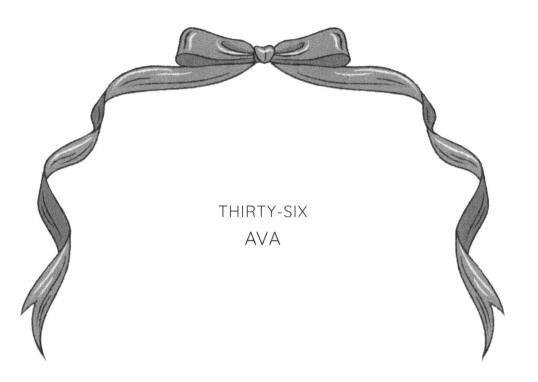

THIRTY-SIX
AVA

We lay like that for long minutes with Jaime's body lying over mine on the arm of the couch while I come down from my high before I whisper, "I should go clean up."

He nods and rolls off of me.

Quickly, I move to the bathroom, cleaning up and fixing my smeared makeup before staring in the mirror, a wash of panic and confusion taking over me.

What's next?

Do I walk back into the living area? Do I go to my room? Do I ignore him? Do I walk in there and kiss him? Was this a one-time, get-it-out-of-our-systems thing?

A million questions run through me, but one is loudest in my mind: What am *I* doing?

I don't *do* self-conscious.

I don't do second-guessing myself. Hell, I barely do *first*-guessing myself.

But that's precisely how I feel right now. What is the expectation now? Do we—

"Ava, get your sweet ass in here," Jaime's rumbly voice calls from his room, and in the mirror, my eyes go wide.

Still, I take a deep breath, nod to myself once, and move back toward the room he's staying in. He's sitting up with his back against the headboard, a sheet pulled up to his waist, a single arm out before his fingers move in a *come here* way.

My body obeys before my mind can process it. When I get close, his hand grabs my hip, the other moving to my waist as his body shifts to lift me with ease until I'm straddling his lap and we're face to face. One hand leaves my hip, gently pushing my hair behind my shoulder.

"What's going through your head?"

I contemplate playing it off, letting the cool-girl version of me click into place and not show him my fears and nerves, but I know he'd see it anyway. That's the downside of Jaime Wilde—he sees everything.

I sigh before answering. "I just...I don't know what I'm supposed to do now that we...you know. I don't know where we stand," I whisper, staring at my hand instead of him before continuing. "What is this now? Did we fuck just once? Are we fuck buddies? Does everything go back to normal in the morning?" His lips tip up, and I wonder momentarily if finally getting some has eviscerated his grumpiness.

"You're saying Ava, the take-no-shit one, the hyper-self-confident one, the one who has told me that I'm in love with her for almost two months now, isn't sure how to act? *My Ava,* who flirted with a rock star just to annoy me," he says, and I let the chill run through me with the way he calls me *his* Ava. "Is suddenly nervous about how to act?"

A blush takes over me, embarrassment and anxiety and doubt rushing through my veins as I bite my lip and turn my head away from him, but his hand moves, rough fingers on my cheek as he moves my face to look at him.

"Where we stand is that you're mine now," he says without hesitation. "You're mine, Ava. It means at every stop from here on out, one of those beds goes untouched because we're sharing one. It means I take care of you, and I sleep next to you, and I get to eat your pussy every night and kiss your sweet lips whenever I want, which is a lot. Besides that, not much changes because we've already been toeing that line for weeks. We're just stomping all over it now."

I take in his words, fighting back the smile and giddiness filling my chest.

I fail spectacularly.

"So we're dating?"

"Yeah, baby," he says, his hand moving to push my hair back again, which he seems to like doing. Maybe he just likes being able to touch me now without it being against some kind of rule, something I can absolutely relate to.

"So you're my *boyfriend*?" I ask, my voice teasing.

He closes his eyes for a moment and sighs. "Boyfriend sounds like we're fifteen, and I'm taking you to prom. But if that's what you want to call me, have at it." My smile goes wider. "We have to make clear lines, though."

I scrunch up my nose, not liking how that sounds, and he smiles as if we've traded places now. He shifts us until I'm on my back, his hands planted in the bed on either side of me.

"Why do I feel like I won't like this?" I grumble.

"Because you hate any rules or constraints when it comes to me trying to make you safer."

"That's not true—" I start, but he glares, and finally, I nod. "Okay, maybe it's a little true."

He takes a deep breath, his hand buried in my hair to hold me in place, to keep my eyes on his.

"We can't be together when you're *on*," he says. "When you're Miss Americana, I'm your bodyguard. When you're Ava, you're mine."

"So this is...just fucking?" My stomach drops to my feet at the thought because, although I could play it cool and what just happened was *amazing*, I don't want *just sex* with Jaime.

"I told you, I'm a decisive man. I see what I want, decide I want it, and I get it, and you're what I want. I'm not letting that go easy." One hand leaves the bed to cup my jaw as he drops down, planting a small kiss on my lips, leaving me lightheaded.

"But..."

"But you're keeping this crown if it kills us both because no one deserves it more than you." Warmth blooms in my belly. "And you're not supposed to date. You would be technically breaking the contract—"

"I don't care about that contract, Jaime. And that *stay single* shit is wildly outdated. They'd get so much backlash if they tried to enforce it. I—"

"They've already threatened to remove me," he says, cutting me off, and my eyes go wide.

"What do you mean?"

"My boss called after the issue in Georgia. The Miss Americana pageant called him and told him to have me keep you in line better, or they might have to replace me." I open my mouth to argue, but he smiles and keeps talking. "I told him I can keep you in line about as much as you can keep a tiger in line. But it means they're watching you, and they aren't happy. We've got five weeks left, and I don't want to be taken off this case."

"You want to make sure you're the only one watching my ass, huh?" His hand travels down my bare back to my ass, grabbing it.

"Absolutely. But mostly, I don't trust anyone else to take care of you."

"You *do* take really good care of me, Jaime." My hand moves to touch his cheek. "Okay," I agree. "We'll keep things under wraps until the tour is over so I don't fuck with your job. But after the tour, we revisit this. I don't want to be a secret forever."

He nods. "Great, now that that's settled, are you ready for me to take care of you some more?" He flips me so my back is to the bed, and he starts to slide down my body.

"I thought you'd never ask," I say with a smile.

I think I'm going to *love* this new version of us.

THIRTY-SEVEN

JAIME

It's been three days since I made Ava mine.

Three amazing days where I don't have to pretend there isn't something so palpable between us, I might explode. Three days where I can act on whatever impulse, tugging her into my body as she walks past me in the hotel, leaning over in the car to press my lips to hers, or sliding my hand over to rest on her leg while I drive.

While I'm still forced to remain professional and act like she doesn't exist to me outside of being my assignment in public, as soon as we're behind closed doors, she's mine, and we have a fuck ton of time to make up for.

But now I have some alone time and need to make a call. That conversation I overheard right before everything went down has been sitting on the outskirts of my mind. Something tells me the pieces of this puzzle I'm missing are absolutely critical, so I leave Ava and Peach safely locked in the hotel room as she gets ready for tonight's event, while I go on a coffee run.

On the drive back, I dial one of the smartest men I know.

"Miles," I say when he picks up, skipping the hellos and jumping right into it. "Got some time?"

Miles is a computer genius with crazy hacking and investigation skills. He worked for Five Star when Hank owned it, doing any research required on potential threats, but was let go when the business changed hands. As I've learned, Greg doesn't believe in spending time and money on preventative security.

"Well, hello to you too, how are you? I'm just fine," he grumbles.

"I don't have time for niceties."

"Does this have anything to do with this pageant queen of yours?" he asks with a laugh, and I groan. I avoided calling Hank because I didn't want to deal with his teasing bullshit, and yet here I am, dealing with it anyway.

"Let me guess, you talked to Hank?"

"He's got a big mouth, and now that he's retired, he gabs more than any chick I've ever met," he says with a laugh. "But I'm just fucking with you. What's going on?"

Scrubbing a hand over my face, I sigh.

"I don't know. Some things aren't adding up over here, and I need to see if you can find any connections not visible to outside eyes." If there's any connection to be found between the hotel break-in, the assault, and whatever the fuck Regina and Anne were talking about, he'd be the one to figure it out. "It could be nothing, but I've got a bad feeling about it."

"I've never known you to be wrong about a bad feeling. If your gut says something is off, I'd trust it." My stomach churns because he's not wrong. I've learned in this business to trust my gut, and when red flags are waving, they're never false alarms.

"Yeah, that's kind of what I'm afraid of." I sigh. "I'm kind of stuck, though, especially since no one seems to be taking this seriously. You know Greg wants to do the bare minimum now. If I send you a list of all of the things that have happened while we've been on tour, can you try to find any kind of connection besides Ava?"

"Of course. Give me the details," he says, any hint of humor gone from his tone, and then I dive into what I've been seeing. It only takes a few minutes to give him all of the details and names I have.

"Can you make sure your search goes deep into Anne Holmes and Regina Miller?" I ask.

"Regina Miller, as in the runner of the Miss Americana pageant?" he asks, keys typing.

"That's the one. She's got it out for Ava, and I can't tell if it's just because she doesn't like her or because there's something more there. A threatening letter was sent to the organization for Ava, and they still haven't mentioned it to me. Regina and Anne were the ones who insisted I not watch Ava the day she was assaulted, and I already told you about the conversation I overheard."

"Got it," he says like he's got everything he needs now. "You're right; red flags are waving." Keys clack a few more times in the background. "I have a few projects I'm working on in the next few weeks, but I'll try and see what I can do."

"I really appreciate it, man," I say as I pull into the hotel parking lot.

"Anytime. So you're in love with the pageant queen?" Miles asks with a laugh, and I groan. "I gotta say, a few weeks ago, Hank called me, told me you'd met your match, and you were head over heels for some chick. I thought he was crazy until I saw a paparazzi photo of you with some tiny little thing. Then it started to make sense."

"Fuck off," I say, feeling suddenly protective of her. Fuck, even before things were concrete between us, I was protective of her in a way that went well past my duties as her bodyguard.

I told Ava that once I make a decision, I don't waver, and I meant it. I've decided Ava is mine, meaning that I need to do whatever I can to make sure she's not just safe, but happy.

"Have you made that official yet?" he asks. I don't speak, trying to decide how to answer, considering things are so new and still under wraps, but I suppose my silence says enough. "Good for you, man. From what I've seen, she's a good one, won't take your shit."

I groan and run a hand through my hair. "She's giving me an ulcer," I say.

"As she should. You need someone to keep you from becoming the most boring person on the planet."

"Oh, fuck off. I won't be boring when Greg finds out I'm dating my assignment and fires me."

"Fuck that job," Miles groans. "I've been telling you for months to quit there, that you should start your own firm. Your references are spectacular, and you know exactly what clients are looking for and are willing to go the extra mile for them. Five Star let me go, and I've had more business since then than I can even manage."

"Sounds great and all, but I'm just three years from my retirement, and I don't want to work in a field until I'm sixty."

"Not everything has to be fieldwork, and that retirement bullshit is negotiable. In my severance, they gave me a portion of it. Hank did us a solid with that contract before he left; put it into the selling agreement so you'll receive what you've earned no matter what. Greg is just holding it over your head because he knows if he loses you, he loses clients."

Interesting, I think, because I had no idea. Maybe it's time I took a look at that contract myself or finally tell Hank what's going on. I hadn't wanted to tell him how shitty things have been since he sold the company so he could enjoy his well-earned retirement, but maybe that was a mistake.

"So what, I just say fuck it and out us?" I ask, joking.

"Absolutely not," he says, voice firm. "You and I both know you have to keep things under wraps for *her* safety. If you out your relationship, from what I'm understanding, you're putting her in danger with the pageant and giving them another reason to fuck with her. We don't know their true intentions right now. And Five Star will take you off the case at the very least. We both know no one can adequately replace you and keep your girl safe."

My gut drops with the confirmation of what I've been thinking this entire time. It's why it took me so long to give in to Ava—this constant thundercloud hanging over us. Greg can pull me from this assignment at any moment, and between Regina and Anne plotting whatever I know they're plotting and Greg being more worried about getting the contract than actually keeping Ava safe, I'm not risking it.

"Gotta say, though, you two going public is going to be hilarious," Miles continues with a laugh.

"What?"

"The way people are obsessed with her every move, they're going to have a blast with the two of you. God, I can't wait for you to have to smile for the cameras. You're gonna love that shit."

"Fuck off," I say, pulling the key from the ignition. "I have to go. Keep me updated on anything you find."

"Aw, come on, I—" he starts, but I grab Ava's coffee and head up to my girl, hanging up before he can say another word.

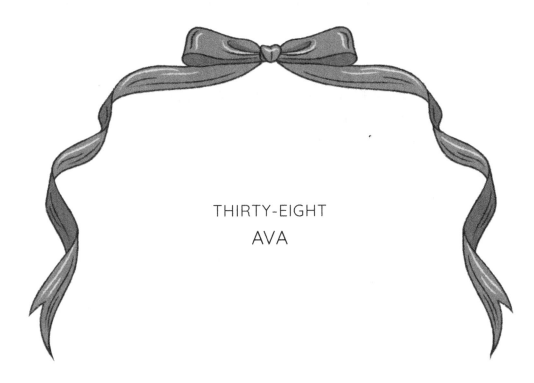

THIRTY-EIGHT
AVA

My phone beeps with a text, and I jump up from where I'm in the bathroom on FaceTime with Harper and Jules, getting ready to let Jaime into the hotel room.

"One sec," I say, then skip to the door, undoing the bar, the deadbolt, and the chain he insists I keep on the door, opening it to see Jaime towering over me with a tray of two coffees in one hand.

"Fuck, Princess," he groans as he steps in, the door slamming behind him, moving to back me into a wall with his body, using his free hand to move to my ass and lift me. Then his lips are on mine, tasting like black coffee and everything Jaime.

My legs wrap around his waist, and I sigh into his lips as his tongue dips into my mouth. Instantly, my hips tip, already wanting him.

I had him this morning; I came at least three times, though the last orgasm got a bit hazy, my mind not able to pinpoint where one started and another stopped, so it could have been more. But still, I want him again.

It's as if my body wants to use every moment we're together to make up for the weeks we denied there being anything between us. Eventually, though, he pulls back, resting his forehead on mine.

"I got your coffee," he says low, and I smile.

"The girls are on FaceTime in the bathroom," I whisper, and slowly, he lowers me.

"And you've gotta be ready to go in." He looks at his watch. "Forty-five minutes." I roll my eyes, knowing we don't have to be at the speed dating event until *at least* an hour from now. "Meaning I don't have time to fuck you now."

My lips tip up, even though I think that's a crying shame.

"But you in your little robe and whatever you're wearing under it," he says of the cream silk robe and the matching silk and lace bra and underwear set I'm wearing to get ready in, "are making it really, really hard for me to make the right choice."

I smile at him, reach for my coffee, and duck under his arm that's braced on the wall.

"Well, it'll just have to wait until after, won't it?" I say with a laugh, moving back to the bathroom, where all of my makeup and hair products are sprawled about.

"Is that him?" Jules asks as I pick up my still-warm curling iron, fixing my bangs one last time.

"Yes, that's Jaime," I say, taking a sip of my coffee before grabbing my primer and starting the process of putting on my makeup base.

"Jaime!" Jules yells from my phone. I turn to him, standing ten feet away from me like a deer in headlights. With a makeup sponge in hand and the straw of my coffee between my lips, I smile at his shocked, panicked face. "Come here."

"Jules, you're going to scare the man," Harper says under her breath. "We need him to like us when she brings him home." Something about that warms me, my friends wanting the new man in my life to like them.

"You've been summoned, Big Guy," I tell Jaime.

"Oh my god, you call him big guy, I can't even."

"Come here," I say to Jaime, tipping my head toward the bathroom.

"I don't think—" he starts, but Jules hears him and jumps on it.

"I don't bite, not through a phone screen at least," she says.

"You really *are* going to scare him off, stop, Jules!" I fully turn to him and fight the laugh at seeing him standing panicked in the other room. "Trust me, it's easier on both of us if you just come here and say hi to them." He stares at me, and I lose the battle of my smile, letting it take over my face. Then he sighs and walks into the bathroom to a round of cheers from me, Jules, and Harper.

"Oh my god, he's even hotter on FaceTime," Jules says under her breath.

"Jules!" Harper shouts.

"Tell me I'm wrong. Do it. You can't!"

"Hi, Jaime, I'm so sorry, please ignore that one. I'm Harper, Ava's *sane* friend."

"Fuck off," Jules says. "I'm Jules, the much more fun one. It's great to meet you. Is our Ava treating you well? Giving you lots of head?"

Now it's *my* turn to turn my head to my phone, a blush coming to my cheeks. "Jules! What the fuck!"

"Oh, don't even *try* to tell me you haven't given that man head. Just *look* at him."

My face burns, and Jaime nods at the disaster that is this interaction and starts to turn away.

"On that note, I'm gonna go," he says.

"No! No, don't go!" Jules yells.

I reach out, grab his arm, and look at my phone screen. I want him to stay, chat with my friends, and spend just a few more minutes with me. It's all I want lately: to spend time with him doing nothing but hanging out, like he's *really* mine and we're not in this very strange arrangement where lines between work and pleasure are much too blurred.

I just want a *hint* of normalcy. A taste of what this could be in a few months.

"If you behave and stop being such a nudge, he'll stay, right?" I say, looking from my phone to Jaime's face in the mirror.

"I promise I'll be good! Nothing weird or anything. I just miss my girl, and she won't tell me any of the juicy details, which probably means she *actually likes you*, and I want the inside scoop. But I'll stop being a pain if you hang out with us."

Jaime sighs. He looks at me, then at the screen of my phone, then moves further into the bathroom, sitting on the closed toilet seat.

"So, how's it going?" Harper asks. "Anything exciting happening?"

"He's teaching me to protect myself!" I say excitedly, remembering I hadn't yet filled them in on this. When we got to the hotel room yesterday, Jaime decided it was a good time to practice our releases again. However, this time, his lesson ended in a *much* more fun way than when we had our first lesson at the dance studio.

"Woooow," Jules says. Then her gaze moves to where Jaime is sitting off-screen. "Prepare for her bullshit, Jaime, because she's a pain in the ass when it comes to that kind of thing. I had to teach her the dance routines, and it was like pulling teeth."

I roll my eyes, putting a hand on my hip. "That's because you're a drill sergeant! I was tired! My feet hurt!"

"I'm just warning the man. If he's going to be teaching you self-defense, he should know how impossible it is to teach literally anything."

Jaime smiles at me before speaking. "Trust me, I know how stubborn she is." I turn to glare at him. "You did good, though, Princess," he says, his voice a bit lower.

I gasp, putting a hand to my chest. "Was that a compliment?" I say facetiously, a wide smile on my lips.

"Well, yeah. I've gotta keep you motivated, so you keep learning," he says.

I see the truth in his words, though—*so we can have more nights like last night.*

"I'm just lucky I have a patient instructor," I say, trying to make him roll his eyes before I lean over with a smile and skim my blush brush on his nose. "Perfect."

"Did you just put makeup on my nose?"

I smile and wink at him as he glares. "Maybe."

He rolls his eyes at me, giving me exactly the reaction I was looking for. I love knowing I got to him, even if it's in a little way.

"God, you two are too cute," Jules says with a sigh right before an alarm goes off. "Fuck, that's my reminder to get out of the house. Gotta go, babe."

"Me too, I have a call in ten I have to get ready for."

"All right. Love you guys!" I say to my friends.

"Love you too. See ya later, Jaime. Keep my girl safe, yeah?" Jules says.

"My only job," he says with a rumble, and I smile at the screen. Jules and Harper's smiles are a reflection of mine right before the screen goes black.

I sigh, missing my friends already.

"They seem nice. A bit crazy, like you, but nice."

"They're the best," I say with another sigh.

"I can't wait to meet them when we get home," Jaime says, his hand reaching out to rub my lower back.

I smile at him, unable to put words to what that means to me that he stays in the bathroom for the rest of the time I get ready like he wants to be near me as much as I want him to be.

THIRTY-NINE
JAIME

Initially, when I was given an itinerary for Ava's stops, I thought going to a speed dating session to promote a matchmaker was a bit of a pain in my ass, but probably meant I could stand in a corner for a few hours in peace while Ava did her thing.

I remember thinking it was a bit odd to put Miss Americana in speed dating when she isn't supposed to *actually date* during her reign, and then I realized it was part of the appeal: the *potential* to have Miss Americana.

The possibility that anyone could date her, this perfect woman.

Where I miscalculated was becoming utterly obsessed with her, and then barely a week after finally claiming her as mine, having to watch her date a dozen men right before my eyes.

It's my own personal version of hell.

We're barely twenty minutes and four dates in when I should probably start getting nervous for the health of my teeth. All this grinding can't be good for them.

When the current man she's sitting with reaches over, touching Ava's hand—a simple, relatively harmless move—I reach into my pocket and grab my phone, tapping on the screen and staring at my girl after I hit send.

Me: *Stop letting these assholes touch you, Ava.*

Her body moves a bit, registering a vibration, but she doesn't reach for her phone until the buzzer sounds, signaling it's time for the men to shift seats.

Ava: Are you jealous?

She sends the response with a smile and her gaze directed at me.

Me: Very.

She sees it and smiles wider before quickly tapping out a response as a new man with a too-white smile sits in front of her.

Ava: Good.

Then she stuffs her phone back into her little bag. I watch this interaction with as much interest as I've watched the past four, my skin prickling with irritation when it happens.

She leans forward, pressing her tits together as she does, and smiles at him. He smiles wide as she does, and I get it. I, too, get utterly enthralled anytime Ava graces me with one of her smiles, but the one spreading on her pink-painted lips isn't for him.

It's directed right at me.

My fingers move on my phone screen.

> Stop being a brat, Ava.

The buzzer rings, time is up, and the douchebags switch positions once more. Ava lifts her phone before smiling again and typing.

> You like it when I'm a brat. You said it gets you hard.

> This would be a very inconvenient place to be hard. Plus, it's difficult to get too excited when you're actively on a date with someone else.

She rolls her eyes at that text.

> Stop rolling your eyes at me, or I'll give you a reason to make them roll.

Promise?

I shake my head at her response, and somehow, despite another man sitting across from her and offering his hand to shake, I feel a twitch in my cock all the same.

What the fuck is this woman doing to me?

She puts her elbows on the table, resting her head in her hands as the man talks, rambling on about himself and never once asking about her. Ava's eyes keep drifting in my direction, a small consolation. Then she tips her head back with a fake laugh, her hand going to her chest, bringing attention to her breasts in the low-cut top.

> Jesus, Ava, try not to draw an arrow to your fucking tits.

She looks at me quickly, a smile on her lips, and I groan internally, knowing that look never means anything good.

As tends to be her way, Ava shocks me. Instead of putting her phone back into her bag, she places it between her legs, crossing one leg over the other, her phone pinned against where I really want to be right now.

> Ava.

It's all I say, but I know it was delivered when her body jolts just a bit. It's not enough for anyone else to notice, but me, so trained to register her every breath, can see it easily.

> Ava, what are you doing?

She pulls her bottom lip between her teeth and then looks at me, her eyes on fire.

> You're being so fucking bad right now.

> Teasing this poor man while I'm getting you wet from across the room.

> That's what's happening, isn't it?

I should feel stupid texting things she's not even reading, but the way her breathing has started to pick up, I know each little buzz is torture.

> I'm going to spank you for teasing me tonight, Princess.

> Such a bad girl.

> My bad girl.

Her hand lifts, and my body freezes and before she even moves much, I know what she's thinking of doing.

She's trying to drive me insane, to make me jealous.

To see if I'll snap.

> Don't you fucking touch that man, Ava.

Her eyes flit to me and then back before she grabs the man's hand, holding it and flipping it like she's reading his palm, her fingers grazing over it.

She doesn't notice it, but I see the instant lust on that man's face, know the thoughts going through his mind, the way he wants her to be lightly touching him somewhere else, and I snap, making a decision.

I move over to the person conducting the speed dating, a sweet elderly woman who, from what I read, started this because she loves the idea of people falling in love, much like my Ava and her romance books.

"Hi, Jane, right?" She nods, looking confused. "I'm the security guard for Ava, and I have to speak with her for a moment. Can we have a bit of a break after this round? Five, ten minutes?"

She smiles sweetly before nodding. "Oh, of course! They're due for some mingling time anyway." The buzzer goes off, and Jane grabs the microphone, telling the crowd they're taking a fifteen-minute break and to remember what seat they were in, but I barely register it as I storm to Ava.

"Ava, a moment," I say, grabbing her by the elbow and lifting and leading her as gently as I possibly can toward an empty room.

"Jaime, what the—"

But she can't speak anymore when I lock the door behind me, press her against a wall, and kiss her.

I kiss Ava with every ounce of pent-up jealousy and irritation running through my veins, frustration that no one knows she's taken, that she's mine, irritation that all of these men think they can have what's *mine*.

I kiss her and taste her, her hand moving up to my hair and pulling me closer as my hand skirts up her waist to her breast, rolling her hard nipple through her bra and shirt.

"What are you doing?" she moans against my lips.

"Reminding you of whose you are," I say, using one hand to free her breast from her low-cut top, pinching her nipple before moving my hand down, gripping the bottom of the short, fitted skirt she's wearing, and tugging it up. Then I slide my hand down the front of her panties.

With my forehead to hers, I gaze down at her, our breaths panting and mingling, my finger circling her clit before dipping down, feeling just how wet she is.

"Jesus. This is from teasing me, isn't it? Making me jealous got you this wet?"

Her head nods against mine. "Yeah," she admits. "I love rattling you." She pants and moans as I slide a finger into her. "I love knowing I get to you."

"All you do is get to me, Ava," I say, starting to fuck her with two fingers. "All I do is think about you, dream about you. Since that very first night, you've completely consumed me." I move, sliding down, kissing the spot on her stomach where her shirt and skirt don't meet, leaving a line of smooth skin before continuing down to my knees, the hand not inside her sliding her underwear down to her ankles. She steps out of them, and I shove the cream-colored lace in my pocket.

Ava moans, her hips rocking in time with my fingers fucking her. "That's it," I say from my knees, looking up at her. "You're fucking magnificent like this, taking what you need."

Her eyes are hooded as she looks down at me, pinching her nipples, her skirt around her waist, hair falling forward.

"Jaime, I... I..."

"Tell me what you need, Ava. I'm here to serve you. Anything you need, it's yours." I crook a finger inside her, her hips bucking as I do, her wetness dripping down my hand.

"I want your mouth," she says quietly, and I groan.

My thumb moves, grazing along her swollen clit. "Where do you want my mouth, baby? Here?" I add a third finger to her wet pussy, sliding them in and feeling her tight body stretch around me. "Or here." My thumb grazes her clit, and she yelps.

"There! Please, please," she begs.

I smile up at her, my thumb moving at a leisurely speed, my fingers sinking deep.

"Quiet, Ava, or everyone will know what a bad little princess you are, letting your bodyguard eat your sweet pussy when there's a room full of people right behind that door."

"Oh, god."

"That's what you want? Right?"

"Yes, yes," she pants, quietly now in a near panic. "Yes, make me come with your mouth."

She doesn't need to ask twice. My free hand moves to lift her leg and place it on my shoulder, leaving her wide open for me before sliding up her leg to her waist to keep her stable. Then I descend, sucking her clit into my mouth while my fingers fuck her. Her hand goes to my hair, tugging me closer, riding my face and fingers.

A fucking queen, taking what she wants.

"Jaime, Jaime, Jaime," she pants, her hips moving with each utterance of my name, her sharp nails digging into my scalp.

I look up at her as she stares down at me. I'd do anything to taste her cum on my tongue, my fingers moving faster now, deeper, crooking to graze her G-spot with each movement.

"Oh!" she yelps, trying to stay quiet as it builds, her pussy tightening on my fingers. "Just like that, just like that. Oh, god, you're going to make me come, Jaime."

I pull my mouth back, and she bemoans the loss, her hand moving on my head to push me closer again.

"Whose are you, Ava?"

She doesn't hesitate.

"I'm yours, Jaime. I'm yours.

"Fuck yeah, you are, Ava. Whose face are you going to come all over?"

"Yours, baby, only yours."

I groan loudly. "Fuck yeah, you are. And after I clean you up with my tongue, when I send you back out there with no panties on, you're going to feel how wet I made you and remember who owns this."

My finger crooks, and she moans.

"Yes, baby, Yes. It's yours."

I smile up at her, her eyes hooded, her lips parted, one hand off her tit, pinching her pink nipple before I move back to her clit, sucking hard. Her hand grips my hair almost painfully, and she rocks her hips on my face once, twice, three times before her entire body stiffens, her pussy tightening around my fingers, my name a quiet prayer on her lips. I continue to fuck her gently until her pussy lets my fingers go, my tongue cleaning her up before I stand.

"Now you?" she asks, eyes barely opened and chest still panting, and I shake my head, moving to right her breast in her bra and tugging her skirt. It's a bit too short to wear without underwear, ending just a few inches above her knees, but it's tight so it should be okay for another hour. Plus, that means on the car ride back, I can play with her pretty pussy until we get to the hotel.

"No, Princess," I say, a finger sliding over her lip to fix her lipstick. "I'm good now."

"Excuse me?" she says, a small smile on her lips.

"I'm good. I just needed to remind you who you belonged to. You make me crazy, you know."

"Yeah, I know," she says with a smile, and I shake my head.

"No more touching, Ava."

She presses off the wall and steps closer to me, seduction on her face as if I didn't have her completely at my mercy moments ago. "Did I make you jealous, Big Guy?"

"You have no fucking idea," I say, groaning as her small hand moves to my hard cock, gripping it gently. I give her one last press of my lips to hers before I step back.

"You first. Go out, tell Jane it's all clear because I told her I had to talk to you about an emergency." She rolls her lips into her mouth. "I'll follow in five. Or however the fuck long it takes for this hard-on to go down."

"All right, Jaime," she says, all sweet.

And then I watch her ass as she opens the door, winking at me over her shoulder before she magically drops her phone, bending down still in the doorway to grab it, showing me the barest glimpse of her swollen, wet cunt. She stands, tugs down her skirt, and walks off to the sweet, older woman like nothing happened.

My woman is going to be the death of me; that much is for certain.

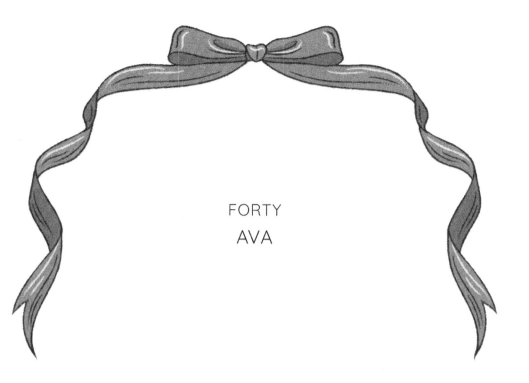

FORTY

AVA

Utah is our next stop, and I'd be lying if I said this state hadn't been way, way, way at the bottom of places I'm excited to go on this tour. Not because Utah isn't gorgeous and exciting and interesting. I'm sure it is. I'm sure it could even be the most interesting of the states we're traveling through.

But I could give two fucks about it because it's the home state of both Regina Miller and Anne Holmes, and I could go an entire lifetime without seeing either of them again, much less with the added bravado of being in their home state.

"It's going to be just fine," Jaime says, running a hand down my back as I spray on some perfume.

He's taken to doing this, hanging out in the bathroom while I get ready, and each time, it makes my belly flip. He'll sit in close quarters watching me do something silly he has no interest in just because he wants to spend time with me or because it makes *me* happy.

"I know. I just think skipping this entire stop would be much more enjoyable," I grumble, leaning in to put a swipe of some lipstick on.

"Yes, but the joy Anne would get from you skipping her home

state would eat at you forever. Imagine having to look at her for the rest of the tour, knowing she knows she gets under your skin."

I scrunch my nose in disgust because that sounds even worse than spending the entire day with Anne. It would be letting her win, even if it's in such a minuscule way, and *that* I won't be doing.

"You're right," I grumble.

"I'm always right," he says, staring, then slaps my ass, walking toward the living area. "Come on, we have to get going."

"Jaime!" I shout through a laugh. Seeing Jaime break out of his rigid shell, goof around with me more, and push my buttons back has been a joy. It's like once he decided we were crossing that line, something in him snapped, letting him be himself completely. It turns out his real self isn't too far from his bodyguard self—uptight, much too careful, and definitely grumpy—but he's also just a tad more fun.

"Gotta go, or you're gonna be late, which Anne and Regina would love to use as yet another reason to hate you."

I pout at the reflection in the mirror. "Ugh, I almost let myself forget she'd be there too. Why can't you ever just let me live in my delusion?"

Grabbing my crown, I carefully place it on my head, pinning it in place and turning left and right to check it from all angles. I don't wear it to every event, but I'd be lying if I said I didn't make an effort to wear it at any event Anne would be attending, too.

"Because one of us has to be grounded in reality, and it's sure as fuck not going to be you."

I smile at him sweetly. He's not wrong.

"Okay, how do I look?" I ask as I walk out of the bathroom. Jaime is scrolling his phone but presses off the wall he's leaning on when I walk in. He slides his phone into his pocket and takes a few steps until he's close enough to pull me into him.

"Fucking beautiful," he murmurs against my lips.

"Don't mess up my lipstick."

His lips tip up, the hand I put to his cheek feeling rather than seeing the dimple emerge.

"Deal. I'll do that later."

"Yes, please," I whisper. He steps back abruptly, a hand on my waist keeping me from toppling over before I get rid of the Jaime-induced vertigo and can stand on my own. "Rude."

"Later, Princess." His hand reaches up, touching one of the gems on my crown. "You know, the first time I saw you in this, I was so fucking pissed."

"Yeah, I know, trust me. You thought I was some chick trying to sneak into the Atlas Oaks section."

"That wasn't why I was pissed."

I look at him, confused, and he steps away, hauling my bag over his shoulder and putting a hand on the door to open it. He looks at me before he does, a small smile on his lips, and I just know whatever he's about to say is going to pack a punch.

"Oh?"

"No, baby, I wasn't pissed because you were trying to get into the section. I was pissed because all I could think about was what it would be like to fuck you wearing nothing but that crown."

A rush of heat runs through my body, making my head light and my toes tingle, but Jaime opens the door, steps out, and holds it open for me.

"After you, Princess."

When we walk into the gymnasium, dozens of preteen and teenage girls start whispering, some excitedly, some with a look of irritation that matches the redhead at the front of the room. For Utah's stop, I'm joining Anne and a few other Miss Americana contestants at an assembly with the Girl Scouts of Utah, an organization for which she was a part of her entire childhood and is now a spokesperson for.

It's strange, considering every other stop we've highlighted *my* mission of supporting small women-owned businesses, but I've come to learn to just let things roll when it comes to the Miss Americana organization.

After I answer a few questions to the dozen or so reporters that are now lining the back of the high school gymnasium, I'm given a mic, and Anne and I stand on the small stage at the front of the room. She's blathering on about how important this is to her, and I'm forcing myself not to zone out when she turns to me.

"So, what have you prepared for us today?" Anne says, a catty smile on her lips, and suddenly, I get the feeling I am being so totally fucked and not in the fun Jaime way.

"I'm sorry?"

"Well, you did prepare something to show the girls, correct? A life lesson you can share with them, something you can teach them...that was the whole point of you coming here, after all." I smile and try to fight the urge to claw her eyes out. "It was all in the email Regina sent you," she says, a stage whisper spoken directly into the microphone she's holding before giving an apologetic look to the girls.

It's one of the fakest looks I've ever seen in my life.

"I'm so sorry, girls. Give us a second. There seems to be an issue with...preparation. Miss New Jersey wasn't a Girl Scout, so she doesn't know our number one rule!" I don't miss how she always *refuses* to call me Miss Americana.

The girls reply in unison, the first cardinal rule of being a Girl Scout or whatever like a creepy little girl army. "Always be prepared!"

"I didn't receive any emails from anyone," I say low to Anne, and she gives me a sad smile.

"Well, I guess you're just going to let all of these girls down," she says, not tampering with her voice to be between just us and waving her arm elegantly to the room.

Irritation and anger brew within me, simmering and simmering until I start to feel my boiling point nearing. My eyes move along the room, trying to bring myself back to reality to figure out what to do next. That's when I see Regina standing in the wings, a smug smile on her face, and somehow, I know.

This is *intentional*.

This is to make me look bad because she can't stand me. She can't stand that I won her precious little contest and don't fit the stupid mold she thinks all women should fit into.

She's so furious I haven't heeded her warnings and haven't fallen into line that she's willing to embarrass me, knowing it won't stay contained to just this event since my every move has become public interest. Reporters in the back of the gym click their cameras, and girls start whispering amongst themselves in the crowd.

But Regina Miller doesn't know me nearly as well as she thinks she does.

Because if there's one thing I am, it's stubborn as fuck.

My eyes shift, my mind moving to try and think of what to do when I see it, the perfect answer to my problems.

He seems to be the answer to everything these days: my happiness, my orgasms, my safety. Jaime stands there, arms crossed on his chest, wearing an olive green T-shirt pulled tight against muscles and his broad chest, and a pair of black cargo pants looking like a real-life GI Joe doll to my Barbie.

God, it's perfect, isn't it?

And he is *so* going to hate this.

I ignore that thought, deciding I can deal with his blowback after I turn and smile wide at Anne, whose own smug smile falters a bit, her perfect forehead creasing as I speak.

"You know, this actually is a wonderful opportunity to share something I've been working on a lot lately," I say excitedly. "Recently, I had an incident where someone put their hands on me without my permission." My eyes move to the crowd, and the girls whisper and nod since the incident was widely publicized. "And it really opened my eyes to how it's become a woman's job to know how to protect herself in any situation. I'm incredibly fortunate nothing terrible happened, but that's not always the case." I hear the shutters of cameras, and I keep my shoulders back, my chin tipped up, my crown on straight.

Shoulders back, tits out, you got this bitch, runs through my mind, and I remember why I'm here, what brought me here.

I'm Ava motherfucking Bordeaux.

I won an entire nationwide pageant on a *whim.*

I can handle a bunch of petty ass bitches who think they're better than everyone.

"After the incident, my security offered to teach me a bit about self-defense, and it's been one of the greatest things I've done. It taught me about how to be more aware of my surroundings and has given me the skills to feel a bit more comfortable and confident. If you're interested, I'd love to teach you guys a few basic moves so you can feel the same." The girls cheer, and slowly, the panic dissipates.

I've got this.

I can do this.

I just need...an assistant.

Finally, I hold a hand out toward the wings of the stage, locking eyes with Regina, her face in an ugly frown now, confirmation that she wanted me to flounder, wanted to teach me some kind of lesson.

But I'm a Jersey girl. I'm gonna bounce back when you give me an obstacle. I'm going to do it looking really fucking good, and I'm going to smile while I do it.

"Jaime, do you mind stepping out onto the stage to help me out?" I say with a smile. His arms move, dropping from his chest, and he shakes his head, mouthing *absolutely not.* I give him wide eyes and try to convey, *come on, Big Guy, help a girl out.*

When he doesn't budge, I turn to the audience, not missing Anne's slight smirk at my attempt at trying to fix this mess I've been pulled into, and place my hands on my hips, showing a faux-disappointed look on my face.

"It seems my friend Jaime is being a bit shy," I say with a cringe, and the girls in the crowd play along with an exaggerated *awww.* "Can you guys help me convince him to come help? Jaime, Jaime." I start the chant, but it doesn't take much more than that to get this crowd in on the fun, and soon, the entire room is loud with chants of Jaime's name.

I turn to where he stands, a slightly entertained look on his face as he looks at his feet and shakes his head. I'm prepared to turn back to the crowd and attempt the presentation on my own or to maybe force Anne into being my attacker (hell, it might even be preferable, considering how much I'd love to kick her ass) when he looks up at me and takes a step forward.

Hot *and* a team player? God, could he be any more perfect?

Instantly, when the girls see him, they start to cheer, and a blush comes over his cheeks.

"Say hello to Jaime, girls!" I shout, and in near unison, one hundred girls all yell *hello, Jaime!*

His arm lifts, and he waves, shifting from embarrassed to a bit of a ham, smiling wide and making me melt.

"Do you mind helping me show these girls a few moves?"

"Anything for you, Princeses," he says. It's a slip of the tongue, our personal comfort behind closed doors, but it plays perfectly into the characters we're playing right now, and I fucking *love* it.

When I look over his shoulder, Regina stands, her jaw tight and irritated.

I wink at her, enjoying my win just a bit too much.

FORTY-ONE
AVA

Jaime and I spent about twenty minutes showing the girls and the crowd in the gymnasium the basic moves he showed me. I encouraged all of the girls to fold up their chairs, stack them up, and partner up to try out the steps while Jaime and I walked around to ensure they were being performed correctly.

The day is a hit, with lots of giggles and excitement, all wrapped up in an afternoon I genuinely feel good about. This is something young people, *especially* girls, should know, and this is the perfect avenue to do it. Ideas start circling in my mind, but I'm distracted when a now-familiar reporter comes up to me, his jaw tight and an iPad in his hands.

"Hey, Miss Bordeaux, do you have a moment?" I turn to Preston Smith, a reporter for the American Star Magazine and an absolute hater of mine. "I'd love to get a few words about your presentation and thoughts on self-defense for young girls."

"Oh, absolutely, I'd love to." He's been at many of the events for the tour, but I'm not exactly excited to chat with him, seeing as most of the articles he writes for his paper haven't been exactly *glowing* about me.

"So you spent today teaching these young girls, ages eight to eighteen, about self-defense," he says.

It's not a question, but I answer it as if it were all the same.

"I did! It was a blast to show these girls how to protect themselves, stay diligent, and make it fun for them." I wave a hand toward where the young girls are all laughing and having a good time. "As you can see, they're all enjoying themselves while learning an important life skill. I'm just so grateful for Regina and Anne, who gave me the opportunity to use this stage as a way to get more education to these girls." Maybe that will get me just a bit more into their good graces. Or maybe it will twist the knife a bit. Either way is a win.

"Do you think that's appropriate, though? Teaching young girls there is some bogeyman out there they need to defend themselves from?"

I frown at his question, both confused and irritated. Still, I put on my pageant face and answer.

"I wish all women learned just a little bit of self-defense. I recently learned just how little I was aware of my surroundings and my safety, even with security around. I'm grateful to know how to protect myself; god forbid anything bad should happen. I, of course, hope and pray nothing happens to these girls, but I'm happy to give them these confidence-building skills everyone should have in their arsenal." A couple of the pageant girls around me nod in agreement, though Anne's jaw goes tight with irritation.

"Personally, I'd love a few more lessons myself," Miss Nevada, one of the other pageant contestants who attended the event, says with a smile. "After seeing what happened to you at that meet and greet, I realized I have no idea what to do in a situation like that."

"Me too!" Miss California says.

I smile at Preston before turning to the girls. "Oh my god, yes, that would be so fun!"

All four of the other Miss Americana contestants in attendance nod except for Anne, who stands there with a tight jaw, her face almost as red as her hair.

"It isn't very *becoming* of women," Anne says through gritted teeth. "Being able to *fight*."

I fight the roll of my eyes, smiling sweetly at her.

"We're just making sure we're prepared for anything. Like you said, '*Always be prepared.*'" My smile goes admittedly catty as she frowns at me and huffs in irritation.

God, it's really great to see her bullshit backfire, and even better to make such delicious lemonade out of her disgusting fucking lemons.

"As for lessons, I'm sure I could set something up either on an upcoming off day or after the tour. We could do an entire Miss Americana self-defense event, live stream it on social media."

"I love this idea! I think most of us will be in California next week," Cara, Miss California, says. "There's a studio downtown that a friend of mine owns. If you all don't have something planned, I bet we could set something up on one of Ava's off days. We could even post it on the official Miss Americana page." She looks over her shoulder with a wide smile at Regina. "Isn't that a great idea, Regina?"

I don't know if it's an unintentional dig or if, somehow, Cara knows about what a bitch Regina has been, but either way, the irritation that crosses Regina's face is *priceless*.

"I don't believe we have anything planned for Thursday. It's a day off for my tour, but I'd be *happy* to sacrifice that time for a good cause." I turn to Jaime. "You into teaching a few more pageant queens about self-defense?"

"Anytime," Jaime says with a small, righteous smile that almost makes me laugh.

"It won't hurt to have a hot instructor, you know?" Cara says with a hip bump, and I nod with a wide, comical smile.

But with the comment, Anne steps closer, listening to the conversation. The reporter's eyes move to her, and she smiles wider before he speaks again.

"About that instructor," the reporter says. I'd completely forgotten he was even there still, my mind rolling with ideas for a self-defense day. "One of your fellow contestants has implied you have a personal relationship with your bodyguard. As we all know, one of the main tenets of the Miss Americana pageant is to remain single. Have you upheld that so far?"

My gut drops to my feet with his words, a clear leading question, and with Anne smiling so close to me, I begin to wonder if this is another setup.

"Kind of an off-topic question, don't you think? We're here to talk Girl Scouts and self-defense, after all," I say with a tight smile.

"I'm interested to know, too," Anne says, and it takes everything in me not to let the irritations show on my face, instead keeping a sweet, pleasant smile on my lips. "Since you're not supposed to be dating anyone while you hold the crown. Would be a shame to lose your title over a *boy.*"

I look at her and smile through the fucking *daggers* I'm sending.

What is this chick's *problem?*

"That's such an outdated rule, Anne, and you know that," Cara says with an annoyed look. "Weren't you bragging about a boyfriend literally days before the pageant? It's misogynistic and stupid."

Anne's mouth opens to argue, but I decide it's time to nip this in the bud before things get out of hand. I turn to Preston with an incredibly fake smile.

"Jaime and I are just good friends," I say with an easy smile and a flick of my hand. "Anytime you spend more than a few days with a person, you're bound to become friends. Unless you have no personal skills, you know?" My eyes shoot to Anne, and I smile one last time. "Now, thank you so much for your time, but I do have to do a few more interviews and would like to chat with some friends before I go," I say, then walk off to literally *anyone* but Anne and this reporter.

"You did good, Princess," Jaime says under his breath.

"I hate this," I whisper. I hate keeping Jaime some secret, hate not being able to claim him as my own, to shout about it from the rooftops. But if today taught me anything, it's that Anne is out for blood.

I spend the next thirty minutes making plans with Cara, who calls her friend to make sure we can use her studio while we're in California, taking photos, and saying our goodbyes before Jaime leads me to the SUV, and I take my very first full breath of air since I walked onto that stage.

"That was a setup," Jaime says once we pull out of the parking lot.

"Yeah," I whisper, because I know he's right. I just don't know *how* or if I won this round. We drive in silence, each of us lost in our thoughts, and before I know it, we're at the hotel.

"Thank you," I say as he helps me out of the car, holding Peach in her carrier in one hand and giving me his other. "For helping me today. Really."

"I'll always come to the rescue for you, Princess."

FORTY-TWO
JAIME

The morning after the Girl Scout presentation, I wake up with the sun to her body curled around me. Slipping out, I get in a workout and a shower before I slide back into bed in sweats and a tee to wake her.

"Good morning," her sleepy, sexy voice groans, her leg hitching up over my hip and pulling herself closer to me before pressing a soft kiss near my lips. Her aim isn't perfect with her eyes closed, so I use a hand to guide her head, to press mine to her for a proper good morning kiss.

"We gotta get up, Princess. Get on the road," I whisper when the kiss breaks.

"I want to lie in bed," she groans, snuggling in closer.

Through my sweats, I can feel the heat of her against me, and it takes everything in me not to take her up on the offer. "We gotta get on the road, Ava."

"Morning quickie."

"Later," I murmur, my lips somehow having found their way to her neck.

"Or we could now..." she says, her words trailing off with insinuation.

"Ava," I groan against her as she lifts her hips to try and get some kind of purchase on me, but I know if I don't get out of this bed now, we are absolutely doomed, as is any hope of getting to our stop in Las Vegas on time. So I roll out of her reach and out of bed, then grab her, lifting her over my shoulder with ease and smacking my hand to her bare ass.

"Come on. We have to go. I'll fuck you as soon as we get to the next stop." She pouts as I set her down in the bathroom, and I laugh. "Five minutes, Ava. Then we've gotta get out the door."

As seems to be her way, Ava takes five more minutes than we have getting ready, something I think she knows I've built into our itinerary at this point, so I only give her enough shit so I get to tease her, but not enough to actually start an argument. She tries to convince me to let her carry her own shit down, but I refuse, and she glares at me as I carry my small bag, her two bags, and Peach's carrier. I put everything in the SUV and then move to the passenger door, opening it for her, but upon looking in, she doesn't *get* in.

I fight a smile.

"What is this?" she asks, staring at me.

One of the reasons I made sure to get up for my workout was because I wanted to make a run to the twenty-four-hour store I spotted down the road, grabbing her a coffee, some new snacks since her stash was pretty well depleted, and a new book.

"Come on, Ava," I say. "Get in."

"You got me flowers," she says, the words filled with awe as she lifts the shitty bouquet of white flowers wrapped in crinkly cellophane from the store I stopped in. I saw them and, for some reason, decided she needed them.

"Yeah, roses or whatever."

Her lips go tight as she fights a smile, moving to her tiptoes and pressing a hand to my cheek before pressing her lips to mine.

"They're carnations, Big Guy."

I shrug. "All the same to me."

"You are *such* a man," she says as if this is news to either of us before sliding them up on the dash and taking in the passenger seat again. "When did you set up my seat?"

Her face is unsure as she takes in her little spot. I laid her blanket out on the seat, her coffee in the cupholder the way she likes it, her devices all charged, and her car bag all packed at her feet. Peach is already snoozing in her carrier in the backseat, though I'm sure she'll make her way up front eventually.

"Ava, I take care of what's mine. Now please, get in so I can get what's mine to her next destination," I say, thinking about the traffic we're bound to hit if we don't leave this hotel five minutes ago.

It only takes a few more seconds of staring her down, of her contemplating arguing and reading me to decide I mean what I say and for her to hop her sweet ass in. She lets me lean over her, pulling the seatbelt and buckling her in, something she stopped bugging me about after we finally got together.

I like taking care of Ava. I like making sure she's safe.

But most of all, I like that she's willing to give me that piece of mind as well.

I stand straight before leaning in once more, pressing a soft kiss to her lips because I just can't fucking help it, her soft hand reaching up to graze my cheek as I do, a small sigh coming from her.

I could do it all day.

But I can't, so I pull back, slam the door shut, get in the driver's seat, and start the car. Leaning to the back, I unzip Peach's carrier so she can explore whenever she wants as Ava lifts the book I bought her, flipping through it. I've pulled out onto the road when she sees it —a dog-eared page she opens up to as we bounce along old back roads leading to the highway.

"What..." she mumbles under her breath, and I know what she

sees. A red tab I borrowed from her clear little pink bag with the pink fuzzy A on it, what she calls her *annotation bag.*

A paragraph is underlined, a detailed description of a woman being fucked against a wall, the man's hand around her neck constricting to reduce blood flow. And in the margins, a single scribbled word: *tonight.*

In my peripheral vision, her head snaps up and looks at me, and though I try to be casual and keep my eyes to the road, I can't fight a smirk. I've been waiting for this moment.

"What—"

"You said you've never tried the stuff in your books because you'd never trust a man to choke you. Think I've proven myself pretty trustworthy."

She stares at me, and I think, for what might be the first time, I've successfully shocked Ava Bordeaux.

An accomplishment, if there ever was one.

She's squirming in her seat, and since we stopped just barely a half hour ago to use the bathroom, stretch our legs, and let Peach do her business, I know it's not that.

"You good over there?" I ask, keeping my eyes to the road.

"Yeah, just fine," she says, her voice a high squeak.

Looking from the road to Ava once more, I catch the blush in her cheeks, the way her eyes are dilated reading the pages of her book, the way she's captured her lip between her teeth, the way her chest is rising...

Fuck.

I'm not ignorant of the types of books Ava reads. Some quick research and flipping through a few of them told me everything I needed to know, and that is that some of Ava's books are absolutely *filthy.*

And I chose this one intentionally after some in-depth research during one of the many times I was waiting around while Ava got ready.

"How's your book?" I ask, fighting a smile and a hard-on at the same time. That's the thing about Ava. She's the only woman I've ever met who can make me laugh and my dick hard in the same millisecond.

"Good," she says, too quick.

She's turned on.

The humor turns to heat, that fire stoked when she crosses and uncrosses her legs again.

"What's happening in it?" I ask, and even to my own ears, it sounds rough.

"What?" she asks, the word even higher this time.

"What's happening in your book?" I feel her eyes rather than see them, and I feel the hesitation that she isn't sure how to answer, suddenly shy.

So unlike my Ava.

"Well, it's about a guy who—" she starts.

"No, what's happening in your book *right now?*"

"Right now?"

"Right now, Princess," I say, the voice stern and heated. When I quickly look at her, there's a flush on her cheeks.

"Uh, he, uh..." She takes a deep breath and shifts a bit in her seat before she speaks, confidence in her words once more. "They're on a bed. She's naked, he's dressed. He's fingering her."

"How does it make you feel?" I ask, my voice gravelly even to my own ears.

"Hot," she whispers. "Really hot."

"Read it to me."

"What?"

The word comes out in a nervous squeak, and I roll my lips into my mouth to stop a smile from coming to my lips. I don't want to discourage her at all, but she's too fucking cute.

"Read your book to me. I can't read it, I'm driving. I could use some entertainment."

"Jaime, I can't—"

"You can, I'll reward you, baby." The unspoken promise hangs in the air, and it must be what she needs to entice her because she takes a deep breath before lifting the book and beginning to read.

"With a guttural moan, one I've never heard, her head tipping further back into the sheets, her back leaving the bed, she comes," Ava reads, her words breathy. *"And with her orgasm comes a gush of liquid, continuing as I refuse to stop rubbing her."* Fuck. I didn't realize there was fucking *squirting* in this book.

"Have you ever done that?" I ask her.

"Done what?"

"Squirt. Has a man ever made you squirt?"

Her head shakes before she answers out loud. "No."

"Mmm. We'll have to fix that sometime, won't we?"

"Oh, god," she breathes out, her legs shifting.

"Spread your legs, baby," I say, my voice low. "Keep reading and spread your legs."

"What?"

"Don't play dumb. You're a smart woman, I know you heard me." Then I reach over, the tips of my fingers moving to the waistband of her loose sweatpants and dipping below them before waiting, my hand stopping on the soft skin of her belly.

And then she spreads her legs like I asked. I don't move until she starts reading again, though.

"'Fuck, Zoe. That's it, baby. Goddamn, you should see yourself. Holy fuck,' he says. 'It's too much, oh god, fuck, I... I need you inside.'" With her words, my fingers slide down, circling her clit gently, and she sighs but keeps reading. *"I oblige, my fingers moving in, pressing against her G-spot once more, and the moan that leaves her lips is pained. 'No, no, just fuck me, please!' Her hips are moving restlessly, lifting to get more despite her words, and I know she's already back on the edge."*

Now I see why she likes to read this stuff. I reward her good behavior by sliding my fingers down, sliding one finger inside her, slowly fucking her. She's soaked already, and I wonder how much of it is the book and how much is the act itself.

"Oh, my god," she whispers, and when I look over, her head is back, eyes closed, and her book is starting to slip in her hands.

"Eyes open, Princess. Keep reading."

"Oh, god, god, god," she says, her hips bucking, but she keeps reading, even though I think she's lost her spot.

"*'That's it baby, fucking gush for me again,' I say low, and I don't think she can even hear me as her head tips back, a loud moan leaving her lips and then cutting out like her lungs couldn't bear to concentrate on working as her cunt squirts once again, soaking my hand and the bedspread.*"

I want that.

I want to make Ava squirt like that. Not here, not in the car, but when she's spread out on a bed before me, her hair a golden halo around her. When I can watch her gush, then fuck her hard after.

Two of my fingers slide inside her now, and I start to fuck her with them, groaning at the wet sound they make.

"Fucking soaked from your book, aren't you? Dirty fucking princess."

"From you," she groans, and I lick my lip, pulling the bottom one in to bite it and fight another groan. I'm hard, dying to slide into her, but I know there are hours before we get to the hotel. She sighs, tipping her hips up. "From you, Jaime. I'm not wet from the book." I crook my finger, a reward for her honesty. "I'm wet from you."

"That's right, Ava. Because whose pussy is this?" My thumb moves and rubs on her clit, hard, her hips bucking as she does.

"It's yours."

God. My fingers move faster now, fucking her with abandon, her hips moving in time to the best of her ability. She's white-knuckling the pages of her book, but it's long forgotten at this point.

"That's right. You can read whatever filthy books you want, Ava, but know it's always me who's going to make you come. Now, are you going to be a good girl and come for me while I drive?"

"Yes, yes," she moans, bucking again, one hand moving to her breast, the book falling to the floor as her back arches.

"Now, Ava. Come on my fingers."

She does, moaning my name as her pussy clamps down on me as I sink them deep and press on her clit. I stay there, caressing her clit until she jolts, the aftershocks over, and the light touch too intense.

Slowly, my hand leaves her pants and underwear, her chest heaving as she comes down from her high. But I know she watches as I bring those fingers to my mouth and clean them.

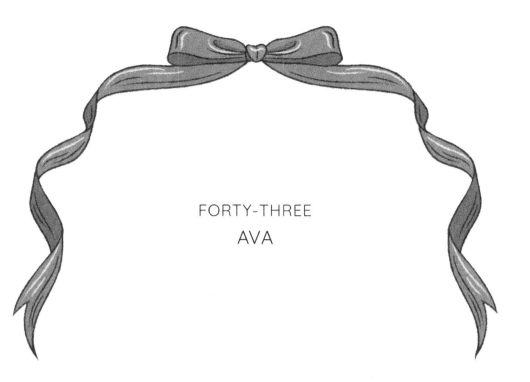

FORTY-THREE

AVA

With five days left in the tour before the final event in California, Jaime wakes me up early, tells me to get dressed with little to no extra information, driving me absolutely insane, and then gets me and Peach into the SUV.

"Where are we going?"

"We'll be there in ten minutes, Ava. I think you can wait that long," Jaime says.

"So it's not too far," I say, tapping a finger to my lips as I try to think. But I know nothing about Washington other than yesterday, when we visited a woman-owned romance bookstore, and I decided I wanted to move and live there forever. Everything was pink and gorgeous, and it was packed to the brim with books—some I'd read, some on my to-be-read list, and others I'd never read.

Jaime's hand reaches out, grabbing mine and pulling it up to his lips before pulling it into his lap, his thumb brushing on the back. "Stop overthinking. We'll be there soon."

I can't argue, instead smiling at him, his head moving to look at me as he rolls to a stop sign before reaching over and pulling me into him, pressing a soft kiss to my lips.

"What was that for?"

"You looked too beautiful not to kiss."

My cheeks heat, and he smiles at me before sitting back once more, his hand in mine gripping tighter as he drives off to a destination unknown.

"What are we doing here?" I ask, staring at the cutesy pink bookstore we were at yesterday, and he puts the car in park ten minutes later.

He doesn't answer, but instead, he steps out of the car and goes into the back to grab Peach in her harness and leash before walking around to my door, opening it, and helping me out.

"Going shopping."

"But..."

"You wanted to spend a decade in here yesterday, Ava."

He's not wrong— we were here for barely an hour, promoting the business, taking pictures, and talking to local press, but all I wanted to do was peruse the aisles for hours. Of course, I didn't because the last thing I needed was some reporter getting a shot of me buying a why choose or an Omegaverse romance and making me out to be some horrific role model. So instead, I looked on in wonder, taking mental notes of books to check up on later.

"Hey, you two," Rosie, the bookstore owner, says as she opens the door, waving us in. I smile at her, still confused, as she closes it behind me and locks the door. "How are you?"

"I'm...I'm great. I..." I pause, looking around again in wonder, before shaking my head. "I'm sorry, I'm so confused." I turn to Jaime, who is setting Peach on her leash on the floor, where she starts rolling around like a goof. "Can someone explain what is happening?"

"Yesterday, your man pulled me aside."

My heart sinks to the floor, and all blood drains from my face as we've not told anyone but Harper and Jules about there being an *us*.

"Oh, we're not—"

"She knows, Princess, it's all good. She's good people," Jaime says, pulling me to his side with an arm on my waist.

"And he made me sign an NDA before we talked."

Now, my eyes go wide, and I push him on the shoulder. "Jaime! I can't believe you made her sign an *NDA!* I'm so sorry, I'm not actually a drama queen, he's just very protective," I say to the smiling owner.

"We are five days from this chaos being over. I'm not risking that now," Jaime grumbles.

"I didn't mind at all. I *love* love. Forbidden romance is a top-tier trope." I fight the blush burning on my cheeks. "So he pulled me aside and asked if I could open later or close for a few hours so you could shop. I, of course, said yes. I'm so grateful for you coming here yesterday and promoting my bookstore. The area isn't the most well-known, and getting the name out there... It meant a lot to me. What you're doing for small businesses is amazing."

I open my mouth but don't speak because I'm unsure of what to say. Whenever someone talks to me like that, I feel wildly uncomfortable, like they think I'm making some grand gesture when I'm just living my life.

"Anyway, I'm going to head into the back, give you two some privacy to wander and shop."

"Two o'clock, right?" Jaime asks, and Rosie nods.

"Yes! We open at three today, and with the press from yesterday, I want to make sure you two have privacy before people come here.

"Perfect. Thank you," Jaime says, and he nods, heading to the back.

"What..." I look around. "What is this?"

"I'm taking you shopping."

"You're...you're taking me shopping?" He smiles wide and nods, crossing his arms on his chest. "You're taking me shopping, and you closed down the entire store so I could buy books in peace?"

"Exactly. Whatever you want, it's yours, Ava. You already filled a duffel bag with the books you've read on this trip. What's a dozen more?"

"I have money, Jaime. I can—"

"This is a date, Ava." The words stick in the air around us, seemingly to twinkle in this pink store with gorgeous books all around. "We haven't had one of those yet. I don't know when we'll get a chance, so I'm taking this one. And I figured." A blush blooms on his cheeks, and he suddenly looks almost...shy. "I figured it would be a good first date to remember, letting you go crazy in your favorite kind of place."

"Oh my god," I whisper, and he suddenly looks on guard.

"What?" I take a step closer to him, closing the gap between us. "What's wrong?"

"Nothing, nothing at all. It's just...you're *so* into me," I whisper, letting a hand trail up his front until my hand is on his shoulder.

"You have no fucking idea," he says before leaning down and pressing his lips to mine. It's a sweet kiss, not completely devoid of the fire that always seems to be burning in the background, but this time just a press of lips on lips. His are soft and warm, the scruff of his chin grating along mine as my hand moves to his neck as his hand moves to my waist, pulling me in tight.

We stand like that, gently kissing like we have all the time in the world, before he finally lets my lips go, pressing his forehead to mine.

"But we don't have all day, so I can't just kiss you in a bookstore indefinitely."

"Bummer," I whisper, and he smiles. "That would be a really good first date."

"Maybe our second one," he says, pushing my hair behind my ear. "Now go shopping."

"How many books can I get?" I ask, stepping back and bouncing on the toes of my shoes in my sneakers.

"However many I can hold, Princess."

"Is that a challenge?" My eyes move to his arms before leaning in to grip his bicep that my hand could barely get a quarter around. "I bet you could hold a *lot* of books."

He shifts closer again, stepping into my space and wrapping an arm around my waist to tug me close. "If you promise to read some of your favorite scenes out loud to me, I'll buy the whole damn store."

Heat runs through me as I remember doing just that. "Deal."

He smiles like there wasn't a doubt in his mind that I'd be game before turning me and smacking my ass.

"Go."

"So... our first date," I say with a smile as we walk through a small suburban park Jaime took us to after the bookstore.

We're hand in hand, Jaime holding Peach's leash as she chases a butterfly. It's hilarious seeing big, bad Jaime Wilde holding a pink, glittery leash attached to a harness with tiny strawberries on it, a kitten prancing around, but somehow, it works.

Everything with Jaime always seems to just *work*.

I can't decide if it's because I'm so damn into him or if we were both made to be right here with one another. Being a hopeless romantic, I've always believed in love at first sight, but maybe in reality, it works a little differently. Maybe my constant need to bug him, his bone-deep desire to protect me is just that: *love at first sight* manifesting in reality. It's been there since the beginning and has refused to be ignored.

"Did I do okay?" A blush creeps over his cheeks and down his neck, and I push my shoulder into him, rolling my eyes.

"You know you did great. Don't go digging for compliments. But it's going to be a hard one to beat."

"Mmm, well, hopefully our next date won't have to be so cloak and dagger."

My belly tumbles at the thought. In five days, the tour will be over, and we'll be headed home. While I'll still have the title of Miss Americana and I'll be expected to attend a handful of events during my reign, it's nothing like this intensive three-month tour.

"So you're saying we're going to have a second date?" I ask with a smile.

"Ava," he says, half irritated, half entertained. "What part of the last month makes you think we won't have a second date?"

I shrug, but decide to give him a real answer. "I don't know. You won't be attached at the hip to me anymore, and you'll probably get a new assignment..." I say, my voice trailing off to his discomfort, but as is his way, Jaime stops walking, seeing it and pulling me into him.

"Ava, I would move in with you tomorrow if it wasn't too much or too fast for you. We've spent three months at each other's side, every waking moment together. The thought of *not* having that when we get back makes me sick, though I'm willing to take this at your pace. So yeah, there will be a second date. And a third date. If I get my way, a one-hundredth date. A *take-my-last-name-and-put-a-ring-on-your-finger*, date down the line if I'm really lucky."

"Oh," I whisper.

"Why are you so surprised by this?" he asks with a laugh.

"I...I don't know. I don't know."

He stops my mumbling by pressing his lips to mine. Taking it deep until it pulls a soft moan from me. When he pulls back, he presses his forehead to mine.

"You so like me," I whisper.

"I really fucking do," he says back.

FORTY-FOUR
JAIME

"Is this okay?" Ava asks, nerves in her words. She turns in the mirror, left and right and forward like she's looking for any imperfection at all she can fix before we leave, but as always, she looks fucking stunning.

Her dress is a pale blue with long sleeves and a higher neckline than normal, fitted until it stops mid-thigh. It's probably one of the most conservative outfits I've seen her wear on this entire trip, but that's because my girl is panicking.

Tonight is our last off night before tomorrow's final event for the Miss Americana organization, and now that we're officially in California, we're having dinner with Hank and his wife.

I put an arm around her waist, tugging her into my body and pressing my lips to hers. She picked out my outfit, one similar to the gala we went to: a black suit and a black dress shirt. *Bodyguard chic,* she told me, giggling when I rolled my eyes, but I can't deny we look damn good together.

"Don't mess up my lipstick, Jaime Wilde!" she shouts, putting her hands to my chest and attempting to push, though it gets her nowhere. "Ugh, you're so annoyingly strong."

"You look perfect, Ava," I say to her, low and reassuring, ignoring her arguing. Her body goes slack in my arms, her eyes going hopeful despite the lingering nerves.

"Really?"

"You always look perfect to me, Princess." That makes her big blue eyes roll, and I smile. Her hand lifts, the nail of her finger pressing into where I never really noticed I had a dimple, but Ava loves to point it out.

"You're so annoying," she says with a sigh.

"They're going to love you."

White teeth come out to bite her bottom lip while her hand plays with the collar of my shirt. "But what if they don't?"

"They will."

"But what if—"

"Then they aren't the good people I thought they were. But I'm telling you, Ava, they're good people."

She lets out a long breath. "I'm nervous," she finally admits.

"No need to be," I say, leaning down and pressing my lips to her gently. "You're perfect, Ava. they're going to love you."

"This feels..." She looks around like she's nervous to say whatever she's about to say. "This feels real."

"Good. It is."

Another roll of her eyes, and my lips tip up in a smile once more as she shakes her head.

"You know what I mean. It feels...it feels like we're a normal couple, even if it's just for a night. Like we're going on a date to meet the people who are essentially your parents."

I'd told Ava how my parents didn't approve of my choice not to go to college, instead choosing to start working for Five Star out of high school. As soon as I was out of the house, they packed everything up and moved to Florida. If you were to ask me, I would say they never really wanted kids to begin with, the typical boomers who had a child because it was the "next step." When I didn't hit all of their big ideals for what a son would be, they stopped putting in the effort, and I'm not one to push a relationship either, so it mostly just fizzled out.

Over the years, Hank had not only become a mentor to me, but he and his wife became parental figures in a way. If something interesting happened in my life, it would be them I called first. While I see my family once or twice a year, it's nothing near the closeness or comfort I have with Hank and Janine. I even spend holidays with them if I'm not on an assignment, but my lifestyle means that, until now, having no real roots to hold me down was a good thing.

"We are," I say. Shifting, I move to sit on the couch, forcing her to straddle me as I do before putting my hands on either side of her face. "Ava. I cannot wait for this tour to be over so I can take you out and show you off everywhere we go. So I can make every man in a ten-mile radius jealous that you're mine. This, us? This is real. We're real. No matter how tonight goes—and Ava, I *know* it's going to go well—we are real, and we will stay the same. Do you understand?"

She stares at me in that way only Ava ever does, reading my face for untruths only she can find before she nods with a smile. "Okay, Jaime. I trust you."

And even though I fucking love it every time she trusts me with something, this time feels the most important.

"Ava," Janine, Hank's wife, says, holding her arm out to Ava as if they're long-lost friends and pulling her in for a hug. "I've heard so many great things about you!"

We barely pulled into the driveway when Janine came running our way, completely ignoring me and making a beeline for Ava. When she pulls back, Ava's cheeks are red, and her smile is nervous.

"Oh, my goodness, you're more gorgeous in person. Isn't she gorgeous, Hank?" Janine asks, turning to her husband, who puts a hand out to me, pulling me into a hug and clapping me on the back.

"Not going to comment on the beauty of Jaime's girl while he's right here, honey."

"Oh, stop it," Janine says, looking at her husband and hooking her arm through Ava's and leading us inside.

"Did you warn her how Janine is?" Hank asks, resting his hand on my shoulder as we follow behind them.

"I probably should have," I say under my breath.

"We're in for a long night," Hank says with a laugh as we follow the women into the kitchen, Janine chatting away at a hundred miles a minute. I'd never realized it, but Janine is a lot like Ava, so I should have known the two would instantly hit it off.

"Well, you know Hank and I met because he was *my* bodyguard, right?" Janine tells Ava after she sets a plate in front of her an hour later.

Ava's mouth drops open, and she turns to me, slapping me on the arm.

"No, I did *not* know that. In fact, he spent almost the entire time we were on tour together telling me just how unprofessional it would be if we were together."

"Oh, don't worry. Hank did the same thing," she says with a laugh. "But once these men make up their minds, it's set."

Ava's lips tip up with humor, her eyes dancing as she turns to me. "This I have learned."

A glass of wine later and some girl talk—Janine's words, not mine —were all it took to get Ava out of her shell, which led to Ava explaining how she spent the first six weeks of her tour trying to "get him to crack."

Janine giggles. "Oh, I absolutely need details," she says, leaning forward.

"No, I think we're good on details," I say with a shake of my head, ready to cover Ava's mouth.

"Agreed, I don't need any kind of details, and I don't need Janine sharing any details."

Both women laugh, but not for the first time, and Hank and I look at one another and sigh deeply.

"So, what are you up to next?" Janine asks, voice sweet. "You've got how many days until you're done?"

"Three," Ava says, nerves in the word as she picks up a fork, pushing some pasta aside. "And I'm not sure. Before all of this." She waves her hand around her. "I was a bartender. I started this all as a way to help out some friends."

"Oh, trust me, I know," says Janine. "I told you, I looked into you."

Ava laughs. "Yeah, well, I didn't think it was going to be much of anything, and it shook my whole world up. But I've always been a go-with-the-flow kind of girl, so we'll see what happens."

"I'm sure Jaime just loves that," Hank says with a snort, and I give him a look to tell him *exactly* how I feel about Ava's go-with-the-flow way of life.

"You know, I saw what you did with those Girl Scouts, teaching them some self-defense moves, then what you did this morning with the pageant girls."

This morning, Ava and I went to the studio Miss California's friend owned alongside about ten pageant contestants and taught them some basic moves of self-defense. Ava had a blast the whole time, teasing me in front of the women and giggling with the girls, but at the end of it all, I think everyone learned some really vital skills in a comfortable environment. The biggest bonus for me was how happy Ava was about it afterward. She seemed more energized and excited than she has been this entire tour.

"That's definitely been a highlight of this tour," Ava says. I knew nothing about self-defense until Jaime decided I needed to learn. It's empowering to feel more confident that I can protect myself, worst-case scenario."

"Have you thought of doing more of that?" Janine asks, taking a sip of her wine. Ava's brow crinkles.

"What do you mean?"

"Teaching basic self-defense, making it trendy. Heck, if there's anyone who could make it fun, it would definitely be you."

Suddenly, Ava's face brightens a bit, and a small smile comes to her lips. "You know, I haven't. But I love the idea of that. I actually had a company reach out to me last week for a sponsorship for a mace keychain."

"Absolutely not," I say at the same time Hank laughs out loud.

"What?"

"Absolutely not," I repeat. "You're not carrying a fucking trial-sized mace around with you on the day-to-day."

Ava turns to me looking annoyed. "Why not?"

"Because you're a disaster waiting to happen, Ava. With your luck, you'll pepper spray yourself by accident, just trying to show someone how it works."

She purses her lips like she wants to argue but can't before she smiles. "You're probably right. What about a taser? They make some really cute pink ones."

I close my eyes and take a deep breath, counting to ten as I do, as if that's going to help with the tiny menace of a woman in front of me.

It doesn't.

Which I'm happy about because I fucking love her, chaos and all.

"Why don't we start smaller, yeah?"

Her lips tip up. "Yeah, that probably makes sense." Then she turns back to Janine. "But I've also had a bunch of people message me every day since Utah, asking if I would think about offering classes near them or in Evergreen Park. I don't think I'd want to have a full-time studio or anything, but today showed me I could do pop-ups or something." She tips her head like she's suddenly building a business plan in there, her lips curving with a smile. "I could probably get them sponsored by different businesses, too. Or maybe even have online videos." She turns to me then. "You'd help me, right?"

I sigh, and Hank laughs.

"Why don't we make it past the end of this tour before you start making a new business plan?" She glares at me, and I can't resist moving a hand to push her hair back over her shoulder, a small smile on my lips. "But yeah, Princess. Whatever you want."

"Thanks, Janine, that was a great idea," Ava says.

"If you do start it, make sure you let me know or have Jaime let us know. I know that we have so many people we know who would be interested, old clients of Hank's who would love to learn more about self-defense. You could even have them co-host pop-ups! Some celebrities to add some pizazz. You could travel all over—"

"Janine," Hank says in warning.

"What?"

"You're gonna give Jaime a fuckin' coronary. Just look at him."

I force myself to unclench my jaw when Ava laughs.

"Yeah, I think Jaime is ready to relax for about ten years after we get back from his tour. I've really been testing his patience."

"Oh, I'm sure he loves it," Janine says with a wave of her hand.

I reach over, putting an arm around Ava's shoulders, then leaning over to press a kiss to her hair. "I'm more than happy to have her test my patience for as long as she wants," I say, and I mean it. Ava blushes, Janine *awws*, but Hank just stares at me thoughtfully before giving me a small, almost imperceptible nod.

After dinner, Ava and Janine make their way to Janine's craft room so she can show Ava some project she's working on when Hank finally sits back on the couch we're sitting on, crossing his arms on his chest.

"Never thought I'd see the day."

"Shut it, Hank."

"Just saying, it's good to see you interested in something other than work. It's been a long time coming."

"I suppose,"

"So what are your plans after all of this? Assuming your plan of disappearing into the Poconos for a life of peace and quiet is off the table," he says.

"Yeah, I don't see Ava being too into living off the grid." I say with a smile, not able to picture her being too far from civilization and shopping and other people for her to socialize with. Though, I bet I could probably convince her to hole up with me for a few weeks at a time. A compromise. We'd have to bring Peach, of course. Peach, who has been trotting around Janine and Hank's house like she owns the place.

"You gonna stay with Five Star?"

"I...I don't know. For one, I'm not sure if they'll want me there after they find out about me and Ava—"

"So, you two are going public?"

"After the tour is done. I'm going crazy as it is, everyone not knowing she's taken," I confess.

He nods his approval. "Good, good. You know I put in provisions for if you get let go or leave early. You and any employee there longer than ten years before the company was sold are covered. There's a different account for your retirement no one can touch."

"Yeah, Miles told me. Wish you'd have informed me of that, I probably wouldn't have waited so fucking long to make things official with Ava."

"Bullshit." Hank laughs, and I stare at him before he leans forward. "You have always been a cautious kid from the moment I met you. Weighing pros and cons past the point of it even making sense. The only way you would have given in earlier is if she pushed your hand."

"She tried to push me," I groan, remembering the weeks of Ava teasing and taunting me.

A unique kind of painful pleasure.

"Oh, I believe it. Her and Janine? Two peas in a fucking pod, could see it a mile away. They're the same woman. So, you know, good luck with that."

I groan, knowing the number of headaches his wife has given him over the years. But I also know the joy greatly outweighs the headaches.

"You'd be good at running your own firm," he says a few beats later.

"What?"

"You can't be in the field forever, but you have the contacts and stellar recommendations. You know how men should act, and they respect you. You'd do well starting your own firm. It would mean you could probably stay at your girl's side more, too."

My mind reels, trying to understand his words. Of course, it had been a passing thought before, occasionally thinking it could be an interesting endeavor, but I also thought I was going to be happy retiring young. Now...I'm not so sure.

Now, I think I wouldn't mind exploring the world with Ava, especially if Janine is putting wild ideas in her mind, ideas that, despite my initial hesitance, make a lot of sense for her.

"Just...think about it. You've got enough saved up, and you could probably not work for the rest of your life even without that retirement account."

He's not wrong—the life I've lived hasn't meant I had much time to throw my money at things, so I've saved most of my paychecks. Hell, I don't even pay rent or mortgage since I'm on the road most of the time, and when I'm not, I'm at the cabin in the Poconos.

"But I know you. You'll get stir-crazy after some time. When you do, you come to talk to me. Let me help you weigh those pros and cons."

From my spot on the couch, I see Janine and Ava walk out of the bathroom, Ava's head tipping back with a laugh.

"Thanks, Hank," I say, my eyes on my girl.

He chuckles, and then his chair scrapes as he stands. "Yeah, you'll do just fine, that one on your arm."

As she gets closer, her eyes locked on me, her smile gets wider and warmer, and I can't do anything but agree with him.

We say our goodbyes and walk out of the front door when it happens: a single reporter with a bright camera flash nearly blinds us at the base of Hank's driveway.

"Ava, so you are having a relationship with your bodyguard?" a voice shouts, a photo being snapped as the words come.

A paparazzi.

At Hank's house.

Seemingly outing Ava and me.

"You're on private property," Hank's voice booms behind me. "Get the fuck out."

The man continues to shout Ava's name, the camera flash never stops, and all I can think about is getting Ava to safety.

"Get in the house, Ava," I snap, not even looking over my shoulder at her. As soon as the first flash came, I pushed her behind me, barely a foot between us and the door we had just stepped out of.

"Jaime, I—"

"*In the house,*" I bark.

"Come on, sweetie," Janine says gently before the door closes behind me, but my eyes are locked on Preston Smith, the fuckwad reporter from the American Star.

"You're on private property," Hank says. "Give me your camera."

"Hell no. Do you know how much these photos are worth? The bodyguard and America's sweetheart having some torrid affair all along? Proof that Ava Bordeaux is nothing like what she's been trying to sell?"

I shake my head at this idiot. "What does it matter to you?" I ask, stepping down off the step and crossing my arms on my chest. He's smaller than me, both in bulk and height, but I won't touch him. I know better, know that it would only hurt Ava more and benefit this jackass.

"She's a fraud, and the world should know."

I stare at him, taking him in and decoding him. "Who sent you?" I ask, taking a step closer.

Suddenly, a flash of something—panic or fear—crosses his face before it's covered again with his smug look. "No one, I work for the American Star."

"Hmm, that much might be true, but there's some other connection," I say, stepping forward again. Now there's maybe five feet between us, his camera still raised, but doubt is in his eyes. "Is it Regina? Is she paying you?"

"No. Why would she pay me? I'm just here to make money on an article."

"You know, I've done a little research on you, since every fucking article you write about Ava is trashing her for no reason. You were also at the event where she was assaulted *and* in Utah, where you made some *interesting* accusations."

"They weren't accusations, though—you're on a date at your old boss's house together."

"And how did you know we were here? You sure as fuck didn't follow me because I would have noticed." Even when it's not a threat, I *always* keep an eye out for tails, and there were none.

His lips tip up. "A little birdie told me."

"You do not want to mess with me, Smith. That much I can promise you."

"You're nobody. You can't do anything, and once this"—he lifts his camera—"is out, you won't even have a job. Five Star, right? I'm sure there's something in their guidelines about fucking your assignment."

I fight to keep my face completely blank before I take another step closer.

"You think you won some game, and honestly, I think you're not even the one playing it, just some poor puppet on someone else's string. But you don't want to fuck with me, that much I can promise you. Because I can know everything about you if I need to. I can know where you went to school, who signs your checks, and the address of your mommy's house you probably live in. I can know everyone you've received cash from, and if any of it seems a little...off, I can know if anyone has ever paid you to write a friendly article or completely trash someone, and I can take all of that and send it to *your* boss because I have a feeling *that's* against some kind of journalist code." I tip my head at him. "And then I can have that information sent to every news outlet in America."

"Are you threatening me?"

I shake my head. "I'm just telling you what can happen if you don't leave Ava alone and if you don't tell me who told you where she was tonight."

The asshole smiles, stepping back. "See you later, Jaime," he says, opening the door to his car, sliding in, and starting the engine.

I stand, arms crossed on my chest watching the journalist as he drives away in a car his salary definitely shouldn't afford before turning and going back into the house and straight to Ava, who is standing with Janine in the foyer.

"Did you post where we were tonight?" I ask.

"What?"

I step into her space, putting one hand on her chin gently and forcing her to look at me.

"Social media. Did you post anywhere about where we would be? Or have you posted anything at all since we got here?" I take a moment before I add, "I won't be mad, I just need to know."

"No," she whispers. "No. I left my phone in the hotel and totally forgot about it. I remember thinking it was funny because it's usually attached to my hip, but..." She wets her lips, and I step away, moving toward the door to go back outside. "Jaime, what's going on? You're freaking me out."

With that and the waver in her words, I turn back around and get in her space again, this time tugging her into me. "Everything is okay." My hand goes to her cheek, cradling it and forcing her to look at me. "Everything is going to be just fine, I promise. You and me? We're good, Ava," I whisper against her lips before kissing them softly in reassurance. When she nods, her eyes looking slightly less concerned, I step back and head to the door once more.

As I step out, I hear Janine squeal, "God, I love this for him!" before Ava giggles as the door slams behind me, a small consolation to hear that noise.

"Tracker," Hank says through a tight jaw, standing near the SUV, a small black rectangle in his hand.

"What?"

"A tracker was on the car. Looks custom, looks expensive. Is the car a rental?" I sigh, looking at my feet and cursing low with a shake of my head. "Let me guess: it's yours."

I look up and nod. It's my SUV, and I know damn well that before we left Jersey, there was absolutely not a tracker on it.

So when was it added?

"Call Miles. Give him everything you can off this tracker, then that fuckwad's info. I got the license plate number. You said he's a journalist?"

I nod, already scrolling to find Miles's number. "A tabloid rag, but a journalist all the same. He's been at a few of the events, and every article he writes, he bashes Ava."

"You think there's something more there."

"I know it," I say, as I hit Miles's number and bring it to my ear.

It's going to be a long fucking night.

FORTY-FIVE
AVA

When I wake up, my bed is empty, and my phone has more notifications than I have since it was announced that I made it into the Miss Americana pageant. That morning, I was flooded with, *oh my fucking god, you crazy person!!* texts and calls from people I hadn't heard from in literal years trying to get the inside scoop.

This time, it's from a dozen or so of the Miss Americana contestants I've become friendly with, a shit ton of reporters who want my commentary on...something, and at least twenty texts from both Harper and Jules, in individual texts as well as our group chat.

I open those first as I squint at the screen.

> **JULES**
>
> Ignore it.
>
> **HARPER**
>
> Don't. Call us right away.
>
> **JULES**
>
> Who the fuck even cares if you're fucking your bodyguard?

HARPER

Since when has being a good down-to-earth person been a bad thing?

HARPER

Don't search your name, Ava. Promise me.

JULES

Oh, stop, don't scare the girl.

HARPER

I'm just saying, some of those comments are feral. Maybe don't read the comments.

JULES

But there are even more good ones. A lot of people agree with us.

I'm lost beyond belief and tap back to my messages, opening the ones from Cara.

CARA

Please tell me you're actually sleeping with that hottie. I'm begging. I'm also begging for all of the details.

And another from Miss New York.

LILY

Babe, call me! I need to know what is happening! Also, good for you!

What the actual fuck is going on?

So I do what any normal person would do: I search my name. And almost instantly, a post from American Star Magazine pops up, the title as concerning as the texts make it seem.

Miss Americana Ava Bordeaux: Disgracing Her Crown and Title
Well.

That's...something. When I scroll, there are a few pictures of me, one at the crowning ceremony, my face covered in genuine shock, but for the first time when I look at it, I see Anne, the crushed look painted on her face, and the absolute *hatred* in her eyes. The rest of the accompanying photos are perfectly timed shots, me with an angry face as I argue with a reporter, a shot of what looks like Jaime assaulting me at the Girl Scout self-defense tutorial, me slapping the man who smacked my ass. A shot of Jaime and me dancing at the benefit, looking much cozier than we should. A photo of Jaime and me walking Peach in the park on our first date both makes ice form in my veins and makes me wonder if this creep would be willing to send me a copy because it's the cutest picture ever.

And finally, there's a snapshot of Jaime leading me out of Hank's house last night, me looking over my shoulder and laughing, Jaime looking down at me with utter adoration in his eyes, his hand on my waist pulling me close.

Each photo is chosen precisely to tell a story, and as I read the article, I realize the story is more of the same.

There's a range of accusations within it, from my not being qualified to be Miss Americana and how the industry needs to add more qualifiers to keep out the riffraff, to my not valuing my position, to my being a bad influence for the many watching young eyes.

It's all bullshit, really, some shitty piece to drag me through the mud, except for one part.

One paragraph that takes the breath from my lungs.

"And it also seems Miss Boudreaux is breaking her contract in more ways than just not upholding the values and tradition of the organization. American Star can officially confirm that she's dating her bodyguard, Jaime Wilde of Five Star Security, assigned by the organization to chaperone her. Because not only does she not uphold traditional values, but she's so self-absorbed, she believes she's in *danger* visiting with the people who voted for her to win her crown."

I don't even let my mind touch on the fact that this article makes it seem like hiring Jaime was *my idea*, like I'm some diva with a self-inflated ego thinking everyone and anyone is out to get me. I don't even care about the accusations that I'm not a good person or that I'm fake.

Whatever.

But I do care that they've dragged Jaime into this.

I feel sick to my stomach, and for a moment, I contemplate hiding in this bed all day.

"What's wrong?" Jaime asks when he walks into the room we're sharing with Peach's food bowl.

I jump, not having heard him, lost in thought as I scroll and read the comments, ignoring all common sense that is *screaming* at me not to. Some were great and supportive, but as you quickly learn when you have any sort of social presence, there are more than a healthy amount that are absolutely scathing.

"Have you seen this?" I ask, pushing my hair back over my shoulder and sitting up straight from where I've been hunched over my phone.

"The article?" I nod. "Yeah. A pile of shit." He tugs his shirt over his head—it seems he not only came back but also showered while I was distracted. Fuck, how long was I lost in that rabbit hole?

"A pile of shit, but it's going *viral*. I have a dozen texts in my inbox right now, all asking me for details."

"Yeah, and so is the video of us teaching the Girl Scouts." My stomach drops to my feet, and suddenly I feel lightheaded. "And the one from teaching the women yesterday morning. Doesn't matter," he says, rooting through a bag for socks before sitting on the side of the bed and pulling them on. Then he stops and looks at me. "You're not letting this get to you, are you?"

My jaw goes tight, but that seems to be enough of an answer for Jaime.

"You're letting it get to you. Why? Are you nervous about repercussions? How it's going to impact you?" He moves closer to me, stopping what he's doing and sitting on the edge of the bed, pushing my hair back with the back of his hand. "Ava, we aren't doing anything wrong. That rule is outdated, and if they really try to enforce it, it would look horrible for them. A PR nightmare. And I have Miles looking into that asshole to find anything we can to discredit him."

I shake my head because he's not understanding.

"I don't care about me. I got to see the country, I got my adventure, and my friends are doing amazing. So what? I lose the crown, and Anne gets it. Who cares? She'll always know that she didn't win, and that's punishment enough."

He looks at me, eyes assessing but not understanding what he's seeing.

"Then what is it?" he asks, his voice soft and gentle.

"They dragged you into it," I whisper, embarrassed that my shit is impacting him this way.

"Yeah, well." That isn't reassuring by any stretch of the imagination.

"Are you going to get in trouble?" I ask. He shrugs like he doesn't even care. "Jaime, this is a big deal."

"It's not, Ava. It's really not. In my world, *you* are a big deal. Everything else is background noise. I told you when we made this official between us that I don't care anymore. I care about you being mine. We were keeping things quiet because I didn't want to be taken off duty as your guard, but we've got just a few days left. I'm not too worried about it."

"But...your job?"

"Not that important."

"Jaime, are you insane? You've only got what, three years before—"

He shakes his head and cuts me off.

"I've got a friend who was let go from Five Star a while ago. A nerd, but a good guy. You'd like him. Turns out, when Hank sold the company, he put stipulations in place so even if we get fired or let go, they have to honor our pension. It's in an account Hank made when we joined up, and Greg and Five Star can't touch it. So fuck it, they fire me, I still get paid out in a few years."

I stare at him for what feels like an eternity, my mouth open with this news.

"Well, that would have been good to know weeks ago, Jaime."

"Why?"

"So I didn't spend every moment *panicking* about what would happen to you if things got out! I've been worried *sick* there would be an article like this"—I lift my phone to indicate what I mean—"exposing us, and you'd regret even *looking* twice at me." It's a confession I don't mean to give, but I do all the same.

"Ava, baby," he says, coming closer to me, his face suddenly soft.

"I don't want you to look back and think you spent your whole life working for something only to throw it away just because of me."

He gets into the bed fully now, pulling me into his lap and brushing a hand down my back.

"That would never happen, Ava," he says, then shifts his hand under my jaw, forcing me to look at him. "Never, okay? If anything, you showed me I've been wasting my life away looking forward to some far-off future I wasn't even excited about. I've been unhappy with Five Star for three years, and you're right, Ava, life is too fucking short. If they let me go because of us, it's for the best. It can give me the opportunity to try my own thing, too."

"Try...try your own thing?"

"I've got good references. I don't want to be in the field forever, but without Hank running Five Star, there's a gap in the industry for a reliable agency. Atlas Oaks won't stay with them if I'm not there, so they're a good place to start. I'd volleyed with the idea a bit in my head for a while, before you were even in the picture, Ava, but Hank mentioned it to me last night, and it's making more and more sense to me."

I bite my lip, staring at him.

"Now, you gotta pack and make sure Peach uses the litter box. Can you do that while I call my buddy? He's looking into things, and I haven't heard from him since I talked to him last night."

I nod, then shift to sit on the edge of the bed, the anxiety still taking over me, my mind spinning from all of the new revelations we've had in such a short amount of time.

Jaime pulls his phone from his pocket, starting to dial before he looks back at me, pauses and comes back. He moves, squatting in front of me until we're face-to-face.

"In case I haven't been clear, Ava. I'm wildly, obsessively, crazy in love with you. A stupid article or a job I don't even like anymore does not change that. My job right now is to keep you safe, keep you happy, and make sure nothing touches you. You understand me?"

My mouth is open as I gape at him and the ease and casualness with which he said that.

"You love me?" I whisper.

"You're a smart girl, Ava. You knew I was in love with you that first night."

I smile, letting the giddy excitement of *Jaime Wilde loving me* crash over me. "You know I love you too, right? Maybe not from the very first night, I'm not a psycho, and you were *really* grumpy, but—" I start, then giggle when he tackles me to the bed hovering over me. "Okay, okay, I have loved you since the moment you told me I was a blonde with a hot body. I love when guys are kind of mean to me. Probably some deep-seated daddy issue, you kn—"

He cuts me off with a deep kiss that takes the breath from my lungs and ends much, much too quickly before he stands up and puts a hand out to me. "All right, come on, Princess. We gotta get on the road."

I grab his hand, letting him pull me up to him. "Can we get coffee on the way?" I ask with a sweet smile.

He sighs. "We're cutting it close, Ava."

"I'm begging you," I say, clasping my hands together. "I would give you my firstborn child if you take me to get an iced coffee so I don't have to sit in a room with fifty shrieking pageant queens uncaffeinated."

The edges of his lips tug up in a small smile before he crosses his arms on his chest. "It's already mine."

My brows furrow before a frown follows suit in confusion. "What?"

"Your firstborn. It's already mine, Ava, whether I get you coffee or not." His hand moves, brushing beneath my chin and tipping it up. "And your second, if you want one of those."

"Oh," I whisper, my eyes wide.

"And because I do want to eventually one day get my shot to give you those kids, who will have your eyes and your hair and my immaculate sense of humor—"

"Oh my god, Jaime, was that...was that a joke?" I ask with a faux-shocked face.

He smiles, but keeps talking. "Because I want to keep you happy and willing to function, if you get out the door in five minutes, I'll make sure we have time to stop."

"You're the best!" I say, then run to get ready and out the door faster than I ever have before, and only half of that reason is because I'm floating on air as I do.

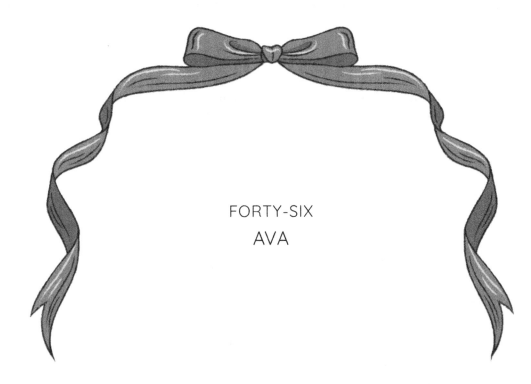

FORTY-SIX
AVA

We drive in silence to the event space where the final part of my tour will be taking place. My mind is stirring with thoughts of the article and worries about what the other Miss Americana contestants will say and what will happen once this event is done. But that silence is broken as soon as we arrive.

When Jaime steps out of the SUV to hand the keys to a valet, shouts start.

I've never felt like I needed an *actual* bodyguard outside of meet and greets or events where I interacted with people. This is the first time I've felt the actual fear of not being able to go out without someone hounding me.

Jaime opens the door, using his body to cover me to the best of his ability, but there are four different cameras all pointed at me and three reporters with phones pointed at me.

"Ava! Ava!" the paparazzi shouts, getting too close for comfort.

"Back up!" Jaime shouts.

"Is this your boyfriend?" someone shouts, and I feel my stomach drop to the floor.

"Is he worth losing the crown for?"

"No comment," I say, feeling silly saying it, like I'm more famous than I actually am, but that seems to make things worse, urging them on as Jaime walks at my side, attempting to create a shield on one side, but the cameras feel like they're everywhere as they follow us to the door.

"Anne told us when she walked in that you should have your crown revoked immediately, and the pageant plans to sue you for breaking the contract."

"I have no comment," I say, this time more confidently. Any of Anne's bullshit, I want nothing to do with.

As we get closer to the building, ten feet away now, the press backs off as a few additional security guards keep them from proceeding any further. I take a deep breath, focusing on the feel of Jaime's hand on my lower back, a grounding point as we walk into peace and quiet, stopping at the security checkpoint. Jaime has my makeup and garment bags slung over his arm, but I start to dig in my purse for my ID.

"Name?" the guard says, not even looking up at us.

"Ava Bordeaux," I say, handing him my license with a pleasant, if not a bit shaken, smile.

"Not you, sweetness," he says, and I fight a cringe at the endearment. "Him." His chin tips to Jaime, and my brow furrows. Never has Jaime had to give information to get into an event with me.

"Oh, that's Jaime, he's my bodyguard." The guard pauses, looks at his clipboard, and then nods with understanding before moving his hand to the walkie-talkie on his shoulder.

"We might have a situation," he says.

"A situation? What kind of situation?" My stomach churns, and I know—I just *know*—this is Regina and Anne taking my crown. I'm blacklisted from the event, I'm no longer invited, I...

"You've been reassigned security for this event. Jaime Wilde is no longer contracted with the Miss Americana organization, and we've been advised to reassign Miss Bordeaux's security personnel."

And suddenly, the room starts to swirl as my world turns into utter chaos.

"I can't fucking believe this," Jaime says under his breath as he walks back into the room they bought us to after the security guard dropped the bomb.

After the initial shock, Jaime made sure the office I was in was secure before he stepped out to figure out what was happening, and my mind started to swirl, trying to put the pieces together.

Jaime was only supposed to take me to and from this last event and then get me home. There wasn't much else for him to do, so why would Five Star bother reassigning someone to me? And when did they get the information? Sending a new guard out and having to pay for what I assume were flights, a hotel stay, and whatever other extras needed for just a day seems counterproductive.

Unless the pageant threw a fit and insisted he be replaced?

But suppose it *was* the Miss Americana pageant who threw a fit— why would they keep the same security company when all along they've been dangling the opportunity of referrals over their head to keep Jaime in line?

A fuck up this big, you'd think they'd hire a new security company or just have the event security take me to and from the room, then throw me on a plane to go home.

And most of all, if Jaime is off the case because I broke the code of conduct, why hasn't anyone said anything to me? Why haven't I been dethroned already?

But these are all things I have to worry about *later*.

Much later.

Right now, I have to calm Jaime down and get to the green room and smile through this final event like nothing has happened because I'll be damned if I let Regina and Anne win.

"What's the update?" I ask because after they brought us here, he stepped out of the room to ask the *new* guard what was going on and called his boss.

"I'm off the case. It seems Five Star sent out a new guard to take over," Jaime says, and my stomach drops at the confirmation that Jaime is done. "He's not one of my favorite guys, but fine enough. I talked to him briefly—he got a call late last night to pack for a few days and get on a plane immediately. He landed three hours ago."

Well, at least this wasn't planned well in advance.

"Apparently, the pageant called Greg and complained. Wanted a new man sent out instantly." That still makes *no sense* to me at all, but I don't mention that right now. It won't fix anything or change anything at this moment. "I helped onboard him, and he worked for Hank for a few years before he sold the business. He's been solid for a few hours, and he's going to let me walk you up to the room with him, so I can see where you are."

A small consolation for him, I'm sure. He's been at my side no matter what since Georgia, so I know not being there is going to mess with him.

I step to him, putting a hand to his jaw, and give him a small smile. "You wouldn't have been able to hover over me while we got ready anyway, Big Guy. All the girls are getting ready in the same giant room, and even if somehow the pageant okayed you being in there, I wouldn't have. That wouldn't be cool, having a random guy in the room while fifty girls are doing their makeup and getting dressed."

"But I could have stood out in the hallway," he grumbles.

"Yeah, you could have, but unfortunately, that's not an option. Right now, we're working with this version of reality."

"I don't like it," he says, and I slide my hand down, resting on his chest.

"I don't either, but with everything they're doing, everything they're *trying* to do, I refuse to let them win. So you're going to agree to walk me up, and when you confirm I'm safe, you'll call Miles, see if he has anything new to tell you. Unfortunately, you'll probably have to call Five Star, then call Hank. I'll take Peach since we don't know exactly where you'll be, okay? Oh, and find whatever you need to take down that fuckwad Preston Smith," I finally add.

His lips tip up with my words.

"Out for blood?"

"Oh, absolutely. But he's just first on my list." I move to my tiptoes, holding his face with both hands and pressing my lips to his. "They'll all pay for fucking with you."

"For fucking with *us*, Ava. They're fucking with you, too. They have this entire time, and we're a team." That makes me smile wide.

"We're a pretty great team, aren't we?" I ask in a whisper, and somehow, despite everything, he smiles wide, something I couldn't have expected thirty minutes ago when everything broke.

"The best team," I whisper against his lips before he kisses me, making all right in the world for just a moment.

All three of us walk in silence up to the green room, where I'll be getting dressed. As I do, I force my mind to empty of everything that just happened in the last hour.

Hell, the last twelve hours since we were at Hank's house and Preston ambushed us.

"This is it," the new Five Star guard, Landon, says. "Sorry you can't stay with her, but I'll be up here while she gets ready, then escort her to dinner."

Jaime's face is hard, and it's strange to see that look again, the one he had in the early days and weeks of this tour, only to move to something much softer for me.

"Ava, you do not leave that room for anything but the event. After, you're being brought to me, and we're headed home. Nothing matters but getting through this in one piece, yeah?"

I roll my eyes. "I'm going to be fine. No need for—"

"I'm serious, Ava. I need you to promise."

I see it then—the nerves, the panic. I step closer and nod.

"Okay, big guy. I'll be on my best behavior." One of his big hands moves to the back of my neck, sinking into my hair and tipping my head back to look at him.

"I love you, Ava."

"And I love you, Jaime."

He stares at me for long moments before he nods, presses his lips to mine, sweet and gentle, then steps back.

Without another word, I turn to the door where giggling and girlish squeals are coming and open it, stepping into utter insanity.

FORTY-SEVEN
JAIME

I walk back down to the lobby of the building, escorted by the security we encountered at the front, and stand there, waiting for one of them to order me to leave. But to my surprise, they let me hang in the lobby and wait, fully planning to stay here the full six hours until Ava is done.

In the meantime, I make some calls.

First, I try Miles, who doesn't answer before I dial Five Star.

Upon calling the Five Star Security offices, I don't get through to Greg, fucking coward that he is, but I do talk to his assistant, who sounds apologetic, at least, as she gives me options for dates to come in and set up a meeting with Greg where, I assume, I'll be fired. I tell her I'll call back and make an appointment when I have a better idea of what we're doing in the next week before hanging up and trying Miles again.

Unfortunately, I get his voicemail this time too, so I hang up before dialing Hank and explaining everything that's happened since I last saw him.

"What I don't get," he says after I fill him in, "is why did they send a new man out from the same agency?"

"Well, I've been fired, so—"

"If I still owned that place, I'd be annoyed, and I might be planning to fire the man, but with only one more event on the job, I wouldn't reassign the position. A waste of time, a waste of resources."

"What are you saying, Hank?"

"Look, I don't know how this man does business. Maybe this is just his style; maybe he does things differently. But it doesn't make sense to send a man across the country for one event, not when you aren't putting Ava at risk. If it were me, I'd have you finish the assignment, come back to the office to explain, and once I heard your story, *then* I'd either fire you or put you on probation."

"Meaning..."

"Meaning, in my opinion, the Miss Americana organization requested a new man be sent out."

My brow furrows in confusion as I try to put those pieces together.

"Why would they want to retain the same agency, though? Why not just hire someone local? Or, even more, since they were never really worried about her safety at all, why even bother? There's event security here, that should have been enough."

"Those are the questions, aren't they?" Hank asks, and nausea roils in my stomach with these new thoughts.

Before I can say anything more, my phone rings in my hand, and I pull it away, seeing Miles's name on the screen and letting Hank know I have to take it.

"See if he's found anything. You have him digging into Regina, right?"

I sigh, then nod. "Yeah."

"Good. Call me back if you learn anything."

"Will do," I say, then hang up and answer Miles's call.

"Hey, man, have you—" I start, but he cuts me off.

"Are you with Ava?" Miles asks without any introduction, his voice brusque and abrupt.

"What?"

"Do you have eyes on your girl, Jaime?"

My stomach sinks to the ground at his question.

"I don't—"

"If you don't, do it. Get your eyes on that woman right now."

My pulse starts to beat in my veins. "Miles, what are you talking about—"

"You've got a good gut, Jaime. I was just looking in the wrong spot. Anne Holmes—you know her?"

"I... yeah, I know her. She's Miss Utah."

"Did you know she's Regina Miller's niece?"

My body goes cold.

"Miles—"

"She was a shoo-in for the crown, apparently. Everyone knew it. I just got some information that she was gunning to be the youngest Miss Americana."

"Okay..." I say.

"I got some IP addresses from Ava's social media accounts, the death threats and stalker shots." My heart stutters, and I wonder if it will start again. "Those messages Ava got? They came from the IP address of Anne Holmes."

My heart starts again, this time pounding. "What?" I ask, the words cold.

"They were a bit scrambled, redirected a few times, but eventually I could find the source, and it's Anne Holmes' phone. She has a dozen burner accounts made from the same location, it seems. Now I'm working on the actual letter sent to the Miss Americana offices—I got a photocopy of it from my source, and apparently, there were a few more sent in and not reported. I'm running a handwriting analysis software now, but at least four of the seven most alarming messages Ava received directly through her social media were sent from Anne Holmes' phone."

"We're just learning this *now*?" I ask, even though I know I'm directing my panic and fury at the wrong person.

"Calm the fuck down, most of this came up in the past few hours or so from the last twelve hours I spent putting pieces together. I didn't need you jumping in and going all Rambo off a hunch. But then I got a call twenty minutes ago that made things a bit more interesting."

I had been moving towards the elevator we took to get Ava to the third floor, but I froze at the way his words hung in the air. "Miles, I swear to fuck—"

"The man who tried to assault Ava in Georgia cut a deal with the DA and spilled everything. Don't lose your shit, but he says he was asked by Anne to try and get Ava riled up, get her some bad press shots, or at least freak her out enough to want to step down. According to him, he was supposed to make her uncomfortable, touch her ass, or whatever, but make it seem like she was exaggerating, crafting something out of nothing. Unfortunately, your girl is a bit of a loose cannon—"

"Watch your fucking mouth," I say, feeling the need even now to protect her.

"I just mean they didn't expect her to snap back the way she did or for the press to lean in her favor. Seems your kitten bites." Despite everything, I can't fight the tip of my lips for just a moment, because he's not wrong. "I'm going to do more digging, particularly on the hotel break-in and any other reports of strange incidents at any of your stops. It could all be unrelated, coincidental, but I don't trust Regina Miller or anyone on her payroll."

"Fuck," I mumble, deciding to skip the elevator, and looking for the stairs. "I gotta go."

"Jaime—" But he doesn't finish because I'm hanging up and sprinting toward the door to the stairs.

"Sir, you need to—" Someone tries to stop me, but I don't listen.

Instead, I'm storming up the stairs, eyes glued to Ava's location on my phone, and praying to whoever the fuck will listen that I didn't make the biggest mistake of my life by leaving her side.

FORTY-EIGHT
AVA

When I walked into the room, I wasn't sure what to expect since I was certain everyone had read or at least heard about the article. A part of me expected utter silence and mean looks, but instead, I was welcomed in with warm hellos and hugs and even a few *hell yeah, girl!*.

I quickly came to the understanding that I am not even close to the first Miss Americana who has been outed for dating someone while reigning, and until now, everyone thought it was some outdated rule no one abided by, like how it's technically illegal to eat a pickle on Sundays in Trenton. No one actually *expects* it to be enforced.

"Hell, I got *engaged* during the last month of my reign, and Regina congratulated me!" Laura, the queen from two years ago says. "And then she asked if I'd be interested in having it televised as a royal wedding."

My eyes widen, and I let out a small laugh at that.

"Regardless of all of *your* opinions, it's a rule that the current reigning Miss Americana must be single or forfeit her crown," Anne says from a corner where I didn't even realize she had been sitting.

I roll my eyes and open my mouth, but Tina speaks instead. "You know, if you put even just half of the energy you put into being a hater into being personable, you might have won, Anne."

I roll my lips into my mouth and fight a laugh. Anne's face goes nearly as red as her hair, and she goes to say something but a head pops in.

"Forty minutes, ladies!" the manager shouts, and I grimace.

"Oh, fuck," I say. Jaime and I spent nearly an hour downstairs trying to figure out what was going on, and then I spent another fifteen minutes once I finally got up here gossiping and now I have almost no time to get ready. I look around and see all of the girls in various states of readiness, but most are nearly finished.

"Okay, ladies, assemble!" Cara says. "I've got her hair."

"Is this your makeup bag?" Emily asks, and I nod.

"Sit, sit! Madison, help me zip this, and then I'll start on Ava's base," Ashleigh says.

And as it seems to be, when you've got girlhood backing you up, we all move into business mode and get shit done.

Thirty five minutes later, Regan is helping me zip into my dress when the door opens, probably one of the event managers here to rush us along to stay on schedule.

"We're almost ready!" I shout with a giggle, and Cara pins my crown into place. "The stagehand told us we had until three fifteen to get ready," I say, only to realize the room has gotten silent, Cara's hands in my hair freezing. "What—"

But then I see it.

A man in all black, a ski mask pulled over his face, walking in and closing the door behind him.

"Oh my god!" I shout and start to back up, looking left and right to see if there's anyone in the room who might be able to help, but unfortunately, it's just a room full of pageant queens in an array of dresses and makeup.

Oh, god, Jaime is going to *kill* me when he realizes we were unguarded.

That's the most I let myself feel before I narrow my eyes on the intruder wearing all black, a black mask covering his face like some shitty villain. Compared to Jaime, he's short, maybe five foot nine, and again, compared to Jaime, he's tiny, has a narrow waist, and scrawny arms. A tattoo peeks out on his arm, and I take note of it before the training Jaime gave me kicks in.

Try and diffuse before you attack, but don't waste much time.

My hand reaches out, grabbing the first thing I can before I say in a brave tone, "Get out of here, you're not authorized to be in here." I tip my head to the side where the door is open. "Just leave, and we won't make a big deal out of this."

"You come with me, and there won't be a big deal," he says, moving closer to me. Over his shoulder, I see Miss New York, a large can of some king of spray in her hands.

She smiles at me, then nods.

Smiles.

You know, maybe my friends and I are just a bit insane.

Unfortunately for him, our intruder doesn't seem to understand just how unhinged we are, and he takes a step closer to me. When he does, my shoulders go back, my feet shifting into the stance Jaime taught me.

"Seriously, I wouldn't get any closer. You're going to regret it." The asshole laughs, his eyes green and somewhat familiar, but I don't have the ability or energy to figure out who it is, needing to concentrate on what's in front of me because this asshole *laughs*.

He *laughs*. "Or what?"

I smile.

God, this is like a bad movie, isn't it?

"Or else we're going to have to kick your ass," I say.

"Fuck this," he says, done with the game. Then he moves, hands out like he's going to grab me, and that's when chaos erupts.

I move the giant can of hair spray I grabbed, spraying it at his face, Regan next to me doing the same, and he starts to scream, covering his eyes.

"Is that glitter spray?!" I ask.

"It's all I could grab!" she shouts back, but then he screams as Peach, deciding for the first time that I've ever seen that someone is a threat, jumps, digging her claws into his arm.

For a moment, I panic for her safety, but then I watch as Emily slams the hair dryer into the back of the man's head until he falls to the ground. Peach jumps next to him, swatting at his face repeatedly, as Madison comes up behind him, using the wire of a hair tool to tie up his hands.

"What the *fuck!*" the man says as she sits on his back. Somewhere near his feet, Ashleigh is tying his legs up with a pair of pantyhose, and then we all stand back, taking in our masterpiece. He tries to get up, but Peach jumps on his ass, claws digging in, and I crouch next to his face.

"I'd stay down if I were you," I say with a sweet smile.

"You bitch—"

I take the hair spray and spray him again, making sure to get it into his eyes.

"I'd also shut the fuck up. To be fair, I *did* tell you we'd kick your ass."

The man opens his mouth, his fabric mask a bit askew, but a quietness takes over the room when the main door opens, and my name is shouted.

"Ava—!"

When I look up, a very flustered, very panicked Jaime is standing in the doorway, and I stand with a smile before putting my foot to the stranger's back like a conquering pirate. "Oh, good timing."

He looks around the room, the intruder lying on the floor, tied up with multiple hair tools, covered in glitter and dry shampoo, and who the fuck knows what else, before closing his eyes and sighing.

FORTY-NINE
JAIME

A million thoughts ran through my mind as I jogged up the stairs and then sprinted down the empty hall to where I last saw Ava, the security guard who was supposed to keep an eye on the room, nowhere to be seen.

Not one of those included Ava standing all dressed up and gorgeous, a man tied up on the floor before her.

Good timing, she said when I walked in, as if she'd been waiting for me, a devilish smile on her lips.

"Can I Scooby Doo him?" Ava asks.

"What?" Walking further into the chaos, I approach the person before Ava. He's tied up with the cords of hair tools and absolutely *covered* in god knows what.

"I want to take off his mask! See who it is!"

"Jesus, Ava,"

"Please, please, please!?"

"You two are adorable," one of the contestants—Miss Wyoming, maybe?—says with a dreamy sigh as if a masked man hadn't entered this room just moments ago.

"Ava, you are not touching any part of this. I think you've done enough." My eyes move to her hands, where a large hair spray can is, and she shifts it behind her like that will help things.

"Won't you like, taint the crime scene or whatever?" Anne says, walking over to where we all stand and worrying her lip. I take her in, reading her and seeing panic all over her face.

"I don't think there's much of a crime scene to taint," Cara says. "He's literally covered in glitter and hair spray."

I sigh, then move, grabbing the man and lifting him under his arms before putting him in a chair. The eyes through the mask look familiar, but I can't quite place them as I step back, crossing my arms on my chest.

"Who are you?" I ask, squatting in front of him.

"Fuck off," the man says, and again, the voice sounds familiar, a bit whiny, but I can't put my finger on it.

"We're going to find out one way or another when the cops come," I say.

As seems to be her way, Ava loses patience and reaches over, grabbing the mask and tugging it off before tossing it to the ground. I stand and turn to argue with her, but her eyes are wide.

"You have *got* to be kidding me," Ava says, standing there with her hands on her hips. Her makeup is impeccable, and she is wearing one of her tiny pink dresses, this one with sequins and feathers, with not a single hair out of place.

A fucking conundrum.

My conundrum.

"Preston?" she says, and I turn to the culprit, looking at him and sighing. Tied up in the chair with red eyes from some kind of irritant, glitter, and white powder all over his cheap black outfit is the reporter who has been following Ava, the one who wrote the article that got me fired.

"Isn't that Anne's boyfriend?" one of the girls asks, and my head swings in her direction.

"Oh my god, yes! That's it! She showed us those pictures of them at the beach last year and was bragging about him," Joy, Miss Montana, says, snapping her fingers.

Faces move to Anne, whose face is ghastly white. "This is *not* how this was supposed to happen," she mumbles.

"You have *got* to be kidding me," Ava repeats, now mildly entertained.

"Look, I was just doing a favor for my girlfriend; this got *way* out of hand," Preston says quickly. "It was all Anne's idea. It wasn't supposed to be this...insane. Just a..." He pauses, looking around with red eyes, his face covered in glitter. "A joke."

"Don't find kidnapping very funny," I say. "And what about the articles?"

"Look, this is a bit—"

Over this charade, I walk over to him, grabbing his arm to bring him out the door to the security. He must think I'm approaching him to harm him, though, because he shakes his head.

"Okay, okay! I'll tell you everything!"

Ava looks at me with humor, fighting a smile because she knows me well enough to know I wasn't going to *attack* him.

"Look, Anne was really upset that you were in the pageant. She asked me to write some articles, do some research, and find some dirt. My bosses liked the reach the articles were getting, so I kept it up, but I wasn't...I wasn't stalking you or anything."

"My man, you put a tracking device on our car," Ava says, even though we have no proof that he put it there. But when his face blanches, I know it wasn't him, though he knew about its existence, obviously.

"Look, that isn't... that isn't what it seems, it's—"

"You followed us on a date in the park, took creepy surveillance photos, then followed us to a friend's house where we had dinner. I don't see how it could be anything but—"

"You weren't even *supposed* to be on a date!" Anne shrieks. "Miss Americana isn't allowed to date!"

"Don't you actively have a boyfriend you've apparently manipulated to try and...what? Get me fired? Bully me until I quit?"

She glares at Ava before crossing her arms on her chest. "Both." Ava nods her head like this makes all the sense in the world. "You weren't even supposed to make it to the final pageant. Aunt Regina *promised me* you would quit before then, that the mean articles and the messages you got telling you to or else would get to you."

The timing is impeccable as the door opens again, three security guards, one of them the Five Star guard, burst into the door. Their steps falter as they see the mess before them.

Behind them, Regina glides in, and instead of panicking like a normal fucking person, she takes in the disaster zone before her and sighs.

"What is going on here?"

"Your niece just tried to have me kidnapped for...some unknown reason."

"If you weren't here for this event, I would take your place, and everyone could see how I was the better fit!" Anne shouts, and I stare at her, shaking my head because that was her plan? To have her boyfriend kidnap Ava so she could wear the crown for *one event*? Never even thinking that it probably would have been at the very least postponed with Ava's disappearance.

"And where were *you*?" Regina asks, glaring at me with her arms crossed on her chest.

"What?"

"Where were you? You're her security, shouldn't you have been here to protect her?"

I stare at her in confusion. "I'm off the case. I was pulled this morning at the request of the pageant. At the request of *you*."

Regina's face morphs into utter confusion. "Why would we do that? That makes no sense." She looks at Landon in his Five Star shirt. "Who are you?"

"I'm the replacement that Five Star sent out, ma'am. I wasn't here because she"—he points at Anne—"told us there was an emergency in the event space, and we ran to check it out, but it was nothing."

"Yes, but why are you *here*? Why is there a replacement?"

Landon's face gets even more confused, and I actually feel bad for the kid.

"My boss told me you insisted he send someone out to replace Jaime before this event because of the article that came out about him being with Ava."

"That's insane, why would..." There's a pause as something starts to click in her mind before her head snaps up to Anne. "Anne." It's a single, chiding word, but when I move to look at the red head, I see it. She's gone pale.

"If he was around, I knew my plan would never work! So I called up Five Star and pretended I was you and told them if they didn't remove him right away, we wouldn't sign a long-term contract." She shrugs. "Honestly, it's a shitty security company if they don't even have any kind of verification process." No one can argue that point, not really. But that explains some of the parts that weren't adding up, at least.

"I'm sorry. Can we go back to the beginning? I feel like I'm missing a few chapters," Cara asks, her arms crossed on her chest.

"Someone has been trying to intimidate Ava for months—since before the crowning event—to quit," I say. "It seems that person has been Anne."

"But it didn't even work because she *didn't quit*, and she *cheated* and stole my crown!" Anne whines.

"How did I cheat?" Ava asks.

"I don't know! But you did. No one would have voted for you—you're a loser! You're a nobody! You're not even pretty!"

"I won because I'm *personable*, Anne. I won because people like me, I'm kind, and I don't act like I'm better than everyone else."

"Of course you don't, because you're *not* better than everybody." Jesus, this chick is really missing the whole point. "Miss Americana isn't supposed to be likable. She's supposed to be *envied*. Perfect.

Unattainable. But then you came and cheated and won. And then I made it my mission to make you quit." She crosses her arms on her chest with a small smile.

"So you wanted to make me quit and got your little boyfriend here to write a bunch of scathing articles?"

"And you trashed Ava's hotel room," I say, jumping in on a hunch.

"That was local—" Regina starts, but Anne cuts her off.

"It was me. But you guys came back too quickly, and I didn't even have time to write a note, so it didn't work."

"And the guy at the Georgia event?"

"She hit that poor man, and everyone cheered for her! How is that pageant queen behavior!?" Regina's eyes go wide, and suddenly, it's clear she didn't realize how much was going on. "He was a fan of mine, and I promised him lunch with me if he just made Ava uncomfortable while her bodyguard wasn't there. I just wanted her to feel unsafe and not want to do this anymore!"

"Anne!" Regina says. "Is that why you threw a fit, wanting Mr. Wilde to accompany you?"

Anne rolls her eyes. "Obviously. He's up her ass all the time. I tried a few things before that, but it didn't work because he's annoyingly good at his job."

"No, it really is kind of annoying, trust me," Ava grumbles, and I glare at her.

"Not the time, Princess."

"Oh, my god, he calls you Princess," Miss Oklahoma whispers, and Ava smiles.

"So the presentation thing? That was..."

"That was supposed to embarrass you," Anne says, pouting. "You were supposed to be unprepared and embarrassed, and then it would go *viral* because you were so boring and stupid. Then it went viral because you did your stupid little self-defense thing. Which is blasphemy because that's, like, the *least* pageant queen thing yet! I don't get it. I kept trying and trying and trying to make everyone hate you, and somehow, every time, it backfired!"

"That's because I'm a decent person, Anne. You should try it sometime."

"What else did you do?" I ask, trying to change the subject. What about the death threats sent to the office?"

"What?" Ava asks with shock. I'd never filled her in on those.

"The death threats Ava has been receiving in her social media and sent to the Miss Americana offices?"

"How do you know about the ones sent to the offices?" Regina asks with confusion on her face. "We didn't tell Five Star about them because Anne was taking it too far, and I needed to keep that under wraps."

"I know about one of them because someone in your mail room had the vague common sense to call security about them but accidentally called my old boss, who informed me of it. I sat on that intel, wondering if and when you would inform me of them, but I never got it. So *you* knew about those all along?"

"Of course, I knew about them. My idiot niece sent them in, and I told my staff to ignore them and give them directly to me." She turns to Anne. "Because if she didn't stop this shit, not only was she going to disgrace the Miss Utah crown, but she was going to ruin any chance of winning next year."

"I'm sorry, Aunt Regina," she says, with big, wide eyes. "I'm sorry, I just...I hate her!"

"So you send death threats? Are you insane?"

"And then she tried to have me kidnapped," Ava says, like she's trying to be helpful. "Still not sure what the point of that one was."

"You weren't supposed to win!" she shrieks, stomping her foot on the ground. "I was supposed to be the youngest Miss Americana. Aunt Regina and I had been planning it for years. It would bring new interest to the event, and I would win a second time in a few years. I was going to make history!" She stops her dramatics for just a moment before taking a deep breath with a pinch of her fingers and smiling wide with her pageant smile.

It's alarming to watch in real time, to watch her go from tantrum to calm in a moment.

"But that's fine. I can still be the first two-time winner. Next year will be my year, and then I'll wait a couple of years and be a dark horse." She turns to Ava. "That's what you did; you were the dark horse no one expected to win. Perfect." She smiles like her plan is set in stone, and everyone in the room stares at her like she has fully lost it.

"You know you're fucked, right?" Ava asks, looking at Anne like she's absolutely insane because she *is*. "There is absolutely *no way* you're winning a pageant after you have multiple charges against you."

Anne rolls her eyes and waves a hand. "The people love me. And Preston is going to take the heat, right, baby?" His eyes go wide like this is news to him. "And then everyone will love me. I'll write a memoir about how I was bamboozled by love after I was unbearably distraught because my crown was stolen and—"

"She's insane," someone whispers.

"Oh, totally."

"Fully delusional," a third pageant queen whispers.

But Ava just shakes her head, a small smile on her lips. "Ooh, so, unfortunately for you, I don't think that's going to happen. But you can have fun writing your silly little memoir from a jail cell, I guess."

"No, I'm not. You have no proof I did anything, and everyone in this room signed NDAs with Aunt Regina, they can't talk bad about me—"

"So, funny story, even if that *was* how NDAs worked, which, I'm so sorry, babe, but it absolutely is not how they work, we were doing a goofy little get ready with us live. You didn't know because you always sit in the corner and avoid us like the plague because you're too good for us. Fortunately for all of us, when this bozo came in, it didn't stop. So, you know. I kind of recorded that whole thing. And." Ava looks at her phone and then shrugs. "It looks like 283,000 people and counting, saw that. So..."

"What?" Anne shrieks.

Ava looks at the phone screen again. "Seems the people are *not* going to be won over very easily now that they know just how horrible of a person you are. The comments are tearing you apart." When Ava moves the phone to show me, I see my own face and do a quick scroll through the list of comments.

What a psycho!

We love you, Ava!

I've been screen-recording this, too! DM me if you need it!

That bitch deserves prison for life.

And then the comments change in nature.

Oooh, is that bodyguard hottie?!

I'd let him guard my body.

I step back, eyes wide and a burning blush on my face, Ava looking at the screen again.

"Oops," Ava says, with a smile as she reads them too, then puts on a chiding look. "Be nice to Jaime, guys, or he's never going to come on one of these again." Then she turns to Anne, whose face is red with anger and panic. "Sorry, Anne. But people love a good true crime story, so maybe write the memoir anyway. It might help pay for your attorney fees."

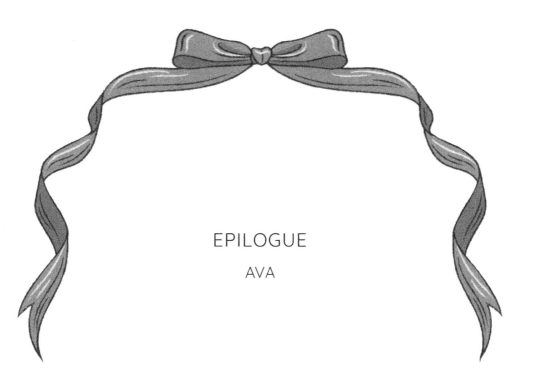

EPILOGUE

AVA

It's been just about a year to the day since I was crowned Miss Americana.

Nine months since Anne went to prison and Regina was forced by the board to step down as head of the Miss Americana pageant, and six months since I started Pretty Strong, the organization I created to travel across the country (world domination imminent, of course), host pop-ups, and teach women basic self-defense.

It's been a crazy year, to say the least.

And now I'm sitting in front of a vanity doing my hair and makeup for my last official task as Miss Americana: announcing this year's winner.

The organization offered to have me get ready with all of the contestants, but considering what happened last time, I opted to get ready in a separate green room on site.

I'm pinning the crown into place before I add finishing touches to my hair when Jaime walks in, a garment bag draped over his arm.

"Ahh! She's here!" I say, running over to grab the bag from his hands and unzipping it to reveal the pale pink rhinestones and sequins all over the bodice. Harper absolutely hit this one out of the park, and I cannot wait to put her on.

Gently, I place the dress on the small couch in my office-slash-get-ready room before moving to my tiptoes to place a kiss on the underside of Jaime's jaw. Then I head back to my vanity before picking up my blush brush.

A moment later, Jaime's lower half is reflected in the mirror behind me. "What's under that robe?"

"What?"

"What's under your robe, Ava?"

I stare at him in the mirror, trying to understand what he's saying.

"A bra and panties," I say.

"Stand up."

I could argue. I could ask what he means.

Instead, I stand, turning toward him, and continuing to do so as his fingers grab the tie on my silky cream-colored robe, the sides falling open, then falling off as one of his hands pushes it off my shoulder until it's pooling around my feet and he's taking a step back to take me in.

"God, you're fucking beautiful."

"I was going for hot," I say, my voice low and scraggy, my lips tipping up with a smile.

"Yeah," he says with a smile before moving closer.

"Jaime, the door—"

"I locked it already. Do you think I'd risk anyone else ever seeing what's mine like this?"

"You do get possessive." A growl rumbles through him, and I can't help but smile. He steps closer, and I put a hand between us, pressing on his chest to keep him from messing up my hard work. "Jaime Wilde, no. I *just* did my makeup!"

"Funny, because I don't need to do anything with your face for what I'm planning.

"What, you're not going to kiss me?"

He rolls his eyes at me before leaning in, pressing a soft kiss to my lips. "I'll kiss you properly when you're done for the night. I won't mess up your face, baby." His fingers move to my back, undoing the clasp of my bra and letting it fall to the floor, one hand moving forward, cupping my breast and rolling the nipple between his fingers.

"Jaime, we don't—"

"We have plenty of time. You don't have to be there until four," he whispers into the curve of my neck, my head tipping a bit as he does, his hand with rough calluses running down my back to my hips tugging down my underwear.

"Four? You told me two!"

"I wanted time to do this," he says.

I open my mouth to argue, but a squeal comes out instead when his hands move to my waist, putting my bare ass on the surface of my vanity. I hear things knock over and roll off, but then Jaime is lowering himself to his knees, pressing kisses to my skin as he does. My neck, my collarbone, between my breasts, right over my belly button, right below...

"What are you doing?" I ask in a whisper, my hands gripping the edges of the vanity as he goes lower, pressing a kiss right above my clit.

One of his hands moves, grabbing my ankle and placing it on the edge of the vanity, my other leg hanging down until I'm wide and bare before him. One of his fingers moves, trailing down my belly, circling my clit but not touching it, then down to my pussy, circling my entrance but never touching where I need him.

"Jaime," I whisper.

"I've been calling you princess, but maybe I should have been calling you queen all along. Let me kneel before your majesty." Then he bends, pressing a kiss to my clit, his eyes looking up at me.

"Oh, god," I whisper, mostly to myself, because then Jaime's tongue is running from my entrance, up until his lips circle my clit. He moves a hand to my hip, holding me down when I try to buck to get more, and he groans against me. His mouth moves down, his tongue moving to my entrance before he starts to fuck me with his tongue, looking up at my body, his eyes locking on mine as he does.

My body sings, pleasure swirling and building in my veins, then his mouth moves back to my clit, sucking hard and grazing it with his teeth as he slides two fingers into me.

"You feel so good, Jaime," I moan, my hand moving to his head and holding him to me as my hips rock a bit, riding his face and his fingers. The wave of pleasure builds as his lips quirk like he has some evil plan.

When I start to come, shouting his name, he stops, sitting back on his heels, stopping the orgasm in its tracks.

"Jaime—" I moan, my hips rocking to get something, more, anything. He just smiles, putting a hand to my belly, and slides three fingers into me, crooking them as he fucks me.

It's a new pleasure that creeps in, all-consuming as it starts in my toes, building up my thighs and down my back like a phantom, unable to grasp it.

"Come on, Ava," he groans, getting pleasure from this too. His face is intense as he stares at his fingers in my pussy, lips parted as he pants, watching his fingers move in me, watching me unravel slowly. He's getting off on this as much as I am, which takes me closer to the edge.

"Jaime," I moan as the hand on my leg moves to my lower belly, pushing and making the pleasure build even more, like a dam ready to collapse. "Fuck!"

"That's it, baby. I want you to make a mess for me; I want you fucking soaked when I slide in there."

I shake my head; everything is too much, too intense. "I can't, I'm going to—" I stutter through trying to tell him that I feel like I'm going to wet myself when he smiles, cutting me off.

"You're going to gush for me, baby. Remember that time in the car when you read your book to me?"

My mind goes back as his fingers crook in me as I try to focus and understand when it finally clicks.

The squirting scene.

"You said you'd never done it. We're going to change that."

"Jaime, it's too much." His fingers leave me, moving to my clit and rubbing there, fast and hard, the pleasure and pressure building and building in my belly as it does. Right as it almost crashes over me, he stops, fingers sliding inside.

"Jaime, please—"

"I know. Just trust me." His fingers fuck me fast, crooking and pressing something inside of me that has my hips bucking. "You're going to feel so fucking good, Ava. So fucking good." Nonsensical words flow from my lips until almost, almost, almost—

He switches back to my clit.

"Ah!" I shout, but this time it's even more intense, the pressure building quicker and faster.

"That's it, Princess. Fuck yes." A wet sound comes from between my legs, splayed on either side of the vanity, as he kneels before me. His hand presses on my belly, and then as his hand continues to work me, it happens.

A gush of liquid and a deep groan comes from me as I scream his name—the most intense orgasm I've ever felt ripping through me. "Jaime!"

"That's it, Ava. Fuck, just look at you, making such a mess for me." His fingers slow, his entire hand rubbing me now, my pussy soaked as I buck with aftershocks. "Such a good fucking girl," he says as he stands, his hands moving to his belt, undoing it, and lowering his pants just enough to pull his cock out.

"Let me—" I start, moving to the crown on top of my head to undo it. It hasn't shifted at all, pinned down expertly, but— a hard slap comes to my wet, swollen pussy, and I shout out, then moan as it radiates through me.

"Absolutely not," he says. "I've been thinking of fucking you with this fucking crown on for a year now, Ava. Now I'm going to make my queen come on my cock."

I moan loudly at his words, then louder as he slides into me with ease.

"Perfect," he moans when he's planted deep. "You were made to be fucked by me."

I nod, agreeing because he's right. You can't convince me I wasn't put on this earth to get fucked by Jaime, to have him give me all-consuming pleasure, and to return the favor.

"Fuck me, Jaime," I whisper, and his eyes flare with heat but he does what I ask, sliding out and slamming into me, hitting deep and hard with each thrust. My tit bounces, my body supported on my elbows. One hand shifts, and I hold my breast, tugging on the nipple.

His eyes watch as I pinch almost too hard, moaning and clamping down on him.

"Youre so fucking tight like this, Ava. Fuck. And all mine."

"Yours," I moan breathily. "I'm yours to fuck, yours to own. Please," I murmur, begging him to make me come, to ease the ache in my stomach he's building higher and higher, adding to with each deep buck of his hips into mine.

My hand moves down from my breast, down my belly, and his eyes burn on me as I do, as I spread my fingers around where he's filling me, feeling him sliding through them and clamping down as I do. The feeling is too intoxicating, and I'm almost there, almost ready to come with him inside of me when he shifts again. His hands are on my ass, lifting me up and taking two steps back before he sits in the large cushioned chair the hotel provided for my vanity, sitting me in his lap.

"Oh, fuck," I moan louder, feeling him slide somehow deeper now, hitting new sensitive spots deep inside. I shift my hips and shout his name.

I'm so fucking close.

He grabs my hands, placing them on his shoulders. "Ride," he says, an order in his words as his hands move to my hips.

He doesn't have to ask me twice. With my shins planted in the cushion of the chair, I move to lift, a low moan leaving my lips as I do.

"Fuck, you feel good," he groans, using his hands to slam me down and grind against me, my hips rocking as his pelvis scrapes against my swollen clit.

"Oh!"

"That's it, Ava. Take what you need from me. Ride my cock."

His hand moves up to my face, gently resting there, forcing me to look into his eyes. We share a breath, our lips barely touching, as he whispers words of encouragement. My hips buck and pleasure— more all-consuming than it's ever been—builds in my belly until I close my eyes with a moan.

"No," I say. "It's too much."

"No, it's not. Open your eyes. I want your eyes when my queen comes for me." I open them, locking on his hazel eyes, and as I move in a downward glide, I erupt, calling out his name as one of his hands moves to my ass, holding me down as his hips buck up, as he buries deep with a groan of satisfaction, filling me.

I sit in his lap like that, panting, trying to come down from what just transpired, feeling him soften inside of me when his hand moves up to my face, pulling me close and kissing me, his tongue sliding into mine, and it's so good, I almost forget I have to finish getting ready and he's probably fucking up my makeup.

"Jaime!" I say, pulling back. "I can't believe you made it through *fucking me* without fucking up my makeup, but now that we're all done and *then* you decide to?!"

He chuckles, his eyes warm and easy as he lifts me off him before standing, towering over me as he does.

His thumb slides along my bottom lip before he says, "Go, Princess. Go fix your lipstick, then get dressed so we can go."

It's reminiscent of our very first kiss, the way he left the room because, in his own words, if he had stayed another moment, he would have fucked me senseless.

I realize then we'll always be like this: impulsive and wildly in love and unable to resist each other.

And even though it's predictable, it's a predictability I am more than happy to fall into.

A year later

"Rosie!" I yell as I enter the small pink bookstore we came to almost two years ago. It's changed a bit—some new decorations and obviously new releases—but it's the same for the most part, and that's strangely comforting.

"Ava! How are you?" the brunette asks, coming over to me and pulling me into a hug.

"I'd be better if you opened up a second location in New Jersey," I say when we pull away. "That way I don't have to convince the big guy to drag me all the way to the West Coast just to go shopping."

It's not *totally* true, but I'd be lying if I said I didn't plan a Pretty Strong pop-up in Washington with the intention of stopping by.

Pretty Strong, my business that consists of weekend-long girls' retreats in different cities where we hang out, have girl talk, do silly crafts, eat good food, and, of course, learn self-defense, has become a raging success.

After my year as Miss Americana was done and once Jaime's own security firm, Wilde Security, was set up and running smoothly to the point where he was able to schedule in a monthly trip with me to help with lessons, I really leaned into the business, hiring a group of four girls to help me run these events as well as the online presence we have, including weekly training videos.

It's funny to think that two years ago, I had no idea what I wanted to do with my life, was joining a pageant just to help my friends, and was slowly coming to terms with the fact that true, all-consuming love might just be in romance books for me.

And here I am: a retired pageant queen business owner dating the prettiest bodyguard on earth. And a cat mom!

Peach trots into the store on her leash like she owns the place, with Jaime trailing behind. He likes to say all the women in his life treat him the same, and seeing him with Peach, I can't say I disagree.

"Maybe one day," she says wistfully. "Until then, you'll just have to keep making the trek out here to see me."

"I'm happy to," I say. "We should do dinner later."

A twinkle is in her eyes like she knows something I don't before she answers. "Yeah, maybe. You looking for anything in particular?"

"Nope, just gonna peruse. See how much the big guy can carry, you know, the norm."

She lets out a tinkling laugh before nodding, and Jaime and I start to wander. I pick up books here and there and read the blurbs. I put some back and ask Jaime to hold others until I'm stopped at a table with just one book propped up on it.

"What is this one?" I ask, approaching a pink book with dark and light stripes on the cover, a big pink bow in a golden frame surrounding the title of the book: *Passenger Princess*. Little icons dot the edges of the book, and I glance at it, confused because I've definitely never seen this book recommended anywhere, but it seems...familiar all the same. Plus, the title is *everything*.

"What's what?" Jaime asks, Peach on her little harness, trotting behind him.

"I've never seen this book, but this cover is to die for," I say, lifting it, then turning it over to look at the back. My body goes tight when I see the name of the female main character, Ava. And the male main character? Jaime.

"What?" Jaime asks, barely interested as he leans on a bookshelf, digging his hand into his pocket and keeping an eye on Peach as she rolls around on the floor.

I flip through the book and see that Ava has an orange cat named Peach. "*Oh my god!*" I shout. "Jaime, this is like an unauthorized biography or something. It's—"

And then I see it.

Smut.

There is a smutty scene in here about Jaime fingering me in the car.

"Oh my god," I whisper, flipping through the pages, then looking at Jaime. "Is this fucking *fanfiction* about *us*?"

"I don't even know what fanfiction is, Ava." I look up at him, unamused.

"Shut up, yes, you do. I know you've been reading that Omegaverse fanfic I sent you." A blush creeps over his cheeks. "I *knew* you'd like it!"

He rolls his eyes, tipping his head toward the book still in my hands. "Who's the author?" he asks. Moving it in my hands, I look, unable to find the name on the cover. "Check the end, there might be an *About the author* page."

My brow furrows, and I flip to the back before the world starts to spin.

A photo of Jaime and me standing together in Maine—a photo that I found out was his phone icon for me months later.

About the author:

Jaime Wilde is the bodyguard of a pageant queen and father to Princess Peach.

His goal in life is to convince the love of his life, Ava Bordeaux, to travel the world with him for the rest of his life as his wife. He went so far as to commission an entire fanfiction (he lied: he totally knows what fanfiction is, and yes, he liked that Omegaverse you sent him) and dragged her to Washington, where they had their first date, so he could ask her to spend forever with him.

"Jaime—" I whisper in panic, but then when I look up again, he's not there.

He's down on the ground.

Down on one knee, a ring in his hand, a nervous smile on his lips.

"*Jaime*—" I whisper, but stop this time because of the lump in my throat.

"I thought about doing this at the club I met you in, the place I probably fell in love with you, if we're being honest. Then I thought about the boardwalk in Atlantic City, where you made me sit with you even though I wanted to be as far from you as I could because I knew even then, I was crazy for you. I thought about Maine, where you ran from me, and I realized I'd always chase you, no matter where you went. Then Georgia, where you were so fucking brave, just like you always are. Florida, where you told me to hold your hand and jump in. Missouri, where I kissed you for the first time and then got scared because I didn't want to stop. Texas, where you yelled at me and I finally gave into what you knew was real all along. Or even Utah, where you got the first kernel of the idea of Pretty Strong. But none of them felt right."

He smiles up at me wide, his dimple coming out, and my eyes start to water, and I fight not to let them fall.

"Eventually, I decided on here. Where we had our first date, surrounded by the stories you love to read, ours in your hands."

"Jaime," I whisper, a single tear escaping to drip down my cheek.

He reaches up to swipe it, leaving his hand there, and the other is still holding the ring I haven't even looked at yet.

"You said you love the idea of falling in love. I don't, Ava. I love *being* in love with you, and I love the idea of you getting your happily ever after every damn day. I love the idea of spending forever making sure you're treated like a queen and that you have everything you want in life. That you'll always have someone at your side cheering you on and watching your ass while you do it."

"Because it's a good ass," I whisper.

"A great ass."

I smile, then kiss him again, this time slightly longer, before he presses his forehead to mine.

"So what do you say? Will you marry me?"

"Of course I will, Jaime. You have a *way* cooler last name than me." He smiles even wider and shakes his head at me. "Plus, do you think I could say no after you wrote an entire fanfiction about us? I cannot wait to read this."

He cringes a bit.

"I hired someone to write it, which was an experience because explaining us fucking so a relative stranger could write it out for you was weird, but...I hope you like it," he whispers.

I shake my head at him, his head shifting along mine as I sigh deeply.

"Oh my god, you so totally love me," I whisper against his lips.

"Yeah, I really do," he agrees.

ACKNOWLEDGMENTS

It's that time again: the time where I get to scream from the rooftops about the amazing, kind, beautiful people who helped make this book a reality and they have to sit there and let me do it. (Or close the book, which, rude, guys. Let me love you.)

First and foremost, thank you Alex, the love of my life, the man who brings me snacks and coffee and drains himself dry so I can live in my silly little fictional worlds without the real one bothering me. I knew 13 years ago I'd spend forever with you and you didn't even blink twice when I told you that way, *way* too early. You are why I'll always believe in love at first sight and the instalove trope. (As well as the grumpy sunshine trope but this is an acknowledgement, not a roast.)

As always, thank you to Ryan, Owen, and Ella, even though you absolutely cannot be reading this. I'm honored I get to raise you guys and every single day you teach me something new. (even if it's just about Nascar or Pokemon or Gabby's Dollhouse, I'm happy to learn it.) I love you guys so much and I don't think you'll ever understand just how proud I am to be your mom.

Thank you to Regan, the best PA in the entire world and I'll die on that hill. Thank you for being the common sense behind my mindless rambling, for taking my silly little ideas and helping me turn them into reality, and for never making me feel stupid for asking questions. Thank you for going with it when I completely shift gears and not giving me shit for having to remind me about something fifteen times. I say I couldn't do this without you and I really mean it down to my soul. I'm so proud of everything you've accomplished even if you don't want to hear it at all.

Thank you to Madi, my cover designer, my person, the creative Jack to my Taylor. It's absolutely wild that I've barely known you for a year and a half, considering when I go, like, two days without talking to you it feels off. I couldn't have done this without you and I'm so, so grateful for you and it's been so amazing to watch you grow. I cannot wait to see what you accomplish next.

Thank you to Salma, who helped make sure this made sense and wasn't a total train wreck. Thank you for your kindness and insightful and for not hating me when I forget to reply to texts.

Thank you to my favorite little influencer girl, Emily, for always keeping me on trend when my boomer tendencies kick in.

Thank you to Ashleigh, our own personal pretty pretty princess. I can't tell you how much it means to me that you let me complain and listen to our meltdowns while working your big girl job. Thanks for always giving us the best rundowns on the most insane stories you read.

Thank you to Christine for helping to edit this beast - you are a lifesaver!

Thank you to my ARC team who always does the absolute most, screaming about my book-babies from the top of the rooftops. You all are the reason this book will find any success, the reason my career even exists, and I'm forever grateful for all of you.

Finally, thank you to the readers. I say it every time, but I started this as a silly goofy little thing to help myself out when I was burnt out and it has transformed my life in so many ways. You've given my family time to be together, me the opportunity to chase my drams, and helped me find some of my absolute best friends. I'll never be able to thank you all enough for all you've done, the way you take my stories and read then, love them, share them. Thank you, thank you, thank you.

ABOUT THE AUTHOR

Morgan is a born and raised Jersey girl, living there with her two sons and daughter, and mechanic husband. She's addicted to iced espresso, barbeque chips, and Starburst jellybeans. She usually has headphones on, listening to some spicy audiobook or Taylor Swift. There is rarely an in between.

Writing has been her calling for as long as she can remember. There's a framed 'page one' of a book she wrote at seven hanging in her childhood home to prove the point. Her entire life she's crafted stories in her mind, begging to be released but it wasn't until recently she finally gave them the reigns.

I'm so grateful you've agreed to take this journey with me.

Stay up to date via TikTok and Instagram

Stay up to date with future stories, get sneak peeks and bonus chapters by joining the Reader Group on Facebook!

ALSO BY MORGAN ELIZABETH

The Springbrook Hills Series

The Distraction

The Protector

The Substitution

The Connection

The Playlist

Season of Revenge Series:

Tis the Season for Revenge

Cruel Summer

The Fall of Bradley Reed

Ick Factor

Big Nick Energy

The Ocean View Series

The Ex Files

Walking Red Flag

Bittersweet

The Mastermind Duet

Ivory Tower

Diamond Fortress

All My Love

Made in the USA
Monee, IL
11 September 2024

65616063R00181